D0503029

Poets on Painters

Poets on Painters

Essays on the Art of Painting
by Twentieth-Century Poets

Edited by

J. D. McClatchy

University of California Press
Berkeley   Los Angeles   London

University of California Press
Berkeley and Los Angeles, California

University of California Press, Ltd.
London, England

©1988 by The Regents of the University of California
First Paperback Printing 1990
The Publisher wishes to acknowledge with gratitude
a generous gift from Deborah and Joseph Goldyne
in support of this project.

Library of Congress Cataloging-in-Publication Data

Poets on painters.

    1. Painting, Modern—20th century—Themes, Motives.
2. Art and literature—United States. 3. Art and
literature—Great Britain. I. McClatchy, J. D.,
1945–
N6490.P5637 1988   759.06   87–10848
ISBN 0-520-05777-5 (alk. paper)
ISBN 0-520-06971-4 (pbk : alk. paper)

Printed in the United States of America

    2   3   4   5   6   7   8   9

For Natalie Charkow and John Hollander

I have ever been too sensible of the labyrinthian path to eminence in Art (judging from Poetry) ever to think I understood the emphasis of Painting. The innumerable compositions and decompositions which take place between the intellect and its thousand materials before it arrives at that trembling delicate and snail-horn perception of Beauty—I know not your many havens of intenseness—nor ever can know them—but for this I hope nought you achieve is lost upon me.

Keats, from a letter
to Benjamin Haydon, 8 April 1818

Contents

CONTENTS

CONTENTS

Introduction

An artist is a person who has invented an artist.

Harold Rosenberg

IT COULD be argued that modern poetry was invented by the painters. Certainly when in 1913 Ezra Pound reviled the mannered blur of Victorian verse and called for the "shock and stroke" of a new poetry based on the *image,* he defined it with a canvas in mind: "An 'Image' is that which presents an intellectual and emotional complex in an instant of time." Only such an image, such a poetry, could give us "that sense of sudden liberation; that sense of freedom from time limits and space limits; that sense of sudden growth, which we experience in the presence of the greatest works of art." (By "greatest," Pound means both oldest and newest, both Giotto and Gaudier-Brzeska.) All the paraphernalia of modernism, in fact, seems largely pictorial. The convulsive energy of the high modernist poetry, its use of collage and cubist fractioning, its *vers libre* expressivity, its sense of the natural object as adequate symbol, of technique as content, of organic form, of dissociation and dislocation—these derive from the example of painters. When Pound demanded "direct treatment of the 'thing,'" and William Carlos Williams urged "no ideas but in things," the *thing* they had in their mind's eye might as well have been the painter's motif.

The impressionists and then the cubists had set the Academy on its ear (and the surrealists next turned the

Academy into an ear), first by challenging the rules and then by making new ones—rules that became a dispensation for the poets. "How shall I be a mirror to this modernity?" Williams asked in an early poem. And it is important to remember that during certain periods painters and poets together form part of a larger group. During the 1920s and 1930s both were part of the avant-garde. "No one knew consistently enough to formulate a 'movement,'" wrote Williams. "We were restless and constrained, closely allied to the painters. Impressionism, dadaism, surealism applied to both painting and the poem." Again in the 1950s and early 1960s there was an alliance, under the banner of the School of New York.

A great deal has been written about "the sister arts," their history and sibling rivalries. The whole heritage of Horace's famous tag *ut pictura poesis* has been analyzed and anthologized: backward to its philosophical and theological sources in a view of experience as an "image" of its own idea or of nature as a divine allegory to be unriddled; forward to the emblem poetry of the Renaissance or to yesterday's concrete poem. The long line of poet-painters is also familiar, from Ben Jonson's court masques to Yosa Buson's calligraphic landscapes, from William Blake to Henri Michaux, all of them artists for whom the text portrays, the picture speaks. In my favorite of Buson's works—"Broom, Poems, and Poet" —the figures and the text not only comment on one another, they are part of one another: in a single brushstroke the broom's straw becomes a line in the haiku beside it.

"One of the characteristic symptoms of the spiritual condition of our age," wrote Baudelaire about Delacroix, is that "the arts aspire, if not to take one another's place, at least reciprocally to lend one another new powers." The nineteenth century forged this alliance of powers: leaving aside Goethe or Baudelaire, in English alone there are poems by Keats, Shelley, Browning, and Rossetti that attest to

it. But it is our own century, the age of mechanical repro-
ductions and of available museums, that is especially rich
not only in poems that seek to "resemble" imaginary
pictures but also in poems that seek to interpret existing
ones. The example of the modernist pioneers has been
taken up and refined by nearly every contemporary poet of
note. In this country the roll call, drawn from every school
of thought, would run from Ashbery and Berryman through
to Gregory Corso, Irving Feldman, Louise Glück, Donald
Hall, Robert Hass, Anthony Hecht, John Hollander, Richard
Howard, Randall Jarrell, Frank O'Hara, Sylvia Plath, W. D.
Snodgrass, May Swenson, Richard Wilbur, and Charles
Wright. For these and for most poets paintings are primal,
as "real" as the bread and wine on the table, as urgent as a
dying parent or concealed lover in the next room.

Poems about paintings may be trying one of several tasks.
It is a way to copy and to learn. The young Delacroix copied
paintings by Poussin to learn the lessons of that master; in a
similar manner, by "describing" a painting a poet may study
figurative problems: the composition of subject matter,
color, and scale, or the relationship between chance occur-
rence and formal patterns. Describing is also homage; to
trace the beloved's body is a traditional poetic feat, and a
painting is as beguiling as any idealized lip or lash, any
fetish. By writing about a contemporary painting, a poet may
cannily have found a useful way to let the poem talk about
itself. Often, writing about an old painting may prove to be
the best way to write about the past, about something at
once over with and ongoing, something framed, distanced,
even miniaturized.

But this collection offers something more unusual: *prose*
by poets about paintings. An altogether different kind of
meditation about art, it is more a Continental tradition.
There one finds intimacies, not just interpretations.
Mallarmé daily visited the studio of his friend Degas. Rilke

served as Rodin's secretary. In England or America, there is nothing comparable to the extraordinary associations, bridged by prose, of Picasso, Braque, or Matisse with Apollinaire, Éluard, Aragon, Char, Reverdy, Marteau, or du Bouchet. In Spain there is Lorca on Dali; in Latin America, Paz on Duchamp.

Most of the writings of these poets are well known; it is an available tradition. What I have sought to assemble here is the Anglo-American tradition that has paralleled the European. It has been a vital and perhaps unrecognized line of force in the arts. One reason for its neglect is that, by contrast with the other tongues, English is more diffident— not least because it has been used to write about an art that is, so to speak, in a foreign language. Not that "our" art is inferior, but it has seemed so to us, at any rate until the Second World War. The essays in this book abound with French and Italian examples, and a distinct sense of *longing*—of north for south, newer for older, near for far—gives a peculiarly haunted edge to many poets' views. That is a measure, too, of the ways in which English and American poets have in this century opened up our literature to new energies and expropriated for their own use the art of other cultures. Much of the groundwork for those transformations can be discovered in these essays.

The first essay in this book begins, "Two days ago I was at the Tate Gallery." The last sentence of the final essay ends, "we become part of what we behold." What are poets looking *at*, looking *for*, when they walk into a room of pictures? Above all, they have their eye on the pictures themselves, on the presence of images, and not on critical fashions. The essays in this book, though sometimes polemical, are rarely theoretical. They avoid both the pedantry of the standard art-historical approach and the fuzziness of conventional "appreciations." They do not offer, in Robert Frost's phrase, merely "copy speech," but "counter-love, original response." The poets bring to their task a fresh eye and a freshened language, vivid with nuance and color and force. Their essays are flecked with poetic asides and startlingly apt phrases, as when Frank O'Hara calls Jackson Pollock's *Number 12* (1952) "a big, brassy gigolo of a painting" or when James Merrill wonders if the women in Corot's lanscapes might be either the last of the Lamias or the first patients of Freud. Image evokes image. Nowhere do we find language about art that is, in Auden's phrase, "pawed at and gossiped over." The paintings, whose appeal is that they both instruct and provoke, work on the poets as a continuous inspiration. Stephen Spender speaks in his essay of "a relationship of love and envy between the arts," and it may be that what focuses the poet's ambivalent emotions and prompts such brilliant speech is the very silence of the paintings.

At the same time, the poets move quickly to context. The paintings in these pages are part of the culture of objects and icons, the society of connoisseurs and consumers. We are offered several eccentric but compelling "histories" of art, such as Gertrude Stein's detailed chronicle of her taste and D. H. Lawrence's inquiry into the industrialization of the human body in painting. Elsewhere a painter is made over, sometimes as a stand-in for the poet, into a type of the bold innovator or of the outsider (Elizabeth Bishop does this). There is an iconography at work too; one can watch, say, St. Cézanne and various donors being painted into the panel depicting the elect.

The point is, the poets are more attracted by the possible meanings of a painting than by the evident means used to make either painting or meaning. The picture as object yields to the subject for interpretation. And the question to ask is, what kind of instruction does the poet seek from the painter's images? When does the picture become a looking glass? Even before they write about it—and prose brings its own set of pressures and reliefs to their writing—the poets have sensed the emblematic value of a picture. First, it represents a portrait of the artist's mind, an image for states of feeling and planes of thought, an embodied temperament. Second, by praising or analyzing the painters, these poets have found a sure way (their objectified correlative, let's say) to describe themselves, or, more generally, to describe the creative process itelf. That is one reason prose is appropriate for these meditations: it catches the simmering, explosive, luxuriating moments in transit—the moment before a painting has been made, the moment after it has been seen. Thus enabled to describe a process so visibly and dramatically objectified, the poets take advantage of it. They give themselves the chance to expand on what their eye remarks. Their essays are not just elaborate captions. Sometimes, in fact, it seems the poet wants to replace what he or she sets out to render. This is true with Williams on Matisse and with Kenneth Rexroth on Léger, and the results are a fascinating superimposition. At other times—I am thinking of John Hollander on Thomas Cole—the poet seems, with a wave of the hand, to have removed the film of misconception obscuring an artist's true ambitions.

If this book has a single, or rather a singular, point of reference, it is this: all these essays are—or should properly be read as being—about *style:* the way artists use art and invent it. The "experience" of any artist—painter or poet—consists of what is *in,* not just in front of, the artist's eye. Life and ideas about life; ideas about ideas; the intention to work on art; and what Yeats defines as the only masterpieces—"the old images, the old emotions, awakened again to overwhelming life by the belief and passion of some new soul": these are what an artist, and in turn an audience, seizes on or is seized by, shapes and is shaped by. And these are the subject of the essays that follow.

A word about my selection: as I have already explained, my purpose is to reveal a tradition, an extensive and a continuing one. Any specialized view is necessarily narrowed, but for that same reason it is less random, richer, and more representative. For lack of space, not all the poets I would like to have included are here; Isaac Rosenberg, David Jones, Stanley Kunitz, and Paul Goodman are among those excluded. But within the compass of one century and one language there is an extraordinary variety. I have, with an anthologist's open arms, tried to gather several different kinds of poet. Where their literary convictions divide them as poets, the opposing points of view they bring to these essays are often exhilarating. Although roughly chronological, the essays have been pointedly juxtaposed. As the reader would expect, the tone of these pieces is highly personal. Even when whimsical or combative, they display an intense imaginative spirit, fixed on the topic and simultaneously freed by it into an absorbing elegance. That spirit drew me to each essay. They have been culled from their fugitive appearances in newspapers, magazines, catalogues, and books. The living poets have given me their second thoughts; these are included in the brief headnotes to each essay. The result is an anthology of forms of tribute—homage, memoir, anecdote, tirade, full-dress study, and cultural dressing-down. That several poets have written about the same artist, or the same sort of artist, though with different emphases, makes the book a form of conversation. It is a marvelous conversation to overhear. Charles Tomlinson speaks up for this entire meeting of poet with painter, of reader with essayist: "You may write with a pencil, but once you come to draw with it, what a diverse end those marks serve. But the fortuitous element is still there—the element of meeting something you didn't expect, something that isn't yourself."

Paul Gauguin, *Contes barbares*, oil on canvas, 51 x 35 in. Folkwang-Museum, Essen. Photograph Bildarchiv Foto Marburg.

Art and Ideas

WILLIAM BUTLER YEATS

Yeats lived in a family of painters. His father, John Butler Yeats, had abandoned a career as a barrister and, while William was a boy, studied to be a painter. He was eventually recognized as a distinguished portraitist, though he refused to paint anyone whose political ideas he disagreed with. Yeats senior illustrated two of William's early books, The Celtic Twilight *(1893) and* The Secret Rose *(1897), and contributed a portfolio of family portraits to* Reveries over Childhood and Youth *(1916). John Butler Yeats's second son and namesake, Jack B. Yeats (1871–1957), followed in his father's brushstrokes and became the most important Irish painter of his generation. Samuel Beckett has praised his paintings in terms that apply to his brother's poems as well: "High solitary art uniquely self-pervaded, one with its wellhead in a hiddenmost of spirit, not to be clarified in any other light." Yeats's two sisters, Lily and Lolly, did watercolors and embroidery, and their involvement with the Dun Emer Press and the Cuala Industries set new standards for Irish craftwork and fine printing. Yeats's own daughter, Anne, also became a painter and stage designer. By the evidence of his drawings and pastels, Yeats himself was a gifted amateur, though one painter-friend, Sir William Rothenstein, complained, "There was something I missed in Yeats—he had no eye.*

Reprinted with permission of Macmillan Publishing Company in New York and A. P. Watt Publishers in London from *Essays and Introductions,* by W. B. Yeats (1937), 346–55. Copyright © 1961 by Mrs. W. B. Yeats.

When he would walk with me in the country, he seemed to notice nothing of the beauty around him; he seemed to keep his eyes on the ground." His eye, Yeats would have countered, was on the unseen, and on the manifestation of the unseen that is the source of art—art itself. It might be said that painters and pictures were the first of those "masks," or second selves, by which in the poet's view we reimagine ourselves. "I seek an image, not a book," he says in "Ego Dominus Tuus." "By the help of an image/I call to my own opposite, summon all/That I have handled least, least looked upon."

I

TWO DAYS ago I was at the Tate Gallery to see the early Millais's, and before his *Ophelia,* as before the *Mary Magdalene* and *Mary of Galilee* of Rossetti that hung near, I recovered an old emotion. I saw these pictures as I had seen pictures in my childhood. I forgot the art criticism of friends and saw wonderful, sad, happy people, moving through the scenery of my dreams. The painting of the hair, the way it was smoothed from its central parting, something in the oval of the peaceful faces, called up memories of sketches of my father's on the margins of the first Shelley I had read, while the strong colours made me half remember studio conversations, words of Wilson, or of Potter perhaps, praise of the primary colours, heard, it may be, as I sat over my toys or a child's story-book. One picture looked familiar, and suddenly I remembered it had hung in our house for years. It was Potter's *Field Mouse.* I had learned to think in the midst of the last phase of Pre-Raphaelitism and now I had come to Pre-Raphaelitism again and rediscovered my earliest thought. I murmured to myself, 'The only painting of modern England that could give pleasure to a child, the only painting that would seem as moving as *The Pilgrim's Progress* or Hans Andersen.' 'Am I growing old,' I thought, 'like the woman in Balzac, the rich bourgeois' ambitious wife, who could not keep, when old age came upon her, from repeating the jokes of the concierge's lodge where she had been born and bred; or is it because of some change in the weather that I find beauty everywhere, even in Burne-Jones's *King Cophetua*, one of his later pictures, and find it without shame?' I have had like admiration many times in the last twenty years, for I have always loved those pictures where I meet persons associated with the poems or the religious ideas that have most moved me; but never since my boyhood have I had it without shame, without the certainty that I would hear the cock crow presently. I remembered that as a young man I had read in Schopenhauer that no man—so unworthy a thing is life seen with unbesotted eyes—would live another's life, and had thought I would be content to paint, like Burne-Jones and Morris under Rossetti's rule, the Union at Oxford, to set up there the traditional images most moving to young men while the adventure of uncommitted life can still change all to romance, even though I should know that what I painted must fade from the walls.

II

Thereon I ask myself if my conception of my own art is altering, if there, too, I praise what I once derided. When I began to write I avowed for my principles those of Arthur Hallam in his essay upon Tennyson. Tennyson, who had written but his early poems when Hallam wrote, was an example of the school of Keats and Shelley, and Keats and Shelley, unlike Wordsworth, intermixed into their poetry no elements from the general thought, but wrote out of the impression made by the world upon their delicate senses. They were of the aesthetic school—was he the inventor of the name?—and could not be popular because their readers could not understand them without attaining to a like delicacy of sensation and so must needs turn from them to Wordsworth or another, who condescended to moral maxims, or some received philosophy, a multitude of things that even common sense could understand. Wordsworth had not less genius than the others—even Hallam allowed his genius; we are not told that Mary of Galilee was more beautiful than the more popular Mary; but certainly we might consider Wordsworth a little disreputable.

I developed these principles to the rejection of all detailed description, that I might not steal the painter's business, and indeed I was always discovering some art or science that I might be rid of: and I found encouragement by noticing all round me painters[1] who were ridding their pictures, and indeed their minds, of literature. Yet those delighted senses, when I had got from them all that I could, left me discontented. Impressions that needed so elaborate a record did not seem like the handiwork of those careless old writers one imagines squabbling over a mistress, or riding on a journey, or drinking round a tavern fire, brisk and active men. Crashaw could hymn Saint Teresa in the most impersonal of ecstasies and seem no sedentary man out of reach of common sympathy, no disembodied mind, and yet in his day the life that appeared most rich and stirring was already half forgotten with Villon and Dante.

---

[1] This thought, which seemed a discovery, was old enough. Balzac derides in a story a certain Pierre Grassou who attained an immense popularity by painting a Chouan rebel going to his death. (1924)

This difficulty was often in my mind, but I put it aside, for the new formula was a good switch while the roads were beset with geese; it set us free from politics, theology, science, all that zeal and eloquence Swinburne and Tennyson found so intoxicating after the passion of their youth had sunk, free from the conventional nobility borne hither from ancient Rome in the galley that carried academic form to vex the painters. Among the little group of poets that met at the Cheshire Cheese I alone loved criticism of Arthur Hallam's sort, with a shamefaced love—criticism founded upon general ideas was itself an impurity—and perhaps I alone knew Hallam's essay, but all silently obeyed a canon that had become powerful for all the arts since Whistler, in the confidence of his American *naïveté*, had told everybody that Japanese painting had no literary ideas. Yet all the while envious of the centuries before the Renaissance, before the coming of our intellectual class with its separate interests, I filled my imagination with the popular beliefs of Ireland, gathering them up among forgotten novelists in the British Museum or in Sligo cottages. I sought some symbolic language reaching far into the past and associated with familiar names and conspicuous hills that I might not be alone amid the obscure impressions of the senses, and I wrote essays recommending my friends to paint on chapel walls the Mother of God flying with Saint Joseph into Egypt along some Connacht road, a Connemara shawl about her head, or mourned the richness or reality lost to Shelley's *Prometheus Unbound* because he had not discovered in England or in Ireland his Caucasus.

I notice like contradictions among my friends who are still convinced that art should not be 'complicated by ideas' while picturing Saint Brandan in stained glass for a Connemara chapel, and even among those exuberant young men who make designs for a Phallic Temple, but consider Augustus John lost amid literature.

III

But, after all, could we clear the matter up we might save some hours from sterile discussion. The arts are very conservative and have a great respect for those wanderers who still stitch into their carpets among the Mongolian plains religious symbols so old they have not even a meaning. It cannot be they would lessen an association with one another and with religion that gave them authority among ancient peoples. They are not radicals, and if they deny themselves to any it can only be to the *nouveau riche*, and if they have grown rebellious it can only be against something that is modern, something that is not simple.

I think that before the religious change that followed on the Renaissance men were greatly preoccupied with their sins, and that to-day they are troubled by other men's sins, and that this trouble has created a moral enthusiasm so full of illusion that art, knowing itself for sanctity's scapegrace brother, cannot be of the party. We have but held to our ancient Church, where there is an altar and no pulpit, and founded, the guide-book tells us, upon the ruins of the temple of Jupiter Ammon, and turned away from the too great vigour of those who, living for mutual improvement, have a pulpit and no altar. We fear that a novel enthusiasm might make us forget the little round of poetical duties and imitations—humble genuflexions and circumambulations as it were—that does not unseat the mind's natural impulse, and seems always but half-conscious, almost bodily.

Painting had to free itself from a classicalism that denied the senses, a domesticity that denied the passions, and poetry from a demagogic system of morals which destroyed the humility, the daily dying of the imagination in the presence of beauty. A soul shaken by the spectacle of its sins, or discovered by the Divine Vision in tragic delight, must offer to the love that cannot love but to infinity, a goal unique and unshared; while a soul busied with others' sins is soon melted to some shape of vulgar pride. What can I offer to God but the ghost that must return undisfeatured to the hands that have not made the same thing twice, but what would I have of others but that they do some expected thing, reverence my plans, be in some way demure and reliable? The turning of Rossetti to religious themes, his dislike of Wordsworth, were but the one impulse, for he more than any other was in reaction against the period of philanthropy and reform that created the pedantic composure of Wordsworth, the rhetoric of Swinburne, the passionless sentiment of Tennyson. The saint does not claim to be a good example, hardly even to tell men what to do, for is he not the chief of sinners, and of how little can he be certain whether in the night of the soul or lost in the sweetness coming after? Nor can that composure of the moralists be dear to one who has heard the commandment, that is for the saint and his brother the poet alike, 'Make excess ever more abundantly excessive', even were it possible to one shaken and trembling from his daily struggle.

IV

We knew that system of popular instruction was incompatible with our hopes, but we did not know how to refute it and so turned away from all ideas. We would not even permit ideas, so greatly had we come to distrust them, to leave their impressions upon our senses. Yet works of art are always begotten by previous works of art, and every master-piece becomes the Abraham of a chosen people. When we delight in a spring day there mixes, perhaps, with our personal emotion an emotion Chaucer found in Guillaume de Lorris, who had it from the poetry of Provence; we celebrate our draughty May with an enthusiasm made ripe by more meridian suns; and all our art has its image in the Mass that would lack authority were it not descended from savage ceremonies taught amid what perils and by what spirits to naked savages. The old images, the old emotions, awakened again to overwhelming life, like the gods Heine tells of, by the belief and passion of some new soul, are the only masterpieces. The resolution to stand alone, to owe nothing to the past, when it is not mere sense of property, the greed and pride of the counting-house, is the result of that individualism of the Renaissance which had done its work when it gave us personal freedom. The soul which may not obscure or change its form can yet receive those passions and symbols of antiquity, certain they are too old to be bullies, too well-mannered not to respect the rights of others.

Nor had we better warrant to separate one art from another, for there has been no age before our own wherein the arts have been other than a single authority, a Holy Church of Romance, the might of all lying behind all, a circle of cliffs, a wilderness where every cry has its echoes. Why should a man cease to be a scholar, a believer, a ritualist before he begin to paint or rhyme or to compose music, or why if he have a strong head should he put away any means of power?

V

Yet it is plain that the casting out of ideas was the more natural, misunderstanding though it was, because it had come to matter very little. The manner of painting had changed, and we were interested in the fall of drapery and the play of light without concerning ourselves with the meaning, the emotion of the figure itself. How many successful portrait-painters gave their sitters the same attention, the same interest they might have given to a ginger-beer bottle and an apple? and in our poems an absorption in fragmentary sensuous beauty or detachable ideas had deprived us of the power to mould vast material into a single image. What long modern poem equals the old poems in architectural unity, in symbolic importance? *The Revolt of Islam, The Excursion, Gebir, Idylls of the King,* even perhaps *The Ring and the Book,* which fills me with so much admiring astonishment that my judgment sleeps, are remembered for some occasional passage, some moment which gains little from the context. Until very lately even the short poems which contained as clearly as an Elizabethan lyric the impression of a single idea seemed accidental, so much the rule were the 'Faustines' and 'Dolores' where the verses might be arranged in any order, like shot poured out of a bag. Arnold when he withdrew his *Empedocles on Etna,* though one had been sorry to lose so much lyrical beauty for ever, showed himself a great critic by his reasons, but his *Sohrab and Rustum* proves that the unity he imagined was a classical imitation and not an organic thing, not the flow of flesh under the impulse of passionate thought.

Those poets with whom I feel myself in sympathy have tried to give to little poems the spontaneity of a gesture or of some casual emotional phrase. Meanwhile it remains for some greater time, living once more in passionate reverie, to create a *King Lear,* a *Divine Comedy,* vast worlds moulded by their own weight like drops of water.

In the visual arts, indeed, 'the fall of man into his own circumference' seems at an end, and when I look at the photograph of a picture by Gauguin, which hangs over my break-fast-table, the spectacle of tranquil Polynesian girls crowned with lilies gives me, I do not know why, religious ideas. Our appreciations of the older schools are changing too, becoming simpler, and when we take pleasure in some Chinese painting of an old man meditating upon a mountain path, we share his meditation, without forgetting the beautiful intricate pattern of the lines like those we have seen under our eyelids as we fell asleep; nor do the Bride and Bridegroom of Rajput painting, sleeping upon a housetop, or wakening when out of the still water the swans fly upward at the dawn, seem the less well painted because they remind us of many poems. We are becoming interested in expression in its first phase of energy, when all the arts play like children about the one chimney, and turbulent innocence can yet amuse those brisk and active men who have paid us so little attention of recent years. Shall we be rid of the pride of intellect, of sedentary meditation, of emotion that leaves us when the book is closed or the picture seen no more; and live amid the thoughts that can go with us by steamboat and railway as once upon horseback, or camel-back, rediscovering, by our reintegration of the mind, our more profound Pre-Raphaelitism, the old abounding, nonchalant reverie?

1913

Wyndham Lewis, *Design for Timon*, watercolor, 16 ⁵/₈ x 10 ³/₄ in. Wadsworth Atheneum, Hartford, Connecticut: Ella Gallup Sumner and Mary Catlin Sumner Collection.

Vorticism

E Z R A   P O U N D

*In a letter to Harriet Monroe written the same month he wrote the
following essay, Pound said his problem was "to keep alive a certain
group of advancing poets, to set the arts in their rightful place as the
acknowledged guide and lamp of civilization." Two months later, in
a letter to John Quinn, he found the answer to his dilemma: "A
great age in painting, a renaissance in the arts, comes when there
are a few patrons who back their own flair and who buy from
unrecognized men." By his own definition, Pound was the "patron"
of modernism. In his view, painting, sculpture, music, and poetry
were all parts of one ideogram it was his career to trace. He set
about, too, to champion the avant-garde not only by promoting it
with the flair of his intelligence and slashing style but also by hold-
ing it and its audience to high standards. He began writing art
criticism as early as 1906 and in his later years kept art as a model
or touchstone in essays, letters, and in* The Cantos. *Most of his art
criticism was written ("for the rent") during his years in London.
He often wrote under the name B. H. Dias, a pseudonym that al-
lowed him to begin one review: "Wyndham Lewis' portrait of Ezra
Pound rises with the dignity of a classic* stele *to the god of gardens
amid the bundles of market-garden produce at the Goupil Gallery
'salon.'" He scorned any sort of top-dressing in art—pictures that
were "made for museums," or the merely "rhetorical" gestures he*

Reprinted with permission of New Directions in New York and Faber & Faber in
London from *Ezra Pound and the Visual Arts,* ed. Harriet Zinnes (1980), 5–10.
Copyright © 1980 by the Ezra Pound Literary Property Trust.

found in Renoir and Rodin. He was drawn to primary sources of energy, and to genius, which he recognized as "an inevitable swiftness and rightness." Sometimes a cause or movement—like vorticism—was shorthand for this sense of genius, but it was more often individual achievement, or embodied genius, that drew out his praise. Henri Gaudier-Brzeska, Wyndham Lewis, Jacob Epstein, Constantin Brancusi—these artists had what he called power in their elbows.

THE NEW AGE permits one to express beliefs which are in direct opposition to those held by the editing staff. In this, *The New Age* sets a most commendable example to certain other periodicals which not only demand that all writers in their columns shall turn themselves into a weak and puling copy of the editorial board, but even try to damage one's income if one ventures to express contrary beliefs in the columns of other papers.

There is perhaps no more authentic sign of the senility of a certain generation of publicists (now, thank heaven, gradually fading from the world) than their abject terror in the face of motive ideas. An age may be said to be decadent, or a generation may be said to be in a state of prone senility, when its creative minds are dead and when its survivors maintain a mental dignity—to wit, the dignity or stationariness of a corpse in its cerements. Excess or even absinthe is not the sure sign of decadence. If a man is capable of creative, or even of mobile, thought he will not go in terror of other men so endowed. He will not call for an inquisition or even a persecution of other men who happen to think something which he has not yet thought, or of which he may not yet have happened to hear.

The public divides itself into sections according to temper and alertness; it may think with living London, or with moribund London, or with Chicago, or Boston, or even with New Zealand; and behind all these there are possibly people who think on a level with Dublin, antiquarians, of course, and students of the previous age. For example, Sir Hugh Lane tried to give Dublin a collection of pictures, Degas, Corot and Manet, and they called him a charlatan and cried out for real pictures "like the lovely paintings which we see reproduced in our city art shops." I have even seen a paper from Belfast which brands J. M. Synge as a "decadent." Is such a country fit for Home Rule? I ask as the merest outsider having not the slightest interest in the question. I have met here in London two men still believing in Watts, and I suppose anything is possible—any form of atavism that you may be willing to name.

I suppose any new development or even any change in any art has to be pushed down the public throat with a ramrod. The public has always squealed. A public which has gushed over the sentimentalities of Rodin adorns Epstein's work with black butterflies, à cause de pudeur. The wickedest and most dashing publisher of "the nineties," of the "vicious, disreputable nineties," demands that our antiseptic works be submitted to ladylike censorship. And the papers in Trieste rejoice that futurism is a thing of the past, that a new god is come to deliver them. Such is the state of the world at the beginning of A.D. 1915.

The political world is confronted with a great war, a species of insanity. The art world is confronted with a species of quiet and sober sanity called Vorticism, which I am for the third or fourth time called upon to define, quietly, lucidly, with precision.

Vorticism is the use of, or the belief in the use of, THE PRIMARY PIGMENT, straight through all of the arts.

If you are a cubist, or an expressionist, or an imagist, you may believe in one thing for painting and a very different thing for poetry. You may talk about volumes, or about colour that "moves in," or about a certain form of verse, without having a correlated aesthetic which carries you through all of the arts. Vorticism means that one is interested in the creative faculty as opposed to the mimetic. We believe that it is harder to make than to copy. We believe in maximum efficiency, and we go to a work of art not for tallow candles or cheese, but for something which we cannot get anywhere else. We go to a particular art for something which we cannot get in any other art. If we want form and colour we go to a painting, or we make a painting. If we want form without colour and in two dimensions, we want drawing or etching. If we want form in three dimensions, we want sculpture. If we want an image or a procession of images, we want poetry. If we want pure sound, we want music.

These different desires are not one and the same. They are divers desires and they demand divers sorts of satisfaction. The more intense the individual life, the more vivid are the divers desires of that life. The more alive and vital the mind, the less will it be content with dilutations; with diluted forms of satisfaction.

I might put it differently. I might say, "I like a man who goes the whole hog." If he wants one sort of, say, "philosophy," he goes to Spinoza. If he wants another sort of "philosophy," he goes to Swedenborg. But nothing under heaven will induce him to have recourse to the messy sort of author who tries to mix up these two incompatible sorts of thought, and who produces only a muddle. Art deals with certitude. There is no "certitude" about a thing which is pretending to be something else.

A painting is an arrangement of colour patches on a canvas, or on some other substance. It is a good or bad painting according as these colour-patches are well or ill arranged. After that it can be whatever it likes. It can represent the Blessed Virgin, or Jack Johnson, or it need not represent at all, it can be. These things are a matter of taste. A man may follow his whim in these matters without the least harm to his art sense, so long as he remembers that it is merely his whim and that it is not a matter of "art criticism" or of "aesthetics." When a man prefers a Blessed Virgin by Watts to a portrait of a nasty pawnbroker by Rembrandt, one ceases to consider him as a person seriously interested in painting. There is nothing very new about that. When a man begins to be more interested in the "arrangement" than in the dead matter arranged, then he begins "to have an eye for" the difference between the good, the bad and the mediocre in Chinese painting. His remarks on Byzantine, and Japanese, and on ultra-modern painting begin to be interesting and intelligible. You do not demand of a mountain or a tree that it shall be like something; you do not demand that "natural beauty" be limited to mean only a few freaks of nature, cliffs looking like faces, etc. The worst symbolist of my acquaintance—that is to say, the most fervent admirer of Watts' pictures—has said to me more than once, quoting Nietzsche most inadvertently, "The artist is part of nature, therefore he never imitates nature." That text serves very well for my side of the case. Is a man capable of admiring a picture on the same terms as he admires a mountain? The picture will never become the mountain. It will never have the mountain's perpetual variety. The photograph will reproduce the mountain's contour with greater exactitude. Let us say that a few people choose to admire the picture on more or less the same terms as those on which they admire the mountain. Then what do I mean by "forms well organised"?

An organisation of forms expresses a confluence of forces. These forces may be the "love of God," the "life-force," emotions, passions, what you will. For example: if you clap a strong magnet beneath a plateful of iron filings, the energies of the magnet will proceed to organise form. It is only by applying a particular and suitable force that you can bring order and vitality and thence beauty into a plate of iron filings, which are otherwise as "ugly" as anything under heaven. The design in the magnetised iron filings expresses a confluence of energy. It is not "meaningless" or "inexpressive."

There are, of course, various sorts or various subdivisions of energy. They are all capable of expressing themselves in "an organisation of form." I saw, some months since, the "automatic" paintings of Miss Florence Seth. They were quite charming. They were the best automatic paintings I have seen. "Automatic painting" means paintings done by people who begin to paint without preconception, who believe, or at least assert, that the painting is done without volition on their part, that their hands are guided by "spirits," or by some mysterious agency over which they have little or no control. "Will and consciousness are our vortex." The friend who sent me to see Miss Seth's painting did me a favour, but he was very much in the wrong if he thought my interest was aroused because Miss Seth's painting was vorticist.

Miss Seth's painting was quite beautiful. It was indeed much finer than her earlier mimetic work. It had richness of colour, it had the surety of articulation which one finds in leaves and in viscera. There was in it also an unconscious use of certain well-known symbols, often very beautifully disguised with elaborate detail. Often a symbol appeared only in a fragment, wholly unrecognisable in some pictures, but capable of making itself understood by comparison with other fragments of itself appearing in other pictures. Miss Seth had begun with painting obviously Christian symbols, doves, etc. She had gone on to paint less obvious symbols, of which she had no explanation. She had no theories about the work, save that it was in some way mediumistic. In her work, as in other "automatic" paintings which I have seen, the structure was similar to the structure of leaves and viscera. It was, that is to say, exclusively *organic*. It is not surprising that the human mind in a state of lassitude or passivity should take on again the faculties of the unconscious or sub-human energies or minds of nature; that the momentarily dominant atom of personality should, that is to say, retake the pattern-making faculty which lies in the flower-seed or in the grain or in the animal cell.

This is not vorticism. They say that an infant six weeks old is both aquatic and arboreal, that it can both swim and hang from a small branch by its fist, and that by the age of six months it has lost these faculties. I do not know whether or no this is true. It is a scientist's report, I have never tried it on a six-weeks-old infant. If it is so, we will say that instinct "revives" or that "memory throws back," or something of that sort. The same phrase would apply to the pattern-making instinct revived in somnolents or in mediumistic persons.

Note especially that their paintings have only organic structures, that their forms are the forms already familiar to us in sub-human nature. Their work is interesting as a psychological problem, not as creation. I give it, however, along with my paragraph on iron filings, as an example of energy expressing itself in pattern.

We do not enjoy an arrangement of "forms and colours" because it is a thing isolated in nature. Nothing is isolated in nature. This organisation of form and colour is "expression"; just as a musical arrangement of notes by Mozart is expression. The vorticist is expressing his complex consciousness. He is not like the iron filings, expressing electrical magnetism; not like the automatist, expressing a state of cell-memory, a vegetable or visceral energy. Not, however, that one despises vegetable energy or wishes to adorn the rose or the cyclamen, which are vegetable energies expressed in form. One, as a human being, cannot pretend fully to express oneself unless one express instinct and intellect together. The softness and the ultimate failure of interest in automatic painting are caused by a complete lack of conscious intellect. Where does this bring us? It brings us to this: Vorticism is a legitimate expression of life.

My personal conviction is as follows: Time was when I began to be interested in "the beauties of nature." According to impressionism I began to see the colour of shadows, etc. It was very interesting. I noted refinements in colour. It was very interesting. Time was when I began to make something of light and shade. I began to see that if you were representing a man's face you would represent the side on which light shone by very different paint from that whereby you would express the side which rested in shadow. All these things were, and are, interesting. One is more alive for having these swift-passing, departmentalised interests in the flow of life about one. It is by swift apperceptions of this sort that one differentiates oneself from the brute world. To be civilised is to have swift apperception of the complicated life of today; it is to have a subtle and instantaneous perception of it, such as savages and wild animals have of the necessities and dangers of the forest. It is to be no less alive or vital than the savage. It is a different kind of aliveness.

And vorticism, especially that part of vorticism having to do with form—to wit, vorticist painting and sculpture—has brought me a new series of apperceptions. It has not brought them solely to me. I have my new and swift perceptions of forms, of possible form-motifs; I have a double or treble or tenfold set of stimulae in going from my home to Piccadilly. What was a dull row of houses is become a magazine of forms. There are new ways of seeing them. There are ways of seeing the shape of the sky as it juts down between the houses. The tangle of telegraph wires is conceivable not merely as a repetition of lines; one sees the shapes defined by the different branches of wire. The lumber yards, the sidings of railways cease to be dreary.

The musical conception of form, that is to say the understanding that you can use form as a musician uses sound, that you can select motives of form from the forms before you, that you can recombine and recolour them and "organise" them into new form—this conception, this state of mental activity, brings with it a great joy and refreshment. I do not wish to convert anyone. I simply say that a certain sort of pleasure is available to anyone who wants it. It is one of the simple pleasures of those who have no money to spend on joy-rides and on suppers at the Ritz.

This "musical conception of form" is more than post-impressionism. Manet took impressions of colour. They say Cézanne began taking "impressions of form." That is not the same thing as conceiving the forms about one as a source of "form-motifs," which motifs one can use later at one's pleasure in more highly developed compositions.

It is possible that this search for form-motif will lead us to some synthesis of western life comparable to the synthesis of oriental life which we find in Chinese and Japanese painting. This lies with the future. Perhaps there is some adumbration of it in Mr. Wadsworth's "Harbour of Flushing."

At any rate I have put down some of my reasons for believing in the vorticist painters and sculptors. I have at least in part explained why I believe in Mr. Wyndham Lewis; why I think him a more significant artist than Kandinsky (admitting that I have not yet seen enough of Kandinsky's work to use a verb stronger than "think"); why I think that Mr. Lewis' work will contain certain elements not to be found in Picasso, whom I regard as a great artist, but who has not yet expressed all that we mean by vorticism.

Note that I am not trying to destroy anyone's enjoyment of the Quattrocento, nor of the Victory of Samothrace, nor of any work of art which is approximately the best of its kind. I state that there is a new gamut of artistic enjoyments and satisfactions; that vorticist painting is not meaningless; and that anyone who cares to may enjoy it.

1915

Henri Matisse, *Blue Nude,* oil on canvas, 36 $^1/_4$ x 55 $^1/_4$ in. The Baltimore
Museum of Art: The Cone Collection, formed by Dr. Claribel Cone and
Miss Etta Cone of Baltimore, Maryland.

A *Matisse* and
Painting in the American Grain

WILLIAM CARLOS WILLIAMS

"An American Place": Alfred Stieglitz named his famous gallery af-
ter an enthusiastic reading of In the American Grain. *Williams*
later said of Stieglitz: "The effect of his life and work has been to
bend together and fuse, against whatever resistance, the split forces
of the two necessary cultural groups: (1) the local effort, well under-
stood in defined detail and (2) the forces from the outside." The fol-
lowing two essays, written at either end of his career, echo that trib-
ute and represent the variety and convergence of Williams's interests.
A friend to painters (Hartley, Demuth, Marin, Sheeler), he learned
from them. The arrangement of words was, in his view, analogous
to the ways pigment is laid on, and French painting showed a new
way. The object of modern painting, he insisted, was not to escape
representation but "to escape triteness, the stupidity of a loose
verisimilitude." He recognized in the new painters, in Matisse par-
ticularly, "a technique along with a stress of experience (the under-
standing, intelligence) that shall not at least be false thought, stale
emotion and lying pretense (of delineation)." But at the same time
Williams claimed that, however avant-garde, the new French paint-
ing was "a local tradition." That is to say, the poet's interest in the
radical was also a claim on the indigenous. In 1954 Art News
asked Williams to respond to the large Garbisch collection of Ameri-
can primitive paintings on exhibit at the National Gallery. For years

Williams had valued these paintings because they were "local" art, and the local—not to be confused with any narrow sense of parochialism—is "the freeing agency to all thought." The very naiveté of these paintings meant they were subject neither to European traditions nor to homegrown academicism. They were for him, one suspects, documents of the American character, and he was attracted to them as he had been, thirty years before, to the "original records" from which he made In the American Grain. *In that work he most strongly calls on the American to come to an "understanding of the ground, his ground,* the ground, *the only ground that he knows, that which is under his feet." And in his essay "French Painting" he spoke of that same ground as a culture: the artist paints or writes with his "whole body (not his eyes), his body, his mind, his memory, his place: himself—that is what he sees—And in America—escape it he cannot—it is an American tree."*

A Matisse

ON THE FRENCH grass, in that room on Fifth Ave., lay that woman who had never seen my own poor land. The dust and noise of Paris had fallen from her with the dress and underwear and shoes and stockings which she had just put aside to lie bathing in the sun. So too she lay in the sunlight of the man's easy attention. His eye and the sun had made day over her. She gave herself to them both for there was nothing to be told. Nothing is to be told to the sun at noonday. A violet clump before her belly mentioned that it was spring. A locomotive could be heard whistling beyond the hill. There was nothing to be told. Her body was neither classic nor whatever it might be supposed. There she lay and her curving torso and thighs were close upon the grass and violets.

So he painted her. The sun had entered his head in the color of sprays of flaming palm leaves. They had been walking for an hour or so after leaving the train. They were hot. She had chosen the place to rest and he had painted her resting, with interest in the place she had chosen.

It had been a lovely day in the air. —What pleasant women are these girls of ours! When they have worn clothes and take them off it is with an effect of having performed a small duty. They return to the sun with a gesture of accomplishment. —Here she lay in this spot today not like Diana or Aphrodite but with better proof than they of regard for the place she was in. She rested and he painted her.

It was the first of summer. Bare as was his mind of interest in anything save the fullness of his knowledge, into which her simple body entered as into the eye of the sun himself, so he painted her. So she came to America.

No man in my country has seen a woman naked and painted her as if he knew anything except that she was naked. No woman in my country is naked except at night.

In the french sun, on the french grass in a room on Fifth Ave., a french girl lies and smiles at the sun without seeing us.

1921

Anonymous (American), *The Cat*, oil on canvas, 16 x 20 in. National Gallery of Art, Washington: Gift of Edgar William and Bernice Chrysler Garbisch.

Painting in the American Grain

HOW *NOT* TO begin an article on American primitives in painting: You don't begin speaking about Giotto and Fra Angelico or even Bosch, but of a cat with a bird in his mouth—a cat with a terrifying enormous head, enough to frighten birds, or of a six-foot Indian in a yellow breech clout. . . . Washington, apart from its official aspect, is a quiet, old-fashioned city, fit home, the only fit home for a collection of primitives such as this that smacks so of the American past.

As you enter the gallery—there are a total of 109 paintings of all sizes—the first thing that hits your eye is the immediacy of the scene, I should say the color! They were putting down what they had to put down, what they saw before them. They had reds to use and greens and flesh tints and browns and blues with which they wanted to surround themselves in shapes which they recognized. A beloved infant had died. If only they could bring it to life again! An artist was employed to paint a counterfeit presentment of the scene as the child stood in the garden by a tombstone near a weeping willow and a cat with arched back. It would bring comfort to the bereaved parents. That is how the artist painted it.

No matter what the skill or the lack of it, someone, somewhere in Pennsylvania—all trace of the painters that we may identify them has been lost—wanted on his walls a picture of Adam and Eve in the garden before the Fall. There is no serpent here, no sign even of God, just the garden and its bountiful blessings. Wild beasts are at Adam's feet or at least one panther is there. The sky is luminous, this was not painted in a potato cellar. The vegetation is luxuriant, huge grape clusters hang from the trees and there at their ease sit together our primordial parents, naked and unashamed, bathed in sunlight. Who shall say the plenty of the New World so evident about them was not the true model that has been recorded?

A head, a head of a young woman in its title designated as "Blue Eyes," caught my eye at once because of the simplicity and convincing dignity of the profile. The hair was black and chopped off short to hang straight at the neck line. The complexion was clear, there was a faint smile to the lips, the look, off to the right, was direct, but the feature of the portrait was for me not the blue eyes but the enormous round chin perfectly in proportion that dominated the face and the whole picture. No one can say that chin was not real and that it was put down to be anything else. It is a world, not a chin that is depicted.

A record, something to stand against, a shield for their protection, the savage world with which they were surrounded; color, color that ran, mostly, to the very edge of the canvas as if they were afraid that something would be left out, covered the whole of their surfaces. One of my first views of the show was of the "Sisters in Red." Both my wife and I were amazed. They were talking to us. The older girl, not more than six, had dark hair and, looking at us directly, was the most serious, even slightly annoyed. The younger sister, holding a flower basket, a blond with wavy hair, wore an alert and daring expression of complete self-assurance, the mark of a typical second-child complex, which made her to me a living individual. I fell in love with her. The brilliant red dresses from which decently projected the snow-white pantalettes, ironed no doubt that morning, and dainty slippers completed the arresting picture.

A view of the burning of Charlestown by the British, with Boston untouched across the harbor, once again emphasized the importance for these people of the recording of events. Titles in this case were superimposed upon the canvas, Charlestown on one side and Boston on the other and between them, incongruously, Bunker Hill. Smoke was billowing to a sky already filled with masses of round clouds that rose above the flame and smoke in the distance.

Intimate scenes of rural life, a scene showing a side view of four cows and two horses, the barn and beyond that a house, a clapboard house, painted white. An obvious pride of possession and of the care which are owed such things.

There is a different pride in a grouping that fills one canvas, again to the very edge, called "The Plantation." Apparently it is near the sea, for a full-rigged ship occupies the foreground. Above rises a hill. The theme is formally treated and not without some skill. The perspective is elementary. Clusters of grapes larger than the ship's sails come in from the right meeting two trees, one on each side, that reach the sky framing the plantation house, with its garden, in the center distance toward the picture's upper edge. Birds are flying about, and down the hill nearer the foreground, linked by paths, are the farm buildings, and at the water's edge a warehouse.

A portrait of a woman past middle life attracted me by the hollow-cheeked majesty of its pose. A plain bonnet from which the two white strings lie symmetrically on either side of her flat breast completes the whole. There is a single tree, formally pruned and cut off only partially shown above her left shoulder. There is a companion portrait of her husband. They are serious individuals; the principal interest for me, apart from the impression they give of pride and reticence, is the colors the unknown artist has used. Nowhere except in El Greco have I seen green so used in the shadows about the face.

31

You will find here another of Hicks's "Peaceable Kingdom," but that hardly needs further comment. The same for "Penn's Treaty with the Indians."

Henry James said it is a complex thing to be an American. Unconscious of such an analysis of their situation, these artists as well as their sitters reacted to it nevertheless directly. They scarcely knew why they yearned for the things they desired, but to get them they strained every nerve.

The style of all these paintings is direct. Purposeful. The artist was called upon to put down a presence that the man or woman for whom the picture was painted wanted to see and remember, the world otherwise was for the moment put aside. That dictated the realist details of the situation and also what was to be excluded.

The kind of people that called for the paintings determined their quality. They demanded something to stand against the crudeness that surrounded them. As Wallace Stevens put it:

> I placed a jar in Tennessee,
> And round it was, upon a hill.
> It made the slovenly wilderness
> Surround that hill.
>
> The wilderness rose up to it,
> And sprawled around, no longer wild.

These were talented, creative painters. They had to be. They had no one to copy from. They were free as the wind, limited only by their technical abilities and driven by the demands of their clients. The very difficulties, technical difficulties, they had to face in getting their images down only added to the intensity of their efforts and to the directness of the results. It gave them a style of their own, as a group they had a realistic style, direct and practical as Benjamin Franklin. Nothing was to daunt them.

The circumstances surrounding the painting of Abraham Clark and his children, 1820, are known. Mr. Clark had just lost his beloved wife. He had gone into his garden with his six small children to read for them from the Bible. There he instructed the artist to paint him with the remainder of his family about him. The father, in profile, his thumb in the Bible no doubt at the passage from which he had been reading, sat to the right under the trees. The boys closely grouped, the baby on the knee of the oldest bareheaded before him. They all look alike, an obvious family. All are serious as befits the occasion. One leans his elbow against the tree. Their colorful faces stand out, no doubt in the clear light of the Resurrection, upon the forested and carefully painted background. The fifth son carries a pet hen in his arm. We are deeply moved by the intimacy.

Across the room is a large portrait of a young woman, Catalynje Post, 1730, wearing a flowered apron. She has a white lace cap on her head. Her arms are bare halfway to the wrist. She wears a low-necked dress and a necklace of pearls. Her hands, crudely painted, are placed one at the waist upon the hem of the colored apron, the other at the throat playing with an ornament which her fingers find there. A four-petaled flower and some carefully placed roses are seen in the background. But the feature of the ensemble is the slippered feet, standing at right angles before the eye; they have high heels and pointed toes and were no doubt the pride of their possessor. The artist had difficulty with the nose, which is presented full face or almost full face; his struggle to master it has not prevented him however from presenting an engaging and realistic portrait of a young woman.

There are still lifes which I wish there were room to comment upon. Fruit, in one case a watermelon with its red flesh, attracts the eye and the palate. One group symmetrically arranged on an oblong table, recognizably Shaker, particularly fascinated me. Curtains hang, always symmetrically, across the top. At either side are plates, with fruit knives. A bowl, it might be that of which Wallace Stevens speaks, stands in the exact center of the picture making of it an obvious decoration, with melons, grapes, apples, perhaps an orange, peaches and pears.

It was the intensity of their vision coupled with their isolation in the wilderness, that caused them one and all to place and have placed on the canvas veritable capsules, surrounded by a line of color, to hold them off from a world which was most about them. They were eminently objective, their paintings remained always things. They drew a line and the more clearly that line was drawn, the more vividly, the better. Color is light. Color is what most distinguishes the artist, color was what these people wanted to brighten the walls of their houses, color to the last inch of the canvas.

It was so with the portrait painted in 1800 of the Sargent family, artist unknown, the gayest and one of the largest pictures in the exhibition. It is the portrait of a cocky little man, in an enormous—to make him look tall—beaver hat (you can't tell me that the artist was not completely wise to the situation), surrounded by his wife and little daughters in white and flouncy dresses. The wife is sitting, sideface, with a new baby in her arms. The room is suffused with light. A toy spaniel frisks joyfully upon the hooked rug, the canaries singing—at least one of them is—in their cages between the pictures on the gaily papered walls. The paneled door is open. Every corner of the painting is distinct and bathed in light. It is a picture of a successful man.

There are in the same gallery two pictures, among the earliest of those shown, 1780, two large canvases of men heavily clad and in top hats, coursing hounds in the half-light of dawn and near sundown: the "Start" and "End of the Hunt." True to the facts the light in both cases is dim, which presented practical difficulties to the artist. These pictures are among the most crudely painted of those shown, but the record they present is filled for all that with something nostalgic and particularly moving. It brings to mind, as it was meant to do, another day which even then was fast vanishing. The artist was faced by the facts and the difficulties they made for him, but he faced them in the only way he knew, head on.

There is also a picture, undated, titled "The Coon Hunt." That, too, presented a scene which must have been familiar to the men of that time. It is moonlight. Half the party, carrying a lighted lantern, is approaching through a forest of partly felled trees; the quarry is on a high limb above their heads. The dogs are bounding into the air at the tree's base. The other half of the party is resting.

It is all a part of their lives that they had to see re-enacted before them to make it real that they could relive it in memory and re-enjoy it and it must be depicted by the artist so that it could be recognized—awkward as he may be.

In the middle gallery, apart from two Rembrandt-like portraits of an ageing burgher and his comfortable and smiling wife, among the best portraits in the exhibition, are two of the most interesting, imaginative pictures of all. I don't quite know what they meant, but suspect that the intention is to represent the travels of a man who has seen much of the world, has made money, perhaps retired from his labors and come home to rest and enjoy his memories. Each of the pictures presents, one overtly, a volcano in the distance, in the background a range of high mountains, perhaps the Andes, before a foreground crowded with all the appurtenances of a commercial civilization to the minutest detail, in the fullest light. The artist means to have you see into every part of his canvas; cities, factories, virtual palaces, railroad trains, alas, giving out smoke, rivers with waterfalls are prominently displayed. It is a pride of wealth which must have decorated a great house now all forgotten.

Many more such pictures showing the lives of the people of the period are displayed in this noteworthy collection. I must not forget to mention a picture labeled "Twenty-two Houses and a Church," depicting just that. The outlines of the buildings, covering several acres, are shown with their surrounding fences, painted white except in the foreground where a darker color is used—the only art displayed aside from the spacing of the buildings. Light, as in all the primitives, is everywhere. Not a single human figure is to be seen in the village, the buildings alone are recorded. The paintings have a definite style of their own which gives them a marked distinction as forthrightness, a candor and a practical skill not to be gainsaid and separate from European schools of painting with which they had not the time or the opportunity to acquaint themselves. So that, collectively, they represent not individual paintings so much as a yearning in the new country for some sort of an expression of the world which they represent.

It was a beginning world, a re-beginning world, and a hopeful one. The men, women and children who made it up were ignorant of the forces that governed it and what they had to face. They wanted to see themselves and be recorded against a surrounding wilderness of which they themselves were the only recognizable aspect. They were lonely. They were of the country, the only country which they or the artist knew and so represented.

This is a collection of paintings, lovingly assembled by a couple, Colonel and Mrs. Edgar William Garbisch, for their home on the eastern shore of Maryland. They found almost at once that the scope of what they had to choose from far exceeded their plans. They are called "American Primitives," the work of gifted artists whose names are largely lost in the shuffle of history.

1954

Robert Andrew Parker, *The Sleeping Dog*. Reproduced from *Arts*, April 1958.

Robert Andrew Parker

MARIANNE MOORE

In 1962 the Museum of Modern Art published a limited edition of
Eight Poems *by Marianne Moore, illustrated with drawings by
Robert Andrew Parker. The poems, reproduced in Moore's crabbed
handwriting, are among her best known and comprise a bestiary of
sorts, if we consider New York City as fabulous a creature as the
pangolin and plumet basilisk. The poems are—to use the same
words she applies to Parker's paintings in the following essay—
"masterpieces of construction plus texture, together with a passion for
accuracies of behavior." Among those poets who were her peers, it has
since emerged that Moore was the best critic of technique. Her stan-
dards for art—painting or poem—were humility (with which artists
arm themselves against the idea of being original), concentration
(which is a precise, persuasive ordering), and gusto. Of gusto, or
art's heightened natural force, she said, "It thrives on freedom, and
freedom in art, as in life, is the result of a discipline imposed by our-
selves." Moore had met Parker at an opening of his in the mid-fifties,
and she wrote this appreciation of his work for* Arts *magazine on the
occasion of an exhibition at the Roko Gallery in 1957. During their
collaboration on* Eight Poems, *Parker would visit Moore at her
house on West Ninth Street. "A very fragile place," Parker recalls,
"very fine, well-waxed, everything treated carefully and shown with
pride. She sent me a photograph of her desk once. On it were a leop-*

ard made of bone with painted spots, an elephant with his legs stretched out like a rocking chair's, an early engraving of a rhinoceros, some candles, a Russian icon, some brass boxes for stamps, some bells, a photo in a round frame of her father. I saw a picture of Francis Bacon's studio once, ankle-deep in torn paper, rags, crushed tubes, cigarette stubs, all sorts of filth. I thought how right and appropriate it was, all connected to his work. I felt the same way about Marianne Moore's house; everything had to do with her work—the quality, the attention to detail, the perfection of it all. And the smell of a particular furniture wax that indicates a rich, well-ordered home."

ROBERT ANDREW Parker is one of the most accurate and at the same time most unliteral of painters. He combines the mystical and the actual, working both in an abstract and in a realistic way. One or two of his paintings—a kind of private calligraphy—little upward-tending lines of actual writing like a school of fish—approximate a signature or family cipher.

His subjects include animals, persons—individually and en masse; trees, isolated and thickset; architecture, ships, troop movements, the sea; an ink drawing of an elm by a stone wall between meadows. His *Sleeping Dog* is the whole in essence: simplicity that is not the product of a simple mind but of the single eye—of rapt, genuine, undeprecatory love for the subject. The dog's pairs of legs curve out parallel, his solid cylinder of tail laid in the same direction, the eye seen as a diagonal slit in the nondescript pallor of whitish skin; they focus thought on treatment, not just on the dog. A cursive ease in the lines suggests a Rembrandt-like relish for the implement in hand; better yet, there is a look of emotion synonymous with susceptibility to happiness. Entwined in a

Beethoven-like Lost Grochen of rhythms, the chalk-gray and dead-grass tones of *Celery and Eggs, No. 2*, have resulted in something elate. The rigidly similar forms, in dark blue, of the audience in *Mario and the Magician* perfectly enunciate the suspense in the story, that one has never known how to define.

His Holiness Pope Pius XI's cloak of flawless violet, lined with ermine, against a black ground, is a triumph of texture, with tinges of lemon defining the four conjoined ridges of the Papal cap. In his satiric tendency and feeling for tones, Robert Parker resembles Charles Demuth; goes further; his wide swaths of paint with a big brush, and washes of clear color touched by some speck or splinter of paint—magenta or indigo—spreading just far enough, are surely in the same category with the Demuth cerise cyclamen and illustrations for Henry James. Robert Parker is not afraid of sweet-pea pink for the face of a soldier in khaki or for the dress of a lady with orange-gold hair. He has plenty of aplomb in his juxtaposings of rust, blood red, shrimp pink and vermilion. He is a specialist in marine blues, blue that could be mistaken for black, faded denim, sapphire-green and—thinking of *Oarsmen*—a Giotto-background blue or telephone-pole-insulator aquamarine. The design of the men and boat (*Oarsmen*) is integrated with the sea as seeds are set in a melon—the men braced by resistance to the mounding weight of deep water; the crisscross of the oars, uninterferingly superimposed on the vastness of a sea without sky. Payne's gray is another specialty of Mr. Parker's, as in the etched-over *Head of a Lady*, and in the fainter gray scene but explicit turrets and rig of the cruiser, *Admiral Hipper*.

Robert Parker is a fantasist of great precision in his studies of troop movements, seen in the *Invasion of an Island*, from the "Gyoncho" series—and in the balanced color pattern, dominated by white, of *East Yorkshire Yeomanry Disembarking from H.M.S. Cressy*—its caraway-seed multitudes pouring down the ship's sides in streams like sand in an hourglass, the sea choked with landing boats repeated to infinity. For this science of tea-leaf-like multitudes, there is an antecedent, if not counterpart, the swarming, seed-compact, arc- or circle-designed battle scenes in central Greece painted by Panaghiotes Zographos (1836–1840) for General Makryannis (reproductions in *Eikones*, April 1956). As multitudinous, although unaware of the Greek scenes, Mr. Parker manages to be epic without being archaic. His *October, 1917* is intensely his own. A platoon—sabers up—seen from the side, reduplicates identical-identical-identical boots that are as black as the men's tunics are flaming vermilion—with an effect resembling the leaves of a partly open book standing upright.

We have here masterpieces of construction plus texture, together with a passion for accuracies of behavior, as where, in the semi-frowning fixity of the eyes, in his portrait of Mrs. Parker, the artist has happily caught her unselfconscious naturalness. Warren Hennrich, moreover, has for his "Field Exercises" (*Wake* magazine, June 1945) the perfect illustration, in Robert Parker's *The Retreat from Caporetto*—a deadly uniformity of faces smothered by their own helmets:

> Harmonious men
> In harmonious masses
>
> Suspend at attention
> Bright, gleaming cuirasses,
>
> And then march away
> In monotonous classes.
>
> They follow the outline
> Of bordering grasses,

Anonymous men
In anonymous masses.

Mr. Parker has an eye: typified by the waiting horse, down on one haunch; by the flick-back of the hoof of a horse in motion, or rearing. *Hussar, 1900, South Africa,* charging with raised saber, down-darting tapered boot, and counterpoint of galloping hoofs, rivals *The Attack, No. 1*'s diversified unity. The excitement here is not all in sabers and furious action. Humor lurks in the beach scenes of distorted perspective; in the slightly over-curled-in claws and rumpled topknot of the *Fairy Shrimp* trundling along like a feather duster; in *Ugly Animal,* and *Another Dog.*

On no account should Mr. Parker's capacity for grandeur be underestimated—as embodied in the reverie at dusk aspect of *An Imaginary Monument to a Lancer, No 1,* and in two rather similar equestrian statues, grand without being accidentally ironic—the rider in one, silhouetted against a glare of magenta fire; the other, massive above an ascending burst of yellowish fire.

Robert Parker is thirty—tall, slender, and meditative—born in Norfolk, Virginia. He is unmistakably American, reliable—in the sense pleasing to Henry James. That his likings and proficiencies should range wide and that, so young, he should have depth and stature unvitiated by egotism, seems remarkable. He is in a sense like Sir Thomas Browne, for whom small things could be great things—someone exceptional—*vir amplissimus.*

1957

Paul Cézanne, *Still Life with Apples* (1895–98), oil on canvas, 27 x 36¹/₂ in.
Collection, The Museum of Modern Art, New York: Lillie P. Bliss Collec-
tion.

From *Introduction*
to These Paintings

D. H. LAWRENCE

"What am I doing, bursting into paint?" Lawrence wrote in 1929. "I am a writer, I ought to stick to ink. I have found my medium of expression: why, at the age of forty in 1926, should I suddenly want to try another?" Years earlier, before he had turned his hand to fiction, the young Lawrence had started both to write poems and to draw and copy paintings (by, among others, Pieter de Hooch and Piero di Cosimo). Those same first artistic stirrings he gave to Paul Morel in Sons and Lovers, *for whom they are at once a refuge and a passion. When Lawrence returned to painting—the return coincides with the years of his slow dying—it was, he said, "because it gave me a form of delight that words can never give. Perhaps the joy in words goes deeper and is for that reason more unconscious. The* conscious *delight is certainly strong in paint." Our interest in Lawrence's paintings is limited to our interest in the artist himself; the canvases are colorful but crude. He did not like high finish in any art—what he called the "would-be"—and he would have insisted he was making pictures, not painting. In a letter to Mark Gertler, he wrote: "One's got to get back to the live, really lovely phallic self, and phallic consciousness. I think I get a certain phallic beauty in my pictures too. I know they're rolling with faults, Sladeily considered. But there's something* there." *His poems and pictures*

kept an odd company toward the end of his life. The police had
intercepted the manuscript of Pansies *(his pun on* pensées*) that*
he had sent to his publisher from Italy, and a bowdlerized edition
appeared in 1929, minus the fourteen poems found to "contain
indecent matter." (Lawrence later had them *printed on Japanese*
vellum.) In that same year, during an exhibition of his pictures at
the Warren Gallery in London, the police raided and seized thirteen
pictures as "obscene." They also confiscated copies of the Mandrake
Press book that reproduced the paintings and for which the following
(truncated) essay was an introduction, "a good peppery foreword
against all that significant form piffle." *His idiosyncratic view of*
art is a gloss on his other views. As he once wrote, "The ordinary
novel would trace the history of the diamond—but I say 'Diamond,
what! This is carbon.'"

...VERY ELEMENTARY in man is his sexual and procreative being, and on his sexual and procreative being depend many of his deepest instincts and the flow of his intuition. A deep instinct of kinship joins men together, and the kinship of flesh-and-blood keeps the warm flow of intuitional awareness streaming between human beings. Our true awareness of one another is intuitional, not mental. Attraction between people is really instinctive and intuitional, not an affair of judgment. And in mutual attraction lies perhaps the deepest pleasure in life, mutual attraction which may make us "like" our travelling companion for the two or three hours we are together, then no more; or mutual attraction that may deepen to powerful love, and last a life-time.

The terror-horror element struck a blow at our feeling of physical communion. In fact, it almost killed it. We have become ideal beings, creatures that exist in idea, to one another, rather than flesh-and-blood kin. And with the collapse of the feeling of physical, flesh-and-blood kinship, and the substitution of our ideal, social or political oneness, came the failing of our intuitive awareness, and the great unease, the *nervousness* of mankind. We are *afraid* of the instincts. We are *afraid* of the intuition within us. We suppress the instincts, and we cut off our intuitional awareness from one another and from the world. The reason being some great shock to the procreative self. Now we know one another only as ideal or social or political entities, fleshless, bloodless, and cold, like Bernard Shaw's creatures. Intuitively we are dead to one another, we have all gone cold.

But by intuition alone can man *really* be aware of man, or of the living, substantial world. By intuition alone can man live and know either woman or world, and by intuition alone can he bring forth again images of magic awareness which we call art. In the past men brought forth images of magic awareness, and now it is the convention to admire these images. The convention says, for example, we must admire Botticelli or Giorgione, so Baedeker stars the pictures, and we admire them. But it is all a fake. Even those that get a thrill, even when they call it ecstasy, from these old pictures are only undergoing cerebral excitation. Their deeper responses, down in the intuitive and instinctive body, are not touched. They cannot be, because they are dead. A dead intuitive body stands there and gazes at the corpse of beauty: and usually it is completely and honestly bored. Sometimes it feels a mental coruscation which it calls an ecstasy or an aesthetic response.

Modern people, but particularly English and Americans, *cannot* feel anything with the whole imagination. They can see the living body of imagery as little as a blind man can see colour. The imaginative vision, which includes physical, intuitional perception, they *have not got.* Poor things, it is

47

dead in them. And they stand in front of a Botticelli Venus, which they know as conventionally "beautiful," much as a blind man might stand in front of a bunch of roses and pinks and monkey-musk, saying: "Oh, do tell me which is red; let me feel red! Now let me feel white! Oh, let me feel it! What is this I am feeling? Monkey-musk? Is it white? Oh, do you say it is yellow blotched with orange-brown? Oh, but I can't feel it! What *can* it be? Is white velvety, or just silky?"

So the poor blind man! Yet he may have an acute perception of alive beauty. Merely by touch and scent, his intuitions being alive, the blind man may have a genuine and soul-satisfying experience of imagery. But not pictorial images. These are for ever beyond him.

So those poor English and Americans in front of the Botticelli Venus. They stare so hard; they do so *want* to see. And their eyesight is perfect. But all they can see is a sort of nude woman on a sort of shell on a sort of pretty greenish water. As a rule they rather dislike the "unnaturalness" or "affectation" of it. If they are high-brows they may get a little self-conscious thrill of aesthetic excitement. But real imaginative awareness, which is so largely physical, is denied them *Ils n'ont pas de quoi,* as the Frenchman said of the angels, when asked if they made love in heaven.

Ah, the dear high-brows who gaze in a sort of ecstasy and get a correct mental thrill! Their poor high-brow bodies stand there as dead as dust-bins, and can no more feel the sway of complete imagery upon them than they can feel any other real sway. *Ils n'ont pas de quoi.* The instincts and the intuitions are so nearly dead in them, and they fear even the feeble remains. Their fear of the instincts and intuitions is even greater than that of the English Tommy who calls: "Eh, Jack! Come an' look at this girl standin' wi' no clothes on, an' two blokes spittin' at 'er." That is his vision of Botticelli's Venus. It is, for him, complete, for he is void of the image-seeing imagination. But at least he doesn't have to work up a cerebral excitation, as the high-brow does, who is really just as void.

All alike, cultured and uncultured, they are still dominated by that unnamed, yet overmastering dread and hate of the instincts deep in the body, dread of the strange intuitional awareness of the body, dread of anything but ideas, which *can't* contain bacteria. And the dread all works back to a dread of the procreative body, and is partly traceable to the shock of the awareness of syphilis.

The dread of the instincts included the dread of intuitional awareness. "Beauty is a snare"—"Beauty is but skin-deep"—"Handsome is as handsome does"—"Looks don't count"—"Don't judge by appearances"—if we only realized it, there are thousands of these vile proverbs which have been dinned into us for over two hundred years. They are all of them false. Beauty is not a snare, nor is it skin-deep, since it always involves a certain loveliness of modelling, and handsome doers are often ugly and objectionable people, and if you ignore the look of the thing you plaster England with slums and produce at last a state of spiritual depression that is suicidal, and if you don't judge by appearances, that is, if you can't trust the impression which things make on you, you are a fool. But all these base-born proverbs, born in the cash-box, hit direct against the intuitional consciousness. Naturally, man gets a great deal of his life's satisfaction from beauty, from a certain sensuous pleasure in the look of the thing. The old Englishman built his hut of a cottage with a childish joy in its appearance, purely intuitional and direct. The modern Englishman has a few borrowed ideas, simply doesn't know *what* to feel, and makes a silly mess of it: though perhaps he is improving, hopefully, in this field of architecture and house-building. The intuitional faculty, which alone relates us in direct awareness to physical things and substantial presences, is atrophied and dead, and we don't know *what* to feel. We know we ought to feel something, but what?—Oh, tell us what! And this is true of all nations, the French and Italians as much as the English. Look at new French suburbs! Go through the crockery and furniture departments in the *Dames de France* or any big shop. The blood in the body stands still, before such *crétin* ugliness. One has to decide that the modern bourgeois is a *crétin.*

This movement against the instincts and the intuition took on a moral tone in all countries. It started in hatred. Let us never forget that modern morality has its roots in hatred, a deep, evil hate of the instinctive, intuitional, procreative body. This hatred is made more virulent by fear, and an extra poison is added to the fear by unconscious horror of syphilis. And so we come to modern bourgeois consciousness, which turns upon the secret poles of fear and hate. That is the real pivot of all bourgeois consciousness in all countries: fear and hate of the instinctive, intuitional, procreative body in man or woman. But of course this fear and hate had to take on a righteous appearance, so it became moral, said that the instincts, intuitions and all the activities of the procreative body were evil, and promised a *reward* for their suppression. That is the great clue to bourgeois psychology: the reward business. It is screamingly obvious in Maria Edgeworth's tales, which must have done unspeakable damage to ordinary people. Be good, and you'll have money. Be wicked, and you'll be utterly penniless at last, and the good ones will have to offer you a little charity. This is sound working morality in the world. And it makes one realize that, even to Milton, the true hero of *Paradise Lost* must be Satan. But by this baited morality the masses were caught and enslaved to industrialism before ever they knew it; the good got hold of the goods, and our modern "civilization" of money, machines, and wage-slaves was inaugurated. The very pivot of it, let us never forget, being fear and hate, the most intimate fear and hate, fear and hate of one's own instinctive, intuitive body, and fear and hate of every other man's and every other woman's warm, procreative body and imagination.

Now it is obvious what result this will have on the plastic arts, which depend entirely on the representation of substantial bodies, and on the intuitional perception of the *reality* of substantial bodies. The reality of substantial bodies can only be perceived by the imagination, and the imagination is a kindled state of consciousness in which intuitive awareness predominates. The plastic arts are all imagery, and imagery is the body of our imaginative life, and our imaginative life is a great joy and fulfilment to us, for the imagination is a more powerful and more comprehensive flow of consciousness than our ordinary flow. In the flow of true imagination we know in full, mentally and physically at once, in a greater, enkindled awareness. At the maximum of our imagination we are religious. And if we deny our imagination, and have no imaginative life, we are poor worms who have never lived.

In the seventeenth and eighteenth centuries we have the deliberate denial of intuitive awareness, and we see the results on the arts. Vision became more optical, less intuitive and painting began to flourish. But what painting! Watteau, Ingres, Poussin, Chardin have some real imaginative glow still. They are still somewhat free. The puritan and the intellectual has not yet struck them down with his fear and hate obsession. But look at England! Hogarth, Reynolds, Gainsborough, they all are already bourgeois. The coat is really more important than the man. It is amazing how important clothes suddenly become, how they *cover* the subject. An old Reynolds colonel in a red uniform is much more a uniform than an individual, and as for Gainsborough, all one can say is: What a lovely dress and hat! What really expensive Italian silk! This painting of garments continued in vogue, till pictures like Sargent's seem to be nothing but yards and yards of satin from the most expensive shops, having some pretty head popped on the top. The imagination is quite dead. The optical vision, a sort of flashy coloured photography of the eye, is rampant.

In Titian, in Velasquez, in Rembrandt the people are there inside their clothes all right, and the clothes are imbued with the life of the individual, the gleam of the warm procreative body comes through all the time, even if it be an old, half-blind woman or a weird, ironic little Spanish princess. But modern people are nothing inside their garments, and a head sticks out at the top and hands stick out of the sleeves, and it is a bore. Or, as in Lawrence or Raeburn, you have something very pretty but almost a mere cliché, with very little instinctive or intuitional perception to it. . . .

Landscape, however, is different. Here the English exist and hold their own. But, for me, personally, landscape is always waiting for something to occupy it. Landscape seems to be *meant* as a background to an intenser vision of life, so to my feeling painted landscape is background with the real subject left out.

Nevertheless, it can be very lovely, especially in water-colour, which is a more bodiless medium, and doesn't aspire to very substantial existence, and is so small that it doesn't try to make a very deep seizure on the consciousness. Water-colour will always be more of a statement than an experience.

And landscape, on the whole, is the same. It doesn't call up the more powerful responses of the human imagination, the sensual, passional responses. Hence it is the favourite modern form of expression in painting. There is no deep conflict. The instinctive and intuitional consciousness is called into play, but lightly, superficially. It is not confronted with any living, procreative body.

Hence the English have delighted in landscape, and have succeeded in it well. It is a form of escape for them, from the actual human body they so hate and fear, and it is an outlet for their perishing aesthetic desires. For more than a century we have produced delicious water-colours, and Wilson, Crome, Constable, Turner are all great landscape-painters. Some of Turner's landscape compositions are, to my feelings, among the finest that exist. They still satisfy me more even than van Gogh's or Cézanne's landscapes, which make a more violent assault on the emotions, and repel a little for that reason. Somehow I don't want landscape to make a violent assault on my feelings. Landscape is background with the figures left out or reduced to minimum, so let it stay back. Van Gogh's surging earth and Cézanne's explosive or rattling planes worry me. Not being profoundly interested in landscape, I prefer it to be rather quiet and unexplosive.

But, of course, the English delight in landscape is a delight in escape. It is always the same. The northern races are so innerly afraid of their own bodily existence, which they believe fantastically to be an evil thing—you could never find them feel anything but uneasy shame, or an equally shameful gloating, over the fact that a man was having intercourse with his wife, in his house next door—that all they cry for is an escape. And, especially, art must provide that escape.

It is easy in literature. Shelley is pure escape: the body is sublimated into sublime gas. Keats is more difficult—the body can still be *felt* dissolving in waves of successive death—but the death-business is very satisfactory. The novelists have even a better time. You can get some of the lasciviousness of Hetty Sorrell's "sin," and you can enjoy condemning her to penal servitude for life. You can thrill to Mr. Rochester's *passion,* and you can enjoy having his eyes burnt out. So it is, all the way: the novel of "passion"!

But in paint it is more difficult. You cannot paint Hetty Sorrell's sin or Mr. Rochester's passion without being really shocking. And you *daren't* be shocking. It was this fact that unsaddled Watts and Millais. Both might have been painters if they hadn't been Victorians. As it is, each of them is a wash-out.

Which is the poor, feeble history of art in England, since we can lay no claim to the great Holbein. And art on the continent, in the last century? It is more interesting, and has a fuller story. An artist *can* only create what he really religiously *feels* is truth, religious truth really *felt,* in the blood and the bones. The English could never think anything connected with the body *religious*—unless it were the eyes. So they painted the social appearance of human beings, and hoped to give them wonderful eyes. But they *could* think landscape religious, since it had no sensual reality. So they felt religious about it and painted it as well as it could be painted, maybe, from their point of view.

And in France? In France it was more or less the same, but with a difference. The French, being more rational, decided that the body had its place, but that it should be rationalized. The Frenchman of today has the most reasonable and rationalized body possible. His conception of sex is basically hygienic. A certain amount of copulation is good for you. *Ça fait du bien au corps!* sums up the physical side of a Frenchman's idea of love, marriage, food, sport, and all the rest. Well, it is more sane, anyhow, than the Anglo-Saxon terrors. The Frenchman is afraid of syphilis and afraid of the procreative body, but not quite so deeply. He has known for a long time that you can take precautions. And he is not profoundly imaginative.

Therefore he has been able to paint. But his tendency, just like that of all the modern world, has been to get away from the body, while still paying attention to its hygiene, and still not violently quarrelling with it. Puvis de Chavannes is really as sloppy as all the other spiritual sentimentalizers. Renoir is jolly: *ça fait du bien au corps!* is his attitude to the flesh. If a woman didn't have buttocks and breasts, she wouldn't be paintable, he said, and he was right. *Ça fait du bien au corps!* What do you paint with, Maître?—With my penis, and be damned! Renoir didn't try to get away from the body. But he had to dodge it in some of its aspects, rob it of its natural terrors, its natural demonishness. He is delightful, but a trifle banal. *Ça fait du bien au corps!* Yet how infinitely much better he is than any English equivalent.

Courbet, Daumier, Degas, they all painted the human body. But Daumier satirized it, Courbet saw it as a toiling thing, Degas saw it as a wonderful instrument. They all of them deny it its finest qualities, its deepest instincts, its purest intuitions. They prefer, as it were, to industrialize it. They deny it the best imaginative existence.

And the real grand glamour of modern French art, the real outburst of delight came when the body was at last dissolved of its substance, and made part and parcel of the sunlight-and-shadow scheme. Let us say what we will, but the real grand thrill of modern French art was the discovery of light, the discovery of light, and all the subsequent discoveries of the impressionists, and of the post-impressionists, even Cézanne. No matter how Cézanne may have reacted from the impressionists, it was they, with their deliriously joyful discovery of light and "free" colour, who really opened his eyes. Probably the most joyous moment in the whole history of painting was the moment when the incipient impressionists discovered light, and with it, colour. Ah, then they made the grand, grand escape into freedom, into infinity, into light and delight. They escaped from the tyranny of solidity and the menace of mass-form. They escaped, they escaped from the dark procreative body which so haunts a man, they escaped into the open air, *plein air* and *plein soleil:* light and almost ecstasy.

Like every other human escape, it meant being hauled back later with the tail between the legs. Back comes the truant, back to the old doom of matter, of corporate existence, of the body sullen and stubborn and obstinately refusing to be transmuted into pure light, pure colour, or pure anything. It is not concerned with purity. Life isn't. Chemistry and mathematics and ideal religion are, but these are only small bits of life, which is itself bodily, and hence neither pure nor impure.

After the grand escape into impressionism and pure light, pure colour, pure bodilessness—for what is the body but a shimmer of lights and colours!—poor art came home truant and sulky, with its tail between its legs. And it is this return which now interests us. We know the escape was illusion, illusion, illusion. The cat had to come back. So now we despise the "light" blighters too much. We haven't a good word for them. Which is nonsense, for they too are wonderful, even if their escape was into *le grand néant,* the great nowhere.

But the cat came back. And it is the home-coming tom that now has our sympathy: Renoir, to a certain extent, but mostly Cézanne, the sublime little grimalkin, who is followed by Matisse and Gauguin and Derain and Vlaminck and Braque and all the host of other defiant and howling cats that have come back, perforce, to form and substance and *thereness,* instead of delicious nowhereness.

Without wishing to labour the point, one cannot help being amused at the dodge by which the impressionists made the grand escape from the body. They metamorphosed it into a pure assembly of shifting lights and shadows, all coloured. A web of woven, luminous colour was a man, or a woman—and so they painted her, or him: a web of woven shadows and gleams. Delicious! and quite true as far as it goes. A purely optical, *visual* truth: which paint is supposed to be. And they painted delicious pictures: a little too delicious. They bore us, at the moment. They bore people like the very modern critics intensely. But very modern critics need not be so intensely bored. There is something very lovely about the good impressionist pictures. And ten years hence critics will be bored by the present run of post-impressionists, though not so passionately bored, for these post-impressionists don't move us as the impressionists moved our fathers. We have to persuade ourselves, and we have to persuade one another to be impressed by the post-impressionists, on the whole. On the whole, they rather depress us. Which is perhaps good for us.

But modern art criticism is in a curious hole. Art has suddenly gone into rebellion, against all the canons of accepted religion, accepted good form, accepted everything. When the cat came back from the delicious impressionist excursion, it came back rather tattered, but bristling and with its claws out. The glorious escape was all an illusion. There *was* substance still in the world, a thousand times be damned to it! There *was* the body, the great lumpy body. There it was. You had it shoved down your throat. What really existed was lumps, lumps. Then paint 'em. Or else paint the thin "spirit" with gaps in it and looking merely dishevelled and "found out." Paint had found the spirit out.

This is the sulky and rebellious mood of the post-impressionists. They still hate the body—hate it. But, in a rage, they admit its existence, and paint it as huge lumps, tubes, cubes, planes, volumes, spheres, cones, cylinders, all the "pure" or mathematical forms of substance. As for landscape, it comes in for some of the same rage. It has also suddenly gone lumpy. Instead of being nice and ethereal and non-sensual, it was discovered by van Gogh to be heavily, overwhelmingly substantial and sensual. Van Gogh took up landscape in heavy spadefuls. And Cézanne had to admit it. Landscape, too, after being, since Claude Lorrain, a thing of pure luminosity and floating shadow, suddenly exploded, and came tumbling back on to the canvases of artists in lumps. With Cézanne, landscape "crystallized," to use one of the favourite terms of the critics, and it has gone on crystallizing into cubes, cones, pyramids, and so forth ever since.

The impressionists brought the world at length, after centuries of effort, into the delicious oneness of light. At last, at last! Hail, holy Light! the great natural One, the universal, the universalizer! We are not divided, all one body we—one in Light, lovely light! No sooner had this paean gone up than the post-impressionists, like Judas, gave the show away. They exploded the illusion, which fell back to the canvas of art in a chaos of lumps. . . .

The actual fact is that in Cézanne modern French art made its first tiny step back to real substance, to objective substance, if we may call it so. Van Gogh's earth was still subjective earth, himself projected into the earth. But Cézanne's apples are a real attempt to let the apple exist in its own separate entity, without transfusing it with personal emotion. Cézanne's great effort was, as it were, to shove the apple away from him, and let it live of itself. It seems a small thing to do: yet it is the first real sign that man has made for several thousands of years that he is willing to admit that matter *actually* exists. Strange as it may seem, for thousands of years, in short, ever since the mythological "Fall," man has been preoccupied with the constant preoccupation of the denial of the existence of matter, and the proof that matter is only a form of spirit. And then, the moment it is done, and we realize finally that matter is only a form of energy, whatever that may be, in the same instant matter rises up and hits us over the head and makes us realize that it exists absolutely, since it is compact energy itself.

Cézanne felt it in paint, when he felt for the apple. Suddenly he felt the tyranny of mind, the white, worn-out arrogance of the spirit, the mental consciousness, the enclosed ego in its sky-blue heaven self-painted. He felt the sky-blue prison. And a great conflict started inside him. He was dominated by his old mental consciousness, but he wanted terribly to escape the domination. He wanted to *express* what he suddenly, convulsedly knew! the existence of matter. He terribly wanted to paint the real existence of the body, to make it artistically palpable. But he couldn't. He hadn't got there yet. And it was the torture of his life. He wanted to be himself in his own procreative body—and he couldn't. He was, like all the rest of us, so intensely and exclusively a mental creature, or a spiritual creature, or an egoist, that he could no longer identify himself with his intuitive body. He wanted to, terribly. At first he determined to do it by sheer bravado and braggadocio. But no good; it couldn't be done that way. He had, as one critic says, to become humble. But it wasn't a question of becoming humble. It was a question of abandoning his cerebral conceit and his "willed ambition" and coming down to brass tacks. Poor Cézanne, there he is in his self-portraits, even the early showy ones, peeping out like a mouse and saying: I *am* a man of flesh, am I not? For he was not quite, as none of us are. The man of flesh has been slowly destroyed through centuries, to give place to the man of spirit, the mental man, the ego, the self-conscious I. And in his artistic soul Cézanne knew it, and wanted to rise in the flesh. He couldn't do it, and it embittered him. Yet, with his apple, he did shove the stone from the door of the tomb.

He wanted to be a man of flesh, a real man: to get out of the sky-blue prison into real air. He wanted to live, really live in the body, to know the world through his instincts and his intuitions, and to be himself in his procreative blood, not in his mere mind and spirit. He wanted it, he wanted it terribly. And whenever he tried, his mental consciousness, like a cheap fiend, interfered. If he wanted to paint a woman, his mental consciousness simply overpowered him and wouldn't let him paint the woman of flesh, the first Eve who lived before any of the fig-leaf nonsense. He couldn't do it. If he wanted to paint people intuitively and instinctively, he couldn't do it. His mental concepts shoved in front, and these he *wouldn't* paint—mere representations of what the *mind* accepts, not what the intuitions gather—and they, his mental concepts, wouldn't let him paint from intuition; they shoved in between all the time, so he painted his conflict and his failure, and the result is almost ridiculous.

Woman he was not allowed to know by intuition; his mental self, his ego, that bloodless fiend, forbade him. Man, other men, he was likewise not allowed to know—except by a few, few touches. The earth likewise he was not allowed to know: his landscapes are mostly acts of rebellion against the mental concept of landscape. After a fight tooth-and-nail for forty years, he did succeed in knowing an apple, fully; and, not quite as fully, a jug or two. That was all he achieved.

It seems little, and he died embittered. But it is the first step that counts, and Cézanne's apple is a great deal, more than Plato's Idea. Cézanne's apple rolled the stone from the mouth of the tomb, and if poor Cézanne couldn't unwind himself from his cerements and mental winding-sheet, but had to lie still in the tomb, till he died, still he gave us a chance.

The history of our era is the nauseating and repulsive history of the crucifixion of the procreative body for the glorification of the spirit, the mental consciousness. Plato was an arch-priest of this crucifixion. Art, that handmaid, humbly and honestly served the vile deed, through three thousand years at least. The Renaissance put the spear through the side of the already crucified body, and syphilis put poison into the wound made by the imaginative spear. It took still three hundred years for the body to finish: but in the eighteenth century it became a corpse, a corpse with an abnormally active mind: and today it stinketh.

We, dear reader, you and I, we were born corpses, and we are corpses. I doubt if there is even one of us who has ever known so much as an apple, a whole apple. All we know is shadows, even of apples. Shadows of everything, of the whole world, shadows even of ourselves. We are inside the tomb, and the tomb is wide and shadowy like hell, even if sky-blue by optimistic paint, so we think it is all the world. But our world is a wide tomb full of ghosts, replicas. We are all spectres, we have not been able to touch even so much as an apple. Spectres we are to one another. Spectre you are to me, spectre I am to you. Shadow you are even to yourself. And by shadow I mean idea, concept, the abstracted reality, the ego. We are not solid. We don't live in the flesh. Our instincts and intuitions are dead, we live wound round with the winding-sheet of abstraction. And the touch of anything solid hurts us. For our instincts and intuitions, which are our feelers of touch and knowing through touch, they are dead, amputated. We walk and talk and eat and copulate and laugh and evacuate wrapped in our winding-sheets, all the time wrapped in our winding-sheets.

So that Cézanne's apple hurts. It made people shout with pain. And it was not till his followers had turned him again into an abstraction that he was ever accepted. Then the critics stepped forth and abstracted his good apple into Significant Form, and henceforth Cézanne was saved. Saved for democracy. Put safely in the tomb again, and the stone rolled back. The resurrection was postponed once more.

As the resurrection will be postponed *ad infinitum* by the good bourgeois corpses in their cultured winding-sheets. They will run up a chapel to the risen body, even if it is only an apple, and kill it on the spot. They are wide awake, are the corpses, on the alert. And a poor mouse of a Cézanne is alone in the years. Who else shows a spark of awakening life, in our marvellous civilized cemetery? All is dead, and dead breath preaching with phosphorescent effulgence about aesthetic ecstasy and Significant Form. If only the dead would bury their dead. But the dead are not dead for nothing. Who buries his own sort? The dead are cunning and alert to pounce on any spark of life and bury *it*, even as they have already buried Cézanne's apple and put up to it a white tombstone of Significant Form.

For who of Cézanne's followers does anything but follow at the triumphant funeral of Cézanne's achievement? They follow him in order to bury him, and they succeed. Cézanne is deeply buried under all the Matisses and Vlamincks of his following, while the critics read the funeral homily.

It is quite easy to accept Matisse and Vlaminck and Friesz and all the rest. They are just Cézanne abstracted again. They are all just tricksters, even if clever ones. They are all mental, mental, egoists, egoists, egoists. And therefore they are all acceptable now to the enlightened corpses of connoisseurs. You needn't be afraid of Matisse and Vlaminck and the rest. They will never give your corpse-anatomy a jar. They are just shadows, minds mountebanking and playing charades on canvas. They may be quite amusing charades, and I am all for the mountebank. But of course it is all games inside the cemetery, played by corpses and *hommes d'esprit*, even *femmes d'esprit*, like Mademoiselle Laurencin. As for *l'esprit*, said Cézanne, I don't give a fart for it. Perhaps not! But the connoisseurs will give large sums of money. Trust the dead to pay for their amusement, when the amusement is deadly!

The most interesting figure in modern art, and the only really interesting figure, is Cézanne: and that, not so much because of his achievement as because of his struggle. Cézanne was born at Aix in Provence in 1839: small, timorous, yet sometimes bantam defiant, sensitive, full of grand ambition, yet ruled still deeper by a naïve, Mediterranean sense of truth or reality, imagination, call it what you will. He is not a big figure. Yet his struggle is truly heroic. He was a bourgeois, and one must never forget it. He had a moderate bourgeois income. But a bourgeois in Provence is much more real and human than a bourgeois in Normandy. He is much nearer the actual people, and the actual people are much less subdued by awe of his respectable bourgeois money.

Cézanne was naïve to a degree, but not a fool. He was rather insignificant, and grandeur impressed him terribly. Yet still stronger in him was the little flame of life where he *felt* things to be true. He didn't betray himself in order to get success, because he couldn't: to his nature it was impossible: he was too pure to be able to betray his own small real flame for immediate rewards. Perhaps that is the best one can say of a man, and it puts Cézanne, small and insignificant as he is, among the heroes. He would *not* abandon his own vital imagination.

He was terribly impressed by physical splendour and flamboyancy, as people usually are in the lands of the sun. He admired terribly the splendid virtuosity of Paul Veronese and Tintoretto, and even of later and less good baroque painters. He wanted to be like that—terribly he wanted it. And he tried very, very hard, with bitter effort. And he always failed. It is a cant phrase with the critics to say "he couldn't draw." Mr. Fry says: "With all his rare endowment, he happened to lack the comparatively common gift of illustration, the gift that any draughtsman for the illustrated papers learns in a school of commercial art."

Now this sentence gives away at once the hollowness of modern criticism. In the first place, can one learn a "gift" in a school of commercial art, or anywhere else? A gift surely is given, we tacitly assume, by God or Nature or whatever higher power we hold responsible for the things we have no choice in.

Was, then, Cézanne devoid of this gift? Was he simply incapable of drawing a cat so that it would look like a cat? Nonsense! Cézanne's work is full of accurate drawing. His more trivial pictures, suggesting copies from other masters, are perfectly well drawn—that is, conventionally: so are some of the landscapes, so even is that portrait of M. Geffroy and his books, which is, or was, so famous. Why these cant phrases about not being able to draw? Of course Cézanne could draw, as well as anybody else. And he had learned everything that was necessary in the art-schools.

He *could* draw. And yet, in his terrifically earnest compositions in the late Renaissance or baroque manner, he drew so badly. Why? Not because he couldn't. And not because he was sacrificing "significant form" to "insignificant form," or mere slick representation, which is apparently what artists themselves mean when they talk about drawing. Cézanne knew all about drawing: and he surely knew as much as his critics do about significant form. Yet he neither succeeded in drawing so that things looked right, nor combining his shapes so that he achieved real form. He just failed.

He failed, where one of his little slick successors would have succeeded with one eye shut. And why? Why did Cézanne fail in his early pictures? Answer that, and you'll know a little better what art is. He didn't fail because he understood nothing about drawing or significant form or aesthetic ecstasy. He knew about them all, and didn't give a spit for them.

Cézanne failed in his earlier pictures because he was trying with his mental consciousness to do something which his living Provençal body didn't want to do, or couldn't do. He terribly wanted to do something grand and voluptuous and sensuously satisfying, in the Tintoretto manner. Mr. Fry calls that his "willed ambition," which is a good phrase, and says he had to learn humility, which is a bad phrase.

The "willed ambition" was more than a mere willed ambition—it was a genuine desire. But it was a desire that thought it would be satisfied by ready-made baroque expressions, whereas it needed to achieve a whole new marriage of mind and matter. If we believed in reincarnation, then we should have to believe that after a certain number of new incarnations into the body of an artist, the soul of Cézanne *would* produce grand and voluptuous and sensually rich pictures—but not at all in the baroque manner. Because the pictures he actually did produce with undeniable success are the first steps in that direction, sensual and rich, with not the slightest hint of baroque, but new, the man's new grasp of substantial reality.

There was, then, a certain discrepancy between Cézanne's *notion* of what he wanted to produce, and his other, intuitive knowledge of what he *could* produce. For whereas the mind works in possibilities, the intuitions work in actualities, and what you *intuitively* desire, that is possible to you. Whereas what you mentally or "consciously" desire is nine times out of ten impossible: hitch your wagon to a star, and you'll just stay where you are.

So the conflict, as usual, was not between the artist and his medium, but between the artist's *mind* and the artist's *intui-*

tion and *instinct.* And what Cézanne had to learn was not humility—cant word!—but honesty, honesty with himself. It was not a question of any gift or significant form or aesthetic ecstasy: it was a question of Cézanne being himself, just Cézanne. And when Cézanne is himself he is not Tintoretto, nor Veronese, nor anything baroque at all. Yet he is something *physical,* and even sensual: qualities which he had identified with the masters of virtuosity.

In passing, if we think of Henri Matisse, a real virtuoso, and imagine him possessed with a "willed ambition" to paint grand and flamboyant baroque pictures, then we know at once that he would not have to "humble" himself at all, but that he would start in and paint with great success grand and flamboyant modern-baroque pictures. He would succeed because he has the gift of virtuosity. And the gift of virtuosity simply means that you don't have to humble yourself, or even be honest with yourself, because you are a clever mental creature who is capable at will of making the intuitions and instincts subserve some mental concept: in short, you can prostitute your body to your mind, your instincts and intuitions you can prostitute to your "willed ambition," in a sort of masturbation process, and you can produce the impotent glories of virtuosity. But Veronese and Tintoretto are real painters; they are not mere *virtuosi,* as some of the later men are.

The point is very important. Any creative act occupies the whole consciousness of a man. This is true of the great discoveries of science as well as of art. The truly great discoveries of science and real works of art are made by the whole consciousness of man working together in unison and oneness: instinct, intuition, mind, intellect all fused into one complete consciousness, and grasping what we may call a complete truth, or a complete vision, a complete revelation in sound. A discovery, artistic or otherwise, may be more or less intuitional, more or less mental; but intuition will have entered into it, and mind will have entered too. The whole consciousness is concerned in every case.—And a painting requires the activity of the whole imagination, for it is made of imagery, and the imagination is that form of complete consciousness in which predominates the intuitive awareness of forms, images, the *physical* awareness.

And the same applies to the genuine appreciation of a work of art, or the *grasp* of a scientific law, as to the production of the same. The whole consciousness is occupied, not merely the mind alone, or merely the body. The mind and spirit alone can never really grasp a work of art, though they may, in a masturbating fashion, provoke the body into an ecstasized response. The ecstasy will die out into ash and more ash. . . .

Which brings us back to Cézanne, why he couldn't draw, and why he couldn't paint baroque masterpieces. It is just because he was real, and could only believe in his own expression when it expressed a moment of wholeness or completeness of consciousness in himself. He could not prostitute one part of himself to the other. He *could* not masturbate, in paint or words. And that is saying a very great deal, today; today, the great day of the masturbating consciousness, when the mind prostitutes the sensitive responsive body, and just forces the reactions. The masturbating consciousness produces all kinds of novelties, which thrill for the moment, then go very dead. It cannot produce a single genuinely new utterance.

What we have to thank Cézanne for is not his humility, but for his proud, high spirit that refused to accept the glib utterances of his facile mental self. He wasn't poor-spirited enough to be facile—nor humble enough to be satisfied with visual and emotional clichés. Thrilling as the baroque masters were to him in themselves, he realized that as soon as he reproduced them he produced nothing but cliché. The mind is full of all sorts of memory, visual, tactile, emotional memory, memories, groups of memories, systems of memories. A cliché is just a worn-out memory that has no more emotional or intuitional root, and has become a habit. Whereas a novelty is just a new grouping of clichés, a new arrangement of accustomed memories. That is why a novelty is so easily accepted: it gives the little shock or thrill of surprise, but it does not *disturb* the emotional and intuitive self. It forces you to see nothing new. It is only a novel compound of clichés. The work of most of Cézanne's successors is just novel, just a new arrangement of clichés, soon growing stale. And the clichés are Cézanne clichés, just as in Cézanne's own earlier pictures the clichés were all, or mostly, baroque clichés.

Cezanne's early history as a painter is a history of his fight with his own cliché. His consciousness wanted a new realization. And his ready-made mind offered him all the time a ready-made expression. And Cézanne, far too inwardly proud and haughty to accept the ready-made clichés that came from his mental consciousness, stocked with memories, and which appeared mocking at him on his canvas, spent most of his time smashing his own forms to bits. To a true artist, and to the living imagination, the cliché is the deadly enemy. Cézanne had a bitter fight with it. He hammered it to pieces a thousand times. And still it reappeared.

Now again we can see why Cézanne's drawing was so bad. It was bad because it represented a smashed, mauled cliché, terribly knocked about. If Cézanne had been willing to accept his own baroque cliché, his drawing would have been perfectly conventionally "all right," and not a critic would have had a word to say about it. But when his drawing was conventionally all right, to Cézanne himself it was mockingly all wrong, it was cliché. So he flew at it and knocked all the shape and stuffing out of it, and when it was so mauled that it was all wrong, and he was exhausted with it, he let it go; bitterly, because it still was not what he wanted. And here comes in the comic element in Cézanne's pictures. His rage with the cliché made him distort the cliché sometimes into parody, as we see in pictures like *The Pasha* and *La Femme*. "You *will* be cliché, will you?" he gnashes. "Then *be* it!" And he shoves it in a frenzy of exasperation over into parody. And the sheer exasperation makes the parody still funny; but the laugh is a little on the wrong side of the face.

This smashing of the cliché lasted a long way into Cézanne's life; indeed, it went with him to the end. The way he worked over and over his forms was his nervous manner of laying the ghost of his cliché, burying it. Then when it disappeared perhaps from his forms themselves, it lingered in his composition, and he had to fight with the *edges* of his forms and contours, to bury the ghost there. Only his colour he knew was not cliché. He left it to his disciples to make it so.

In his very best pictures, the best of the still-life compositions, which seem to me Cézanne's greatest achievement, the fight with the cliché is still going on. But it was in the still-life pictures he learned his final method of *avoiding* the cliché: just leaving gaps through which it fell into nothingness. So he makes his landscape succeed.

In his art, all his life long, Cézanne was tangled in a twofold activity. He wanted to express something, and before he could do it he had to fight the hydra-headed cliché, whose last head he could never lop off. The fight with the cliché is the most obvious thing in his pictures. The dust of battle rises thick, and the splinters fly wildly. And it is this dust of battle and flying of splinters which his imitators still so fervently imitate. If you give a Chinese dressmaker a dress to copy, and the dress happens to have a darned rent in it, the dressmaker carefully tears a rent in the new dress, and

darns it in exact replica. And this seems to be the chief oc-
cupation of Cézanne's disciples, in every land. They absorb
themselves reproducing imitation mistakes. He let off vari-
ous explosions in order to blow up the stronghold of the
cliché, and his followers make grand firework imitations of
the explosions, without the faintest inkling of the true at-
tack. They do, indeed, make an onslaught on representa-
tion, true-to-life representation: because the explosion in
Cézanne's pictures blew them up. But I am convinced that
what Cézanne himself wanted *was* representation. He *wanted*
true-to-life representation. Only he wanted it *more* true to
life. And once you have got photography, it is a very, very
difficult thing to get representation *more* true-to-life: which it
has to be.

Cézanne was a realist, and he wanted to be true to life. But
he would not be content with the optical cliché. With the
impressionists, purely optical vision perfected itself and fell
at once into cliché, with a startling rapidity. Cézanne saw this.
Artists like Courbet and Daumier were not purely optical,
but the other element in these two painters, the intellectual
element, was cliché. To the optical vision they added the
concept of force-pressure, almost like an hydraulic brake,
and this force-pressure concept is mechanical, a cliché,
though still popular. And Daumier added mental satire, and
Courbet added a touch of a sort of socialism: both cliché
and unimaginative.

Cézanne wanted something that was neither optical nor
mechanical nor intellectual. And to introduce into our
world of vision something which is neither optical nor me-
chanical nor intellectual-psychological requires a real
revolution. It was a revolution Cézanne began, but which
nobody, apparently, has been able to carry on.

He wanted to touch the world of substance once more
with the intuitive touch, to be aware of it with the intuitive

awareness, and to express it in intuitive terms. That is, he wished to displace our present mode of mental-visual consciousness, the consciousness of mental concepts, and substitute a mode of consciousness that was predominantly intuitive, the awareness of touch. In the past the primitives painted intuitively, but *in the direction* of our present mental-visual, conceptual form of consciousness. They were working away from their own intuition. Mankind has never been able to trust the intuitive consciousness, and the decision to accept that trust marks a very great revolution in the course of human development.

Without knowing it, Cézanne, the timid little conventional man sheltering behind his wife and sister and the Jesuit father, was a pure revolutionary. When he said to his models: "Be an apple! Be an apple!" he was uttering the foreword to the fall not only of Jesuits and the Christian idealists altogether, but to the collapse of our whole way of consciousness, and the substitution of another way. If the human being is going to be primarily an apple, as for Cézanne it was, then you are going to have a new world of men: a world which has very little to say, men that can sit still and just be physically there, and be truly non-moral. That was what Cézanne meant with his: "Be an apple!" He knew perfectly well that the moment the model began to intrude her personality and her "mind," it would be cliché and moral, and he would have to paint cliché. The only part of her that was not banal, known *ad nauseam,* living cliché, the only part of her that was not living cliché was her appleyness. Her body, even her very sex, was known, nauseously: *connu, connu!* the endless chance of known cause-and-effect, the infinite web of the hated cliché which nets us all down in utter boredom. He knew it all, he hated it all, he refused it all, this timid and "humble" little man. He knew, as an artist, that the only bit of a woman which nowadays escapes being ready-made and ready-known cliché is the appley part of her. Oh, be an apple, and leave out all your thoughts, all your feelings, all your mind and all your personality, which we know all about and find boring beyond endurance. Leave it all out—and be an apple! It is the appleyness of the portrait of Cézanne's wife that makes it so permanently interesting: the appleyness, which carries with it also the feeling of knowing the other side as well, the side you don't see, the hidden side of the moon. For the intuitive apperception of the apple is so *tangibly* aware of the apple that it is aware of it *all round,* not only just of the front. The eye sees only fronts, and the mind, on the whole, is satisfied with fronts. But intuition needs all-aroundness, and instinct needs insideness. The true imagination is for ever curving round to the other side, to the back of presented appearance.

So to my feeling the portraits of Madame Cézanne, particularly the portrait in the red dress, are more interesting than the portrait of M. Geffroy, or the portraits of the housekeeper or the gardener. In the same way the *Card-Players* with two figures please me more than those with four.

But we have to remember, in his figure-paintings, that while he was painting the appleyness he was also deliberately painting *out* the so-called humanness, the personality, the "likeness," the physical cliché. He had deliberately to paint it out, deliberately to make the hands and face rudimentary, and so on, because if he had painted them in fully they would have been cliché. He *never* got over the cliché denominator, the intrusion and interference of the ready-made concept, when it came to people, to men and women. Especially to women he could only give a cliché response— and that maddened him. Try as he might, women remained a known, ready-made cliché object to him, and he *could not* break through the concept obsession to get at the intuitive awareness of her. Except with his wife—and in his wife he did at least know the appleyness. But with his housekeeper he failed somewhat. She was a bit cliché, especially the face. So really is M. Geffroy.

With men Cézanne often dodged it by insisting on the clothes, those stiff cloth jackets bent into thick folds, those hats, those blouses, those curtains. Some of the *Card-Players,* the big ones with four figures, seem just a trifle banal, so much occupied with painted stuff, painted clothing, and the humanness a bit cliché. Nor good colour, nor clever composition, nor "planes" of colour, nor anything else will save an emotional cliché from being an emotional cliché, though they may, of course, garnish it and make it more interesting.

Where Cézanne did sometimes escape the cliché altogether and really give a complete intuitive interpretation of actual objects is in some of the still-life compositions. To me these good still-life scenes are purely representative and quite true to life. Here Cézanne did what he wanted to do: he made the things quite real, he didn't deliberately leave anything out, and yet he gave us a triumphant and rich intuitive vision of a few apples and kitchen pots. For once his intuitive consciousness triumphed, and broke into utterance. And here he is inimitable. His imitators imitate his accessories of tablecloths folded like tin, etc.—the unreal parts of his pictures—but they don't imitate the pots and apples, because they can't. It's the real appleyness, and you can't imitate it. Every man must create it new and different out of himself: new and different. The moment it looks "like" Cézanne, it is nothing.

But at the same time Cézanne was triumphing with the apple and appleyness he was still fighting with the cliché. When he makes Madame Cézanne most *still*, most appley, he starts making the universe slip uneasily about her. It was part of his desire: to make the human form, the *life* form, come to rest. Not static—on the contrary. Mobile but come to rest.

And at the same time he set the unmoving material world into motion. Walls twitch and slide, chairs bend or rear up a little, cloths curl like burning paper. Cézanne did this partly to satisfy his intuitive feeling that nothing is really *statically* at rest—a feeling he seems to have had strongly—as when he watched the lemons shrivel or go mildewed, in his still-life group, which he left lying there so long so that he *could* see that gradual flux of change: and partly to fight the cliché, which says that the inanimate world *is* static, and that walls *are* still. In his fight with the cliché he denied that walls are still and chairs are static. In his intuitive self he *felt* for their changes.

And these two activities of his consciousness occupy his later landscapes. In the best landscapes we are fascinated by the mysterious *shiftiness* of the scene under our eyes; it shifts about as we watch it. And we realize, with a sort of transport, how intuitively *true* this is of landscape. It is *not* still. It has its own weird anima, and to our wide-eyed perception it changes like a living animal under our gaze. This is a quality that Cézanne sometimes got marvellously.

Then again, in other pictures he seems to be saying: Landscape is not like this and not like this and not like this and not . . . etc.—and every *not* is a little blank space in the canvas, defined by the remains of an assertion. Sometimes Cézanne builds up a landscape essentially out of omissions. He puts fringes on the complicated vacuum of the cliché, so to speak, and offers us that. It is interesting in a *repudiative* fashion, but it is not the new thing. The appleyness, the intuition has gone. We have only a mental repudiation. This occupies many of the later pictures: and ecstasizes the critics.

And Cézanne was bitter. He had never, as far as his *life* went, broken through the horrible glass screen of the mental concepts, to the actual *touch* of life. In his art he had touched the apple, and that was a great deal. He had intuitively known the apple and intuitively brought it forth on the tree of his life, in paint. But when it came to anything beyond the apple, to landscape, to people, and above all to nude woman, the cliché had triumphed over him. The cliché had triumphed over him, and he was bitter, misanthropic. How not to be misanthropic when men and women are just clichés to you, and you hate the cliché? Most people, of course, love the cliché—because most people *are* the cliché. Still, for all that, there is perhaps more appleyness in man, and even in nude woman, than Cézanne was able to get at. The cliché obtruded, so he just abstracted away from it. Those last water-colour landscapes are just abstractions from the cliché. They are blanks, with a few pearly-coloured sort of edges. The blank is vacuum, which was Cézanne's last word against the cliché. It is a vacuum, and the edges are there to assert the vacuity.

And the very fact that we can reconstruct almost instantly a whole landscape from the few indications Cézanne gives, shows what a cliché the landscape is, how it exists already, ready-made, in our minds, how it exists in a pigeon-hole of the consciousness, so to speak, and you need only be given its number to be able to get it out, complete. Cézanne's last water-colour landscapes, made up of a few touches on blank paper, are a satire on landscape altogether. *They leave so much to the imagination!*—that immortal cant phrase, which means they give you the clue to a cliché and the cliché comes. That's what the cliché exists for. And that sort of imagination is just a rag-bag memory stored with thousands and thousands of old and really worthless sketches, images, etc., clichés.

We can see what a fight it means, the escape from the domination of the ready-made mental concept, the mental consciousness stuffed full of clichés that intervene like a complete screen between us and life. It means a long, long fight, that will probably last for ever. But Cézanne did get as far as the apple. I can think of nobody else who has done anything.

When we put it in personal terms, it is a fight in a man between his own ego, which is his ready-made mental self which inhabits either a sky-blue, self-tinted heaven or a black, self-tinted hell, and his other free intuitive self. Cézanne never freed himself from his ego, in his life. He haunted the fringes of experience. "I who am so feeble in life"—but at least he knew it. At least he had the greatness to feel bitter about it. Not like the complacent bourgeois who now "appreciate" him!

So now perhaps it is the English turn. Perhaps this is where the English will come in. They have certainly stayed out very completely. It is as if they had received the death-blow to their instinctive and intuitive bodies in the Elizabethan age, and since then they have steadily died, till now they are complete corpses. As a young English painter, an intelligent and really modest young man, said to me: "But I do think we ought to begin to paint good pictures, now that we know pretty well all there is to know about how a picture should be made. You do agree, don't you, that technically we know almost all there is to know about painting?"

I looked at him in amazement. It was obvious that a new-born babe was as fit to paint pictures as he was. He knew technically all there was to know about pictures: all about two-dimensional and three-dimensional composition, also the colour-dimension and the dimension of values in that view of composition which exists apart from form: all about the value of planes, the value of the angle in planes, the different values of the same colour on different planes: all about edges, visible edges, tangible edges, intangible edges: all about the nodality of form-groups, the constellating of mass-centres: all about the relativity of mass, the gravitation and the centrifugal force of masses, the resultant of the complex impinging of masses, the isolation of a mass in the line of vision: all about pattern, line pattern, edge pattern, tone pattern, colour pattern, and the pattern of moving planes: all about texture, impasto, surface, and what happens at the edge of the canvas: also which is the aesthetic centre of the canvas, the dynamic centre, the effulgent centre, the kinetic centre, the mathematical centre, and the Chinese centre: also the points of departure in the foreground, and the points of disappearance in the background, together with the various routes between these points, namely, as the crow flies, as the cow walks, as the mind intoxicated with knowledge reels and gets there: all about spotting, what you spot, which spot, on the spot, how many spots, balance of spots, recedence of spots, spots on the explosive vision and spots on the co-ordinative vision: all about literary interest and how to hide it successfully from the policeman: all about photographic representation, and which heaven it belongs to, and which hell: all about the sex-appeal of a picture, and when you can be arrested for solicitation, when for indecency: all about the psychology of a picture, which section of the mind it appeals to, which mental state it is intended to represent, how to exclude the representation of all other states of mind from the one intended, or how, on the contrary, to give a hint of complementary states of mind fringing the state of mind portrayed: all about the chemistry of colours, when to use Winsor & Newton and when not, and the relative depth of contempt to display for Lefranc: on the history of colour, past and future, whether cadmium will really stand the march of ages, whether viridian will go black, blue, or merely greasy, and the effect on our great-great-grandsons of the flake white and zinc white and white lead we have so lavishly used: on the merits and demerits of leaving patches of bare, prepared canvas, and which preparation will bleach, which blacken: on the mediums to be used, the vice of linseed oil, the treachery of turps, the meanness of gums, the innocence or the unspeakable crime of varnish: on allowing your picture to be shiny, on insisting that it should be shiny, on weeping over the merest suspicion of gloss and rubbing it with a raw potato: on brushes, and the conflicting length of the stem, the best of the hog, the length of bristle most to be desired on the many varying occasions, and whether to slash in one direction only: on the atmosphere of London, on the atmosphere of Glasgow, on the atmosphere of Rome, on the atmosphere of Paris, and the peculiar action of them all upon vermilion, cinnabar, pale cadmium yellow, mid-chrome, emerald green, Veronese green, linseed oil, turps, and Lyall's perfect medium: on quality, and its relation to light, and its ability to hold its own in so radical a change of light as that from Rome to London—all these things the young man knew—and out of it, God help him, he was going to make pictures.

Now, such innocence and such naïveté, coupled with true modesty, must make us believe that we English have indeed, at least as far as paint goes, become again as little children: very little children: tiny children: babes: nay, babes unborn. And if we have really got back to the state of the unborn babe, we are perhaps almost ready to be born. The English *may* be born again, pictorially. Or, to tell the truth, they may begin for the first time to be born: since as painters of composition pictures they don't really exist. They have reached the stage where their innocent egos are entirely and totally enclosed in pale-blue glass bottles of insulated inexperience. Perhaps now they *must* hatch out!

"Do you think we may be on the brink of a Golden Age again in England?" one of our most promising young writers asked me, with that same half-timorous innocence and naïveté of the young painter. I looked at him—he was a sad young man—and my eyes nearly fell out of my head. A golden age! He looked so ungolden, and though he was twenty years my junior, he felt also like my grandfather. A golden age! in England! a golden age! now, when even money is paper! when the enclosure in the ego is final, when they are hermetically sealed and insulated from all experience, from any *touch*, from anything *solid*.

"I suppose it's up to *you*," said I.

And he quietly accepted it.

But such innocence, such naïveté must be a prelude to something. It's a *ne plus ultra*. So why shouldn't it be a prelude to a golden age? If the innocence and naïveté as regards artistic expression doesn't become merely idiotic, why shouldn't it become golden? The young might, out of a sheer sort of mental blankness, strike the oil of their live intuition, and get a gusher. Why not? A golden gush of artistic expression? "Now we know pretty well everything that can be known about the technical side of pictures." A golden age!

1929

Jean-François Millet, *Man with a Hoe*, oil on canvas, 31 1/2 x 39 in. The J. Paul Getty Museum.

Pictures

GERTRUDE STEIN

*For her 1934 American tour—during which she decided the country
had no sky, just air, "and that makes religion and wandering and
architecture"—Stein prepared six public lectures. The first was
"Pictures," sponsored by the Museum of Modern Art and delivered
to an overflow crowd at the Colony Club on November 1. The next
morning the* Herald Tribune *reported the lecture had "variously
pleased, mystified and infuriated her audience" and had been spo-
ken in "the same slightly monotonous voice that mothers use to read
to sick children." This particular Mother of Us All hated lecturing:
"Sooner or later," she told an interviewer, "you hear your voice, and
you do not hear what you say. You just hear what they hear you say.
As a matter of fact, as a writer I write entirely with my eyes." Few
writers have taken more delight and instruction from painting than
Gertrude Stein. Her flat on the rue de Fleurus was both gallery and
salon. Her close artist friends ranged from Matisse and Picasso to
Pavel Tchelitchew and Francis Rose; and once, when she gave a
lunch party for some painters, she rearranged the pictures on her
wall so that each guest would be seated opposite his own work,
thereby ensuring his happiness. "Pictures" records, especially in her
discussion of the concepts of "resemblance" and "framing," how and
what she had learned from art. It is characteristic of Stein that it
was the flatness of pictures that first attracted her; that, on her first*

visit to the Louvre, she mainly noticed the frames and liked looking out the windows; and that, in the Italian museums, she would lie down on the red benches so that she could both sleep and wake in front of the Tintorettos and Botticellis. Later, her more serious study of cubist methods led to her sense that "in composition one thing is as important as another thing. Each part is as important as the whole." Her style, that always seems to count to a hundred by ones, is a new way to old accounts and owes a debt to the painters: the modeling of Three Lives, *the still lifes of objects in* Tender Buttons, *or the abstracting "continuous present" in her series of "Portraits." If she is not one of this century's greatest writers, she is surely one of its great stylists. What she says to define the genius of Picasso in her 1938 biographical study might summarize her own work as well: "Picasso only sees something else, another reality. Complications are always easy but another vision than that of all the world is very rare. That is why geniuses are rare, not to complicate things in a new way that is easy, but to see things in a new way that is difficult, everything prevents one, habits, schools, daily life, reason, necessities of daily life, indolence, everything prevents one, in fact there are very few geniuses in the world."*

IT IS NATURAL that I should tell about pictures, that is, about paintings. Everybody must like something and I like seeing painted pictures. Once the Little Review had a questionnaire, it was for their farewell number, and they asked everybody whose work they had printed to answer a number of questions. One of the questions was, what do you feel about modern art. I answered, I like to look at it. That was my real answer because I do, I do like to look at it, that is at the picture part of modern art. The other parts of it interest me much less.

As I say everybody has to like something, some people like to eat some people like to drink, some people like to make money some like to spend money, some like the theatre, some even like sculpture, some like gardening, some like dogs, some like cats, some people like to look at things, some people like to look at everything. Any way some one is almost sure to really like something outside of their real occupation. I have not mentioned games indoor and out, and birds and crime and politics and photography, but anybody can go on, and I, personally, I like all these things well enough but they do not hold my attention long enough. The only thing, funnily enough, that I never get tired of doing is looking at pictures. There is no reason for it but for some reason, anything reproduced by paint, preferably, I may even say certainly, by oil paints on a flat surface holds my attention. I do not really care for water colors or pastels, they do not really hold my attention.

I cannot remember when I was not so.

I like sign paintings and I do regret that they no longer paint the signs on the walls with oil paints. Paper with the things reproduced plastered on the wall does not do the same thing to me, it does not hold my attention. Neither does wall paper although wall paper does sometimes give the illusion of paint. But it does not do so enough, no not enough. I like to look at anything painted in oil on a flat surface although for nothing in the world would I want to be a painter or paint anything.

I have often wondered why I like the representation or the presentation of anything in oil on a flat surface but I have never been able to find out the reason why. It is simply a fact. I even like a curtain or a sign painted as they often do in Europe painted in oil of the things to be sold inside and I like a false window or a vista painted on a house as they do so much in Italy. In short anything painted in oil anywhere on a flat surface holds my attention and I can always look at it and slowly yes slowly I will tell you all about it.

When I look at landscape or people or flowers they do not look to me like pictures, no not at all. On the other hand pictures for me do not have to look like flowers or people or landscapes or houses or anything else. They can, they often do, but they do not have to. Once an oil painting is painted, painted on a flat surface, painted by anybody who likes or is hired or is interested to paint it, or who has or has not been taught to paint it, I can always look at it and it always holds my attention. The painting may be good it may be bad, medium or very bad or very good but any way I like to look at it. And now, why does the representation of things that being painted do not look at all like the things look to me from which they are painted why does such a representation give me pleasure and hold my attention. Ah yes, well this I do not know and I do not know whether I ever will know, this. However it is true and I repeat that to give me this interest the painting must be an oil painting and any oil painting whether it is intended to look like something and looks like it or whether it is intended to look like something and does not look like it it really makes no difference, the fact remains that for me it has achieved an existence in and for itself, it exists on as being an oil painting on a flat surface and it has its own life and like it or not there it is and I can look at it and it does hold my attention.

That the oil painting once it is made has its own existence this is a thing that can of course be said of anything. Anything once it is made has its own existence and it is because of that that anything holds somebody's attention. The question always is about that anything, how much vitality has it and do you happen to like to look at it.

By anything here I really mean anything. Anything that happens anything that exists anything that is made has of course its own vitality and presumably some one or if not yet then there could presumably be sometime someone who would like to look at it. But does it really, that is is it true of everything does everything that is anything does it hold somebody's attention. Yes perhaps so. One certainly may say so. And so it comes back to the fact that anything having its own existence how much vitality has it and do you happen to like to look at it and does it hold your attention.

Now most of us live in ourselves that is to say in one thing and we have to have a relief from the intensity of that thing and so we like to look at something. Presidents of the United States of America are supposed to like to look at baseball games. I can understand that, I did too once, but ultimately it did not hold my attention. Pictures made in oil on a flat surface do, they do hold my attention, and so to go further into this matter.

The first thing I ever saw painted and that I remember and remembered seeing and feeling as painted, no one of you could know what that was, it was a very large oil painting. It was the panorama of the battle of Waterloo. I must have been about eight years old and it was very exciting, it was exciting seeing the panorama of the battle of Waterloo. There was a man there who told all about the battle, I knew a good deal about it already because I always read historical novels and history and I knew about the sunken road where the french cavalry were caught but though all that was exciting the thing that was exciting me was the oil painting. It was an oil painting a continuous oil painting, one was surrounded by an oil painting and I who lived continuously out of doors and felt air and sunshine and things to see felt that this was all different and very exciting. There it all was the things to see but there was no air it just was an oil painting. I remember standing on the little platform in the center and almost consciously knowing that there was no air. There was no air, there was no feeling of air, it just was an oil painting and it had a life of its own and it was a scene as an oil painting sees it and it was a real thing which looked like something I had seen but it had nothing to do with that something that I knew because the feeling was not at all that not at all the feeling which I had when I saw anything that was really what the oil painting showed. It the oil painting showed it as an oil painting. That is what an oil painting is.

Later when I was about eighteen I saw the actual battle field of the Battle of Gettysburg and the difference in emotion in seeing the actual battle field of the battle of Gettysburg and the panorama of the Battle of Waterloo is a thing that I very well remember. I knew of course I knew all about the battle of Gettysburg. When we were there it was a wonderful early summer day, and it was an entirely different thing from an oil painting. There were so many things back present and future, and a feeling of enjoying oneself and there it was and the whole thing was very complicated. I know what the battle field of the Battle of Gettysburg looks like in general and in detail and I know what I felt and I know what was said by us and what we said and the states that were represented but I do not know exactly what it looked like as I know exactly what the battle of Waterloo looked like at the Panorama of the battle of Waterloo which was an enormous circular oil painting. Do you begin to see a little bit what it is to be an oil painting. I have always liked looking at pictures of battle scenes but as I say I always like looking at pictures and then once after the war I saw the battle field of the battle of Metz. For a moment as I looked at it, it was a grey day and we were on our way back from Alsace to Paris and we had seen so many battle fields of this war and this one was so historical, it almost it did almost look like an oil painting. As I say things do not generally look to me like an oil painting. And just then into this thing which was so historical that it almost did look like an oil painting a very old couple of people a man and woman got out of an automobile and went to look at a grave at the way-side and the moment of its existence as an oil painting ceased, it became a historical illustration for a simple historical story. In connection with the Panorama of the Battle of Waterloo there was a description of the battle of Waterloo as told by Victor Hugo. If it had not rained on the twenty-sixth of March 1814 the fate of Europe would have been changed. I never really believed this because of course I had read so many English novels and so much English history about the battle of Waterloo but it was a perfectly definite picture of the battle of Waterloo and it had nothing whatever to do with an oil painting. It was the complete other thing of an oil painting. And now to go on with what an oil painting is.

The next thing I remember about an oil painting were the advent, in San Francisco I was still a child, of two very different paintings. One was by a man I think named Rosenthal who had been sent to Europe to develop his talent and he came back with a very large painting of a scene from Scott's Marmion the nun being entombed in a wall as a punishment. The other painting was Millet's Man with a Hoe. Both the pictures interested me equally, but I did not want a photograph of the Rosenthal picture but I did of the Man with a Hoe. I remember looking at it a great deal. And then we that is my brother and myself very moved not knowing exactly why but very moved showed the photograph to my eldest brother and he looked at it equally solemnly and then he said very decidedly, it is a hell of a hoe, and he was right.

But I still know exactly how the picture of the Man with a Hoe looked. I know exactly how it looked although having now lived a great deal in the french country I see the farmers constantly hoeing with just that kind of a hoe. The hoeing with just that kind of a hoe as I see them all the time and meet them all the time have nothing to do with Millet's Man with a Hoe but that is natural because I know the men as men, the hoe as a hoe and the fields as fields. But I still do know Millet's Man with a Hoe, because it was an oil painting. And my brother said it was a hell of hoe but what it was was an oil painting. Millet's pictures did have something that made one say these things. I remember not so many years ago at Bourg going through the monastery next to the cathedral of Brou. There unexpectedly in a little room was a cow, almost a real cow and it was an oil painting by Millet, and it did not startle me but there it was it was almost a cow but it was an oil painting and though I had not thought of a Millet for years, I did like it.

After this experience with Millet's Man with a Hoe and the Rosenthal picture I began to become educated aesthetically, first etchings, they were in those days reproduced in magazines and we used to cut them out and then we began to collect real etchings, not many but still a few, all this was still in San Francisco, Seymour Hayden, Whistler, Zorn and finally Meryon, but these two were much later, and Japanese prints. I took on all this earnestly but inevitably as they were not oil paintings they did not hold my attention. I do remember, still in San Francisco, a sign painting of a man painting a sign a huge sign painting and this did hold my attention. I used to go and look at it and stand and watch it and then it bothered me because it almost did look like a man painting a sign and one wants, one likes to be deceived but not for too long. That is a thing to remember about an oil painting. It bothered me many years later when I first looked at the Velasquez's in Madrid. They almost looked really like people and if they kept on doing so might it not bother one as wax works bother one. And if it did bother one was it an oil painting, because an oil painting is something that looking at it it looks as it is, an oil painting.

All this has to be remembered but to go back again.

The next thing that interested me in the way of an oil painting, still in San Francisco, were some paintings by a frenchman named Cazin. Of course perhaps none of you have ever heard of him.

He was one of the then new school of painters who being accepted officially in the salons were the commonplace end of the then still outlawed school of impressionists. Cazin made a field of wheat look almost like a field of wheat blowing in the wind. It did look like a field of wheat blowing in the wind and I was very fond of looking at fields of wheat blowing in the wind. In a little while I found myself getting a little mixed as to which looked most like a field of wheat blowing in the wind the picture of the field of wheat or the real field of wheat. When that happens one naturally gets discouraged. I may say one finally gets discouraged. One is not discouraged at first, one is confirmed in one's feeling about a field of wheat blowing in the wind and then gradually one is less pleased and at last one is discouraged. One does not like to be mixed in one's mind as to which looks most like something at which one is looking the thing or the painting. And so I rather lost interest in both.

There was another painting also by Cazin called Juan and Juanita or at least that is what I called it to myself because at that time I was reading a story that had these two names, I think actually it was called something biblical. Anyway it was a picture of two children lost in the desert and the desert was like the California deserts I knew. The desert this painted desert looked very like the desert but the children did not look really very much like children and so finally I preferred that picture to the field of wheat. I suppose I concluded that since the children did not really look as children looked to me probably neither did the blowing wheat nor the desert. All this of course was very dim inside me.

The next thing that impressed me in the way of oil painting was in Baltimore at the Walters Art Gallery the pictures of the Barbizon school, not Millet any longer but Daubignys and Rousseaus. Here once more the blue sky behind the rocks was the blue sky I knew behind rocks, and particularly the Rousseaus solidifying for me the blue sky behind rocks held me. As the pictures were small and the blue sky was small the question of the real sky did not bother me, and beside although it pleased me and I liked it it did not really excite me. Then I went to Boston and there I saw the first big Corots. The one in the Boston Museum the evening star. There again I felt peaceful about it being a sky because after all it was filled with association, it was not a thing in itself. It looked like the evening star it looked as Tannhauser felt and more than that one could feel how it looked and so there was no bother. Later on, Corots always pleased me but that I think was largely because they were so gentle. I never was much troubled by anything in connection with them.

Then I bought myself my first oil painting. It was painted by an American painter called Shilling and I wanted it because it looked like any piece of American country and the sky was high and there was a cloud and it looked like something in movement and I remember very well what it was like, and then again it bothered me because after all which did I like most the thing seen or the thing painted and what was a thing in movement. I began to be almost consciously bothered.

Then I went to Europe first Antwerp then Italy then France then Spain and then later again France. Of course all this in successive years, I naturally looked at a great many pictures.

In Antwerp I only remember the colour of the Rubens' and that they were religious. I liked their colour. I liked pretty well liked their religion.

Then we went through France to Italy.

The Louvre at first was only gold frames to me gold frames which were rather glorious, and looking out of the window of the Louvre with the gold frames being all gold behind within was very glorious. I always like, as well as liked looking out of windows in museums. It is more complete, looking out of windows in museums, than looking out of windows anywhere else.

Then we went to Italy and my brother and I spent a long hot summer in Italy, in Florence and in Venice and in Perugia and I began to sleep and dream in front of oil paintings.

I did look out of the windows of the museums but it was really not necessary.

There were very few people in the galleries in Italy in the summers in those days and there were long benches and they were red and they were comfortable at least they were to me and the guardians were indifferent or amiable and I could really lie down and sleep in front of the pictures. You can see that it was not necessary to look out of the windows.

In sleeping and waking in front particularly of the Tintorettos the Giottos and the Castagnas, the Botticellis were less suited to that activity, they little as one can think it they bothered me because the Italian flowers were just like the flowers in the Botticelli pictures. I used to walk in the country and then I concluded that the Botticellis being really so like the flowers in the country they were not the pictures before which one could sleep, they were to my feeling, being that they looked so like the flowers in the country, they were artificial. You know what I mean artificial flowers. And I literally mean just that. At least that is the way I felt then about it. I liked Mantegna then because he made me realize that white is a colour, and in a way he made me feel something about what oil paintings were that prepared me for much that was to come later.

As I say in sleeping and waking in front of all these pictures I really began to realize that an oil painting is an oil painting. I was beginning after that to be able to look with pleasure at any oil painting.

I had another curious experience concerning oil painting at about that same time.

I went into Italian churches a great deal then and I began to be very much interested in black and white marble. Even other colored marbles. I went in Rome to Saint John without the walls and I did not like the marble and then I looked at the marble I did like and I began to touch it and I found gradually that if I liked it there was always as much imitation oil painted marble as real marble. And all being mixed together I liked it. It was very hard to tell the real from the false. I spent hours in those hot summer days feeling marble to see which was real and which was not. I found that granite pillars if they were four were some of them make believe if they gave me pleasure, some could be real but some had to be painted, of course they did, if it was all marble or if it was all granite there was nothing to content the eye by deceiving it. Of course anybody could come to know that.

And so I began to look at all and any oil painting. I looked at funny pictures in churches where they described in a picture what had happened to them, the ex-voto pictures. I remember one of a woman falling out of a high two wheeled cart, this a picture of what happened to her and how she was not killed. I looked at all oil paintings that I happened to see and not consciously but slowly I began to feel that it made no difference what an oil painting painted it always did and should look like an oil painting.

And so one comes to any oil painting through any other oil painting.

Then we went to Spain and there I looked and looked at pictures. I do not think there were any windows to look out of in the Prado museum in those days. Any way I only remember looking and looking at pictures. The gallery was not arranged in those days and you found your pictures. It was my first real experience in finding pictures. I then for the first time really began to think about them. I liked Rubens landscapes because they all moved together, people landscape animals and color. I liked Titians because they did not move at all and as they did not move they were noble. The Velasquez bothered me as I say because like the Cazins of my youth they were too real and yet they were not real enough to be real and not unreal enough to be unreal.

And then I found Greco and that really excited me.

There the oil painting was pure it neither moved nor was still nor was it real. I finally came to like them best. I liked them because every thing in them was so long and I liked them because they were so white. I have never forgotten what white is since.

Then I came back to France and there at once I forgot Greco because there was the Louvre and somehow there with the gold frames and all, there was an elegance about it all, that did not please me, but that I could not refuse, and in a way it destroyed oil paintings for me.

I completely for a while forgot about oil paintings.

I did not care at that time for elegance and since oil painting, so the Louvre had decided for me, were fundamentally elegant I lost interest in oil paintings. I did not get back any interest in them until the next year.

To finish a thing, that is to keep on finishing a thing, that is to be one going on finishing so that something is a thing that any one can see is a finished thing is something. To finish a thing so that any one can know that that thing is a finished thing is something.

To make a pretty thing so that any one can feel that the thing is a pretty thing is something.

To begin a thing that any one can see is begun is something. To begin a pretty thing so that any one can see that a pretty thing has been begun is something.[1]

I remember much later than that being very bothered by Courbet. I had commenced looking at later oil paintings, that is later than old museum pictures. I liked David then because he was so dry and Ary Sheffer because he was so tender and Greuze because he was so pretty and they all painted people to look like people that is more or less to look like people, to look like people more or less, and it did not make any difference.

But Courbet bothered me. He did really use the color that nature looked like that any landscape looked like when it was just like itself as you saw it in passing. Courbet really did use the colors that nature looked like to anybody, that a water-fall in the woods looked like to anybody.

And what had that to do with anything, in fact did it not destroy a little of the reality of the oil painting. The paintings of Courbet were very real as oil paintings, they existed very really as oil painting, but did the colors that were the colors anybody could see trees and water-falls naturally were, did these colors add or did they detract from the reality of the oil painting as oil painting. Perhaps and most likely perhaps it did not really make any difference. There was a moment though when I worried about the Courbets not being an oil painting but being a piece of country in miniature as seen in a diminishing glass. One always does like things in

---

[1]Gertrude Stein, *Portraits and Prayers* (New York: Random House, 1934), p. 54.

little. Models of furniture are nice, little flower pots are nice, little gardens are nice, penny penny peep shows are nice, magic lanterns are nice and photographs and cinemas are nice and the mirrors in front of automobiles are nice because they give the whole scene always in little and yet in natural colors like the receiver of a camera. As I say one does quite naturally like things in small, it is easy one has it all at once, and it is just like that, or in distorted mirrors when one has it even more all at once, and as I say I worried lest Courbet was like that. But soon I concluded that no, it only seemed so, no the Courbets were really oil paintings with the real life of oil paintings as oil paintings should have. Only the Courbets being nearly something else always keeps them from being really all they are. However. To come back to pictures that is oil paintings.

I began to feel that as a different thing from Courbet, nobody or nothing looked now any more like the people in the old pictures in the museums and the old pictures were alright. Did anything one saw look really like the new pictures and were they alright.

You see it gets to be a bother but still if oil paintings are oil paintings and you really like to look at them it is not really a bother.

Should a picture look like anything or does it, even a Courbet, or a Velasquez, or does it make any difference if it does or if it does not as long as it is an oil painting.

And if it is less like anything does it make any difference and if it is more like anything does it make any difference and yet if it is not like anything at all is it an oil painting.

You see it does get complicated because after all you have to like looking at an oil painting.

And then slowly through all this and looking at many many pictures I came to Cezanne and there you were, at least there I was, not all at once but as soon as I got used to it. The landscape looked like a landscape that is to say what is yellow in the landscape looked yellow in the oil painting, and what was blue in the landscape looked blue in the oil painting and if it did not there still was the oil painting, the oil painting by Cezanne. The same thing was true of the people there was no reason why it should be but it was, the same thing was true of the chairs, the same thing was true of the apples. The apples looked like apples the chairs looked like chairs and it all had nothing to do with anything because if they did not look like apples or chairs or landscape or people they were apples and chairs and landscape and people. They were so entirely these things that they were not an oil painting and yet that is just what the Cezannes were they were an oil painting. They were so entirely an oil painting that it was all there whether they were finished, the paintings, or whether they were not finished. Finished or unfinished it always was what it looked like the very essence of an oil painting because everything was always there, really there.

Cezanne

The Irish lady can say, that to-day is every day. Caesar can say that every day is to-day and they say that every day is as they say.

In this way Cezanne nearly did nearly in this way Cezanne nearly did nearly did and nearly did. And was I surprised. Was I very surprised. Was I surprised. I was surprised and in that patient, are you patient when you find bees. Bees in a garden make a specialty of honey and so does honey. Honey and prayer. Honey and there. There where the grass can grow nearly four times yearly.[2]

This then was a great relief to me and I began my writing.

[2]Stein, *Portraits and Prayers,* p. 11.

This sounds as if it might have been an end of something as being in the nature of a solution but it was not it was just something going on.

Up to this time I had been getting acquainted with pictures I had been intimate with a number of them but I had not been really familiar with them.

I once wrote something called Made A Mile Away, which was a description of all the pictures that had influenced me, all the pictures up to this moment the moment when I became familiar with pictures.

From this time on familiarity began and I like familiarity. It does not in me breed contempt it just breeds familiarity. And the more familiar a thing is the more there is to be familiar with. And so my familiarity began and kept on being.

From that time on I could look at any oil painting. That is the essence of familiarity that you can look at any of it.

Having thus become familiar with oil paintings I looked at any and at all of them and I looked at thousands and thousands of them. Any year in Paris if you want to look at any and all paintings you can look at thousands and thousands of them, you can look at them any day and everywhere. There are a great great many oil paintings in Paris.

Once a picture dealer told me and he knew that there were sixty thousand people in Paris painting pictures and that about twenty thousand of them were earning a living at it. There are a great many oil paintings to be seen any year in Paris.

Gradually getting more and more familiar with oil paintings was like getting gradually more and more familiar with faces as you look very hard at some of them and you look very hard at all of them and you do all of this very often. Faces gradually tell you something, there is no doubt about that as you grow more and more familiar with any and all faces and so it is with oil paintings. The result was that in a way I slowly knew what an oil painting is and gradually I realized as I had already found out very often that there is a relation between anything that is painted and the painting of it. And gradually I realized as I had found very often that that relation was so to speak nobody's business. The relation between the oil painting and the thing painted was really nobody's business. It could be the oil painting's business but actually for the purpose of the oil painting after the oil painting was painted it was not the oil painting's business and so it was nobody's business.

But still one always does like a resemblance.

A resemblance is always a pleasurable sensation and so a resemblance is almost always there.

That is not the business so to speak of the oil painting, that is just a pleasant human weakness. Anybody and so almost everybody pleasantly likes anything that resembles anything or any one.

Then there is another thing another pleasant human weakness. There is another thing about an oil painting. It makes you see something to which it is resembling makes you see the thing in the way it the oil painting resembles it. And that too and that again is a pleasant thing. But then really and this everybody knows, very soon anybody that is everybody really forgets about this resemblance. They naturally do do so because things change at least they seem so to do or any way they look as if they did change that is they look different and so the resemblance of the oil painting that is to anybody that is to anything is only a thing that has become historical.

And so we are once more back to the life in and for itself of an oil painting.

As I say having in this way become more and more familiar with any kind of an oil painting I of course became more and more familiar with many particular oil paintings with a great many particular oil paintings, and as I say when you have looked at many many faces and have become familiar with them, you may find something new in a new face you may be surprised by a different kind of a face you may be even shocked by a different kind of a face you may like or not like a new kind of a face but you cannot refuse a new face. You must accept a face as a face. And so with an oil painting. You can now see that when it came first to Matisse and then to the cubism of Picasso nothing was a bother to me. Yes of course in a way it was a bother to me but not the bother of a refusal. That would not have been possible being that I had become familiar with oil paintings, and the essence of familiarity being that you can look at any of it.

Matisse

One was quite certain that for a long part of his being one being living he had been trying to be certain that he was wrong in doing what he was doing and then when he could not come to be certain that he had been wrong in doing what he had been doing, when he had completely convinced himself that he would not come to be certain that he had been wrong in doing what he had been doing he was really certain then that he was a great one and he certainly was a great one. Certainly every one could be certain of this thing that this one is a great one.[3]

If I Told Him
A COMPLETED PORTRAIT OF PICASSO

If I told him would he like it. Would he like it if I told him.

Would he like it would Napoleon would Napoleon would would he like it.

[3]Stein, *Portraits and Prayers*, p. 12.

If Napoleon if I told him if I told him if Napoleon. Would he like it if I told him if I told him if Napoleon. Would he like it if Napoleon if Napoleon if I told him. If I told him if Napoleon if Napoleon if I told him. If I told him would he like it would he like it if I told him.

Shutters shut and open so do queens. Shutters shut and shutters and so shutters shut and shutters and so and so shutters and so shutters shut and so shutters shut and shutters and so. And so shutters shut and so and also. And also and so and so and also. Let me recite what history teaches, History teaches.[4]

The Life of Juan Gris

As a Spaniard he knew cubism and had stepped through into it. He had stepped through it. There was beside this perfection. To have it shown you. Then came the war and desertion. There was little aid. Four years partly illness much perfection and rejoining beauty and perfection and then at the end there came a definite creation of something. This is what is to be measured. He made something that is to be measured. And that is that something.[5]

Anything may be a surprise to you even a shock to you but nothing can be a bother to you if you are really familiar with it. This is a natural thing.

And then having gotten so far I began often to think a great deal about oil paintings. They were familiar to me they were never really a bother to me but sometimes they were an annoyance to me.

Having now accepted all oil paintings as oil paintings I naturally sometimes began to feel something else about

---

[4]Stein, *Portraits and Prayers*, p. 21.
[5]Stein, *Portraits and Prayers*, p. 49.

them. I wondered what they would be if some day they would be different. But could they be different. I often wondered in those days if oil paintings ever could be different.

This led me back to the question in oil paintings the question one might call it the eternal question for painters of oil paintings the question of the subject of the oil painting.

I naturally did not talk to painters about what they painted in their oil paintings. Painters real painters never really ever talk about that. But I told about how every picture affected me. And in a way that is what I can say. But now to go on with the difficult question why when and in which way can a painter have a subject for his pictures. And if he does and of course he does why does he. Why does he paint what he does paint.

There are first of all three things, people, objects which include flowers and fruits, landscapes which included the sea and complications of these things which may if you like be called painters' thoughts.

Beside this there are all these things staying still and then there are all these things not staying so still, even sometimes almost moving, and somehow sometime almost any painter paints them all.

And if he does is it annoying.

And is it really that that which the painter paints that in an oil painting is its element of annoyance.

Yes I think so.

Most people think that the annoyance that they feel from an oil painting that annoys them and a great many oil paintings annoy a great many people, the annoyance then that these people that anybody feels from an oil painting they think comes from the way the oil painting represents these things, the things represented in the oil painting. But I myself do not think so. I think the annoyance comes from the fact that

the oil painting exists by reason of these things the oil paint-
ing represents in the oil painting, and profoundly it should
not do so, so thinks the oil painting, so sometime thinks the
painter of the oil painting, so instinctively feels the person
looking at the oil painting. Really in everybody's heart there
is a feeling of annoyance at the inevitable existence of an oil
painting in relation to what it has painted people, objects
and landscapes. And indeed and of course as I have already
made you realize that is not what an oil painting is. An oil
painting is an oil painting, and these things are only the way
the only way an oil painter makes an oil painting.

One might say almost all oil painters spend their life in
trying to get away from this inevitability. They struggle and
the result is what everybody naturally likes or dislikes de-
pending upon whether they think the struggle is hopeless or
whether it is not. And then everybody almost everybody likes
a resemblance even when there is none. Does the painter
like the resemblance, oh yes he does. He does like a resem-
blance. That is a naturally pleasant human thing, to like a
resemblance. And does this naturally pleasant human thing
the liking a resemblance make everything difficult very diffi-
cult. Yes it certainly does. And it makes an oil painting an-
noying.

You see how this brings one to anything, to everything that
any one has ever tried to do in painting.

And then there is another trouble. A painting is painted as
a painting, as an oil painting existing as an oil painting, it
may be in or it may be out of its frame, but an oil painting
and that is a real bother always will have a tendency to go
back to its frame, even if it has never been out of it. That is
one of the things that an oil painting any oil painting has a
very great tendency to do. And this is a bother sometimes to
the painter and sometimes to any one looking at an oil
painting.

Does an oil painting tend to go back into its frame because after all an oil painting belongs in its frame.

Or does it not.

It does and does not. But mostly it does and that may make for elegance that, that it does belong in its frame but it may also be a bother to the quality in it that makes it an oil painting.

And if it does belong in its frame, must it the oil painting be static.

If it tries to move and there have been good attempts to make it move does it move. Leonardo, in the Virgin child and Sainte Anne tried to make it move, Rubens in his landscapes, Picasso and Velasquez in their way, and Seurat in his way.

The trouble is always, is it the people in it who move or does the picture move and if so should it. I myself like it to do so but then I like a picture, that is an oil painting to do anything it likes to do.

The first thing that ever interested me in that way as the picture moving was the Leonardo in the Louvre, the Virgin, the child and Sainte Anne. Before this the moving in a picture was the effect of moving, but in this picture there was an internal movement, not of the people or light or any of these things but inside in the oil painting. In other words the picture did not live within the frame, in other words it did not belong within the frame. The Cezanne thing was different, it went further and further into the picture the life of the oil painting but it stayed put.

I have thought a great deal about all this and I am still thinking about it. I have passionately hoped that some picture would remain out of its frame, I think it can even while it does not, even while it remains there. And this is the problem of all modern painting just as it has been the problem of all old painting. That is to say the first hope of a painter who really feels hopeful about painting is the hope that the painting will move, that it will live outside its frame.

On the other hand most elegant painting does not move does not live outside its frame and one does like elegance in painting.

I wonder if I have at all given you an idea of what an oil painting is. I hope I have even if it does seem confused. But the confusion is essential in the idea of an oil painting.

There it is the oil painting in its frame, a thing in itself. There it is and it has to look like people or objects or landscapes. Besides that it musts not completely only exist in its frame. It must have its own life. And yet it may not move nor imitate movement, not really, nor must it stay still. It must not only be in its frame but it must not, only, be in its frame. This whole question of a picture being in its frame returning to its frame or not returning to its frame is the question that has latterly bothered me the most. Modern pictures have made the very definite effort to leave their frame. But do they stay out, do they go back and if they do is that where they belong and has anybody been deceived. I think about that a great deal these days.

You see it is difficult to describe exactly what an oil painting is, it is difficult for those who like to look at oil paintings presumably also difficult for those who paint oil paintings and it leads painters to the thing the last thing of which I wish to speak, the literary ideas so called of the painter.

I hope you all begin to feel with me what an oil painting is and granted that an oil painting is that that one likes to look at it and granted that one likes to look at it even it it is not that. Also that you do understand that what really annoys people that is anybody who is at all annoyed by an oil painting is not its being an oil painting, but the subject that is to say what it paints as an oil painting. I know I myself and mostly I am not bothered by certain things oil paintings do that is by the things oil paintings always have to paint. For instance taking all the later oil paintings. Is it true that they are alright when the painting is the painting of objects and are they not alright when they are the painting of people. In spite of everything can that be a bother. May it not be a bother to you. May it not bother you. I remember so well some one saying of Van Gogh, it was a great many years ago, I like his pictures of people but not of flowers, and then adding reflectively, because of course I never do look at people and so I do not know what people look like but I do look at flowers and I do know what flowers look like. As I say persistently the thing that really annoys that deeply annoys people, that is, anybody who is annoyed by oil paintings, is not the way they are painted, that they can always get accustomed to more or less and reasonably quickly, but the subject of the oil painting. Of course it is always the same subject but even so it takes so much longer for the one looking at an oil painting to accustom himself to the subject in spite of it always being the same subject than to accustom himself to the oil painting itself. At least that is the way I feel about it.

And now there is one more subject in connection with oil paintings, the literary ideas painters have and that they paint.

The literary ideas painters have and that they paint are not at all the literary ideas writers have.

Of course the best writers that is the writers who feel writing the most as well as the best painters that is the painters who feel painting the most do not have literary ideas. But then a great many writers and a great many painters do have literary ideas. The thing that has often interested me is that the painters' literary idea is not the same kind of an idea as the writers' literary idea although they call it the same thing.

The painter has an idea which he calls a literary idea and it is to him that is he thinks it is the same kind of an idea as a writer has but it is not. And its being not makes the essential thing that makes an oil painting.

A painter's literary idea always consists not in the action but in the distortion of the form. That could never be a writer's literary idea. Then a painter's idea of action always has to do with something else moving rather than the center of the picture. This is just the opposite of the writer's idea, everything else can be quiet, except the central thing which has to move. And because of all this a painter cannot really write and a writer cannot really paint, even fairly badly.

All this is very important because it is important. It is important not for the painter or for the writer but for those who like to look at paintings and who like to know what an oil painting is and who like to know what bothers them in what an oil painting is. I hope I have been making it slowly clear to you. I might have told you more in detail but in that case you would that is to say I would not have as clearly seen as I do now what an oil painting is.

1935

Henri Lebasque, *Paysage avec femme,* oil on canvas, 19 x 23 1/2 in. Formerly Wallace Stevens's collection. Montgomery Gallery, San Francisco.

The Relations between
Poetry and Painting

WALLACE STEVENS

*At the invitation of Monroe Wheeler, Stevens delivered the following
address at the Museum of Modern Art on January 15, 1951.
Thirty-five years earlier, no longer a young man but still a begin-
ning poet, he had frequented Walter Arensberg's apartment and his
circle of "advanced" poets and painters in New York. One evening
he dined with Marcel Duchamp and went afterward to look at his
"things." "I made very little of them," he wrote to his wife. "But nat-
urally, without sophistication in that direction, and with only a very
rudimentary feeling about art, I expect little of myself." In time, he
came to expect a great deal. Pictures became an avocation, and his
avocation yielded crucial metaphors. When in New York on business
he was an inveterate gallery-goer; in Hartford there were the
Wadsworth Atheneum (its brilliant director, A. Everett Austin, was
a neighbor) and his own collection. When he spoke of the painters he
liked, he spoke of Braque and Klee and Kandinsky. When he col-
lected for himself, his purchases were far less adventurous than his
taste —Maurice Brianchon, Jean Labasque, Pierre Tal Coat. His
selections, a friend remarked, "all belonged to a certain sort of gallery
right down from the Madeleine." But Stevens's collecting (from the
1930s he used the Parisian bookseller Anatole Vidal as his agent,
and after Vidal's death his daughter Paule) was of a peculiar order.
"When he talked about painting," said James Johnson Sweeney, his*

Reprinted with permission of Random House in New York and Faber & Faber in
London from *The Necessary Angel,* by Wallace Stevens (1951), 159–76. Copyright © 1951
by Wallace Stevens.

friend and onetime director of the Guggenheim Museum, "I thought he looked at contemporary painting much as he looked at French poetry, not as something native to him but which attracted him. I found it was always what was interesting to him as a stimulant, not as a document." Picasso stimulated "The Man with the Blue Guitar." And one of Tal Coat's still lifes prompted "Angel Surrounded by Paysans," where Stevens gives voice to a muse who is also a painter: "In my sight, you see the earth again, / Cleared of its stiff and stubborn, man-locked set." In an earlier poem called "The Latest Freed Man" (which mentions the portrait of Vidal that Stevens kept in his bedroom), he predicts and celebrates the subject of his museum lecture. What he says of reality he is saying too of art, in the poem's moment the same term:

> *It was everything being more real, himself*
> *At the centre of reality, seeing it.*
> *It was everything bulging and blazing and big in itself,*
> *The blue of the rug, the portrait of Vidal,*
> Qui fait fi des joliesses banales, *the chairs.*

1

ROGER FRY concluded a note on Claude by saying that "few of us live so strenuously as never to feel a sense of nostalgia for that Saturnian reign to which Virgil and Claude can waft us." He spoke in that same note of Corot and Whistler and Chinese landscape and certainly he might just as well have spoken, in relation to Claude, of many poets, as, for example, Chénier or Wordsworth. This is simply the analogy between two different forms of poetry. It might be better to say that it is the identity of poetry revealed as between poetry in words and poetry in paint.

Poetry, however, is not limited to Virgilian landscape, nor painting to Claude. We find the poetry of mankind in the figures of the old men of Shakespeare, say, and the old men of Rembrandt; or in the figures of Biblical women, on the one hand, and of the madonnas of all Europe, on the other; and it is easy to wonder whether the poetry of children has not been created by the poetry of the Child, until one stops to think how much of the poetry of the whole world is the poetry of children, both as they are and as they have been written of and painted, as if they were the creatures of a dimension in which life and poetry are one. The poetry of humanity is, of course, to be found everywhere.

There is a universal poetry that is reflected in everything. This remark approaches the idea of Baudelaire that there exists an unascertained and fundamental aesthetic, or order, of which poetry and painting are manifestations, but of which, for that matter, sculpture or music or any other aesthetic realization would equally be a manifestation. Generalizations as expansive as these: that there is a universal poetry that is reflected in everything or that there may be a fundamental aesthetic of which poetry and painting are related but dissimilar manifestations, are speculative. One is better satisfied by particulars.

No poet can have failed to recognize how often a detail, a propos or remark, in respect to painting, applies also to poetry. The truth is that there seems to exist a corpus of remarks in respect to painting, most often the remarks of painters themselves, which are as significant to poets as to painters. All of these details, to the extent that they have meaning for poets as well as for painters, are specific instances of relations between poetry and painting. I suppose, therefore, that it would be possible to study poetry by studying painting or that one could become a painter after one had become a poet, not to speak of carrying on in both métiers at once, with the economy of genius, as Blake did. Let me illustrate this point of the double value (and one might well call it the multifold value) of sayings for painters that mean as much for poets because they are, after all, sayings about art. Does not the saying of Picasso that a picture is a horde of destructions also say that a poem is a horde of destructions? When Braque says "The senses deform, the mind forms," he is speaking to poet, painter, musician and sculptor. Just as poets can be affected by the sayings of painters, so can painters be affected by the sayings of poets and so can both be affected by sayings addressed to neither. For many examples, see Miss Sitwell's *Poet's Note-Book*. These details come together so subtly and so minutely that the existence of relations is lost sight of. This, in turn, dissipates the idea of their existence.

2

We may regard the subject, then, from two points of view, the first from the point of view of the man whose center is painting, whether or not he is a painter, the second from the point of view of the man whose center is poetry, whether or not he is a poet. To make use of the point of view of the man whose center is painting let me refer to the chapter in Leo Stein's *Appreciation* entitled "On Reading Poetry and Seeing Pictures." He says that, when he was a child, he became aware of composition in nature and gradually realized that art and composition are one. He began to experiment as follows:

I put on the table . . . an earthenware plate . . . and this I looked at every day for minutes or for hours. I had in mind to see it as a picture, and waited for it to become one. In time it did. The change came suddenly when the plate as an inventorial object . . . a certain shape, certain colors applied to it . . . went over into a composition to which all these elements were merely contributory. The painted composition on the plate ceased to be *on* it but became a part of a larger composition which was the plate as a whole. I had made a beginning to seeing pictorially.

What had been begun was carried out in all directions. I wanted to be able to see anything as a composition and found that it was possible to do this.

He improvised a definition of art: that it is nature seen in the light of its significance, and recognizing that this significance was one of forms he added "formal" to "significance."

Turning to education in hearing, he observed that there is nothing comparable to the practice in composition that the visible world offers. By composition he meant the compositional use of words: the use of their existential meanings. Composition was his passion. He considered that a formally complete picture is one in which all the parts are so related to one another that they all imply each other. Finally he said, "an excellent illustration is the line from Wordsworth's Michael . . . 'And never lifted up a single stone.'" One might say of a lazy workman, "He's been out there, just loafing, for an hour and never lifted up a single stone," and no one would think this great poetry. . . . These lines would have no existential value; they would simply call attention to the lazy workman. But the compositional use by Wordsworth of his line makes it something entirely different. These simple words become weighted with the tragedy of the old shepherd, and are saturated with poetry. Their referential importance is slight, for the importance of the action to which they refer is not in the action itself, but in the meaning; and that meaning is borne by the words. Therefore this is a line of great poetry.

The selection of composition as a common denominator of poetry and painting is the selection of a technical characteristic by a man whose center was painting, even granting that he was not a man whom one thinks of as a technician. Poetry and painting alike create through composition.

Now, a poet looking for an analogy between poetry and painting and trying to take the point of view of a man whose center is poetry begins with a sense that the technical pervades painting to such a degree that the two are identified. This is untrue, since, if painting was purely technical, that conception of it would exclude the artist as a person. I want to say something, therefore, based on the sensibility of the poet and of the painter. I am not quite sure that I know what is meant by sensibility. I suppose that it means feeling or, as we say, the feelings. I know what is meant by nervous sensibility, as, when at a concert, the auditors, having composed themselves and resting there attentively, hear suddenly an outburst on the trumpets from which they shrink by way of a nervous reaction. The satisfaction that we have when we look out and find that it is a fine day or when we are looking at one of the limpid vistas of Corot in the pays de Corot seems to be something else. It is commonly said that the origins of poetry are to be found in the sensibility. We began with the conjunction of Claude and Virgil, noting how one evoked the other. Such evocations are attributable to similarities of sensibility. If, in Claude, we find ourselves in the realm of Saturn, the ruler of the world in a golden age of innocence and plenty, and if, in Virgil, we find ourselves in the same realm, we recognize that there is, as between Claude and Virgil, an identity of sensibility. Yet if one questions the dogma that the origins of poetry are to be found in the sensibility and if one says that a fortunate poem or a fortunate painting is a synthesis of exceptional concentration (that degree of concentration that has a lucidity of its own, in which we see clearly what we want to do and do it instantly and perfectly), we find that the operative force within us does not, in fact, seem to be the sensibility, that is to say, the feelings. It seems to be a constructive faculty, that derives its energy more from the imagination than from the sensibility. I have spoken of questioning, not of denying. The mind retains experience, so that long after the experience, long after the winter clearness of a January morning, long after the limpid vistas of Corot, that faculty within us of which I have spoken makes its own constructions out of that experience. If it merely reconstructed the experience or repeated for us our sensations in the face of it, it would be the memory. What it really does is to use it as material with which it does whatever it wills. This is the typical function of the imagination which always makes use of the familiar to produce the unfamiliar. What these remarks seem to involve is the substitution for the idea of inspiration of the idea of an effort of the mind not dependent on the vicissitudes of the sensibility. It is so completely possible to sit at one's table and without the help of the agitation of the feelings to write plays of incomparable enhancement that that is precisely what Shakespeare did. He was not dependent on the fortuities of inspiration. It is not the least part of his glory that one can say of him, the greater the thinker the greater the poet. It would come nearer the mark to say the greater the mind the greater the poet, because the evil of thinking as poetry is not the same thing as the good of thinking in poetry. The point is that the poet does his job by virtue of an effort of the mind. In doing so, he is in rapport with the painter, who does his job, with respect to the problems of form and color, which confront him incessantly, not by inspiration, but by imagination or by the miraculous kind of reason that the imagination sometimes promotes. In short, these two arts, poetry and painting, have in common a laborious element, which, when it is exercised, is not only a labor but a consummation as well. For proof of this let me set side by side the poetry in the prose of Proust, taken from his vast novel, and the painting, by chance, of Jacques Villon. As to Proust, I quote a paragraph from Professor Saurat:

> Another province he has added to literature is the description of those eternal moments in which we are lifted out of the drab world. . . . The madeleine dipped in tea, the steeples of Martinville, some trees on a road, a perfume of wild flowers, a vision of light and shade on trees, a spoon clinking on a plate that is like a railway man's hammer on the wheels of the train from which the trees were seen, a stiff napkin in an hotel, an inequality in two stones in Venice and the disjointment in the yard of the Guermantes' town house. . . .

As to Villon: shortly before I began to write these notes I dropped into the Carré Gallery in New York to see an exhibition of paintings which included about a dozen works by him. I was immediately conscious of the presence of the enchantments of intelligence in all his prismatic material. A woman lying in a hammock was transformed into a complex of planes and tones, radiant, vaporous, exact. A tea-pot and a cup or two took their place in a reality composed wholly of things unreal. These works were *deliciae* of the spirit as distinguished from *delectationes* of the senses and this was so because one found in them the labor of calculation, the appetite for perfection.

3

One of the characteristics of modern art is that it is un-compromising. In this it resembles modern politics, and perhaps it would appear on study, including a study of the rights of man and of women's hats and dresses, that every-thing modern, or possibly merely new, is, in the nature of things, uncompromising. It is especially uncompromising in respect to precinct. One of the De Goncourts said that nothing in the world hears as many silly things said as a pic-ture in a museum; and in thinking about that remark one has to bear in mind that in the days of the De Goncourts there was no such thing as a museum of modern art. A really modern definition of modern art, instead of making conces-sions, fixes limits which grow smaller and smaller as time passes and more often than not come to include one man alone, just as if there should be scrawled across the façade of the building in which we now are, the words *Cézanne deli-neavit.* Another characteristic of modern art is that it is plausible. It has a reason for everything. Even the lack of a reason becomes a reason. Picasso expresses surprise that people should ask what a picture means and says that pic-tures are not intended to have meanings. This explains ev-erything. Still another characteristic of modern art is that it is bigoted. Every painter who can be defined as a modern painter becomes, by virtue of that definition, a freeman of the world of art and hence the equal of any other modern painter. We recognize that they differ one from another but in any event they are not to be judged except by other mod-ern painters.

We have this inability (not mere unwillingness) to com-promise, this same plausibility and bigotry in modern poetry. To exhibit this, let me divide modern poetry into two classes,

117

one that is modern in respect to what it says, the other that is modern in respect to form. The first kind is not interested primarily in form. The second is. The first kind is interested in form but it accepts a banality of form as incidental to its language. Its justification is that in expressing thought or feeling in poetry the purpose of the poet must be to subordinate the mode of expression, that, while the value of the poem as a poem depends on expression, it depends primarily on what is expressed. Whether the poet is modern or ancient, living or dead, is, in the last analysis, a question of what he is talking about, whether of things modern or ancient, living or dead. The counterpart of Villon in poetry, writing as he paints, would concern himself with like things (but not necessarily confining himself to them), creating the same sense of aesthetic certainty, the same sense of exquisite realization and the same sense of being modern and living. One sees a good deal of poetry, thanks, perhaps, to Mallarmé's *Un Coup de Dés,* in which the exploitation of form involves nothing more than the use of small letters for capitals, eccentric line-endings, too little or too much punctuation and similar aberrations. These have nothing to do with being alive. They have nothing to do with the conflict between the poet and that of which his poems are made. They are neither "bonne soupe" nor "beau langage."

What I have said of both classes of modern poetry is inadequate as to both. As to the first, which permits a banality of form, it is even harmful, as suggesting that it possesses less of the artifice of the poet than the second. Each of these two classes is intransigent as to the other. If one is disposed to think well of the class that stands on what it has to say, one has only to think of Gide's remark, "Without the unequaled beauty of his prose, who would continue to interest himself in Bossuet?" The division between the two classes, the division, say, between Valéry and Apollinaire, is the same division into factions that we find everywhere in modern painting. But aesthetic creeds, like other creeds, are the certain evidences of exertions to find the truth. I have tried to say no more than was necessary to evince the relations, in which we are interested, as they exist in the manifestations of today. What, when all is said and done, is the significance of the existence of such relations? Or is it enough to note them? The question is not the same as the question of the significance of art. We do not have to be told of the significance of art. "It is art," said Henry James, "which makes life, makes interest, makes importance . . . and I know of no substitute whatever for the force and beauty of its process." The world about us would be desolate except for the world within us. There is the same interchange between these two worlds that there is between one art and another, migratory passings to and fro, quickenings, Promethean liberations and discoveries.

Yet it may be that just as the senses are no respecters of reality, so the faculties are no respecters of the arts. On the other hand, it may be that we are dealing with something that has no significance, something that is the result of imitation. Quatremère de Quincy distinguished between the poet and the painter as between two imitators, one moral, the other physical. There are imitations within imitations and the relations between poetry and painting may present nothing more. This idea makes it possible, at least, to see more than one side of the subject.

4

All of the relations of which I have spoken are themselves related in the deduction that the vis poetica, the power of poetry, leaves its mark on whatever it touches. The mark of poetry creates the resemblance of poetry as between the most disparate things and unites them all in its recognizable virtue. There is one relation between poetry and painting which does not participate in the common mark of common origin. It is the paramount relation that exists between poetry and people in general and between painting and people in general. I have not overlooked the possibility that, when this evening's subject was suggested, it was intended that the discussion should be limited to the relations between modern poetry and modern painting. This would have involved much tinkling of familiar cymbals. In so far as it would have called for a comparison of this poet and that painter, this school and that school, it would have been fragmentary and beyond my competence. It seems to me that the subject of modern relations is best to be approached as a whole. The paramount relation between poetry and painting today, between modern man and modern art is simply this: that in an age in which disbelief is so profoundly prevalent or, if not disbelief, indifference to questions of belief, poetry and painting, and the arts in general, are, in their measure, a compensation for what has been lost. Men feel that the imagination is the next greatest power to faith: the reigning prince. Consequently their interest in the imagination and its work is to be regarded not as a phase of humanism but as a vital self-assertion in a world in which nothing but the self remains, if that remains. So regarded, the study of the imagination and the study of reality come to appear to be purified, aggrandized, fateful. How much stature, even vatic stature, this conception gives the poet! He need not exercise this dignity in vatic works. How much authenticity, even orphic authenticity, it gives to the painter! He need not display this authenticity in orphic works. It should be enough for him that that to which he has given his life should be so enriched by such an access of value. Poet and painter alike live and work in the midst of a generation that is experiencing essential poverty in spite of fortune. The extension of the mind beyond the range of the mind, the projection of reality beyond reality, the determination to cover the ground, whatever it may be, the determination not to be confined, the recapture of excitement and intensity of interest, the enlargement of the spirit at every time, in every way, these are the unities, the relations, to be summarized as paramount now. It is not material whether these relations exist consciously or unconsciously. One goes back to the coercing influences of time and place. It is possible to be subjected to a lofty purpose and not to know it. But I think that most men of any degree of sophistication, most poets, most painters know it.

When we look back at the period of French classicism in the seventeenth century, we have no difficulty in seeing it as a whole. It is not so easy to see one's own time that way. Pretty much all of the seventeenth century, in France, at least, can be summed up in that one word: classicism. The paintings of Poussin, Claude's contemporary, are the inevitable paintings of the generation of Racine. If it had been a time when dramatists used the detailed scene directions that we expect today, the directions of Racine would have left one wondering whether one was reading the description of a scene or the description of one of Poussin's works. The practice confined them to the briefest generalization. Thus, after the list of persons in *King Lear,* Shakespeare added only two words: "Scene: Britain." Yet even so, the directions of Racine, for all their brevity, suggest Poussin. That a common quality is to be detected in such simple things exhibits the extent of the interpenetration persuasively. The direction for *Britannicus* is "The scene is at Rome, in a chamber of the palace of Nero"; for *Iphigénie en Aulide,* "The scene is at Aulis, before the tent of Agamemnon"; for *Phèdre,* "The scene is at Trézène, a town of the Peloponnesus"; for *Esther,* "The scene is at Susa, in the palais of Assuérus"; and for *Athalie,* "The scene is in the temple of Jerusalem, in a vestibule of the apartment of the grand priest."

Our own time, and by this I mean the last two or three generations, including our own, can be summed up in a way that brings into unity an immense number of details by saying of it that it is a time in which the search for the supreme truth has been a search in reality or through reality or even a search for some supremely acceptable fiction. Juan Gris began some notes on his painting by saying: "The world from which I extract the elements of reality is not visual but imaginative." The history of this attitude in literature and particularly in poetry, in France, has been traced by Marcel Raymond in his *From Baudelaire to Surrealism.* I say particularly in poetry because there are associated with it the names of Baudelaire, Rimbaud, Mallarmé and Valéry. In painting, its history is the history of modern painting. Moreover, I say in France because, in France, the theory of poetry is not abstract as it so often is with us, when we have any theory at all, but is a normal activity of the poet's mind in surroundings where he must engage in such activity or be extirpated. Thus necessity develops an awareness and a sense of fatality which give to poetry values not to be reproduced by indifference and chance. To the man who is seeking the sanction of life in poetry, the namby-pamby is an intolerable dissipation. The theory of poetry, that is to say, the total of the theories of poetry, often seems to become in time a mystical theology or, more simply, a mystique. The reason for this must by now be clear. The reason is the same reason why the pictures in a museum of modern art often seem to become in time a mystical aesthetic, a prodigious search of appearance, as if to find a way of saying and of establishing that all things, whether below or above appearance, are one and that it is only through reality, in which they are reflected or, it may be, joined together, that we can reach them. Under such stress, reality changes from substance to subtlety, a subtlety in which it was natural for Cézanne to say: "I see planes bestriding each other and sometimes straight lines seem to me to fall" or "Planes in color. . . . The colored area where shimmer the souls of the planes, in the blaze of the kindled prism, the meeting of planes in the sunlight." The conversion of our *Lumpenwelt* went far beyond this. It was from the point of view of another subtlety that Klee could write: "But he is one chosen that today comes near to the secret places where original law fosters all evolution. And what artist would not establish himself there where the organic center of all movement in time and space—which he calls the mind or heart of creation—determines every function." Conceding that this sounds a bit like sacerdotal jargon, that is not too much to allow to those that have helped to create a new reality, a modern reality, since what has been created is nothing less.

This reality is, also, the momentous world of poetry. Its instantaneities are the familiar intelligence of poets, although it has been the intelligence of another ambiance. Simone Weil in *La Pesanteur et La Grâce* has a chapter on what she calls decreation. She says that decreation is making pass from the created to the uncreated, but that destruction is making pass from the created to nothingness. Modern reality is a reality of decreation, in which our revelations are not the revelations of belief, but the precious portents of our own powers. The greatest truth we could hope to discover, in whatever field we discovered it, is that man's truth is the final resolution of everything. Poets and painters alike today make that assumption and this is what gives them the validity and serious dignity that become them as among those that seek wisdom, seek understanding. I am elevating this a little, because I am trying to generalize and because it is incredible that one should speak of the aspirations of the last two or three generations without a degree of elevation. Sometimes it seems the other way. Sometimes we hear it said that in the eighteenth century there were no poets and that the painters—Chardin, Fragonard, Watteau—were élégants and nothing more; that in the nineteenth century the last great poet was the man that looked most like one and that the whole Pierian sodality had better have been fed to the dogs. It occasionally seems like that today. It must seem as it may. In the logic of events, the only wrong would be to attempt to falsify the logic, to be disloyal to the truth. It would be tragic not to realize the extent of man's dependence on the arts. The kind of world that might result from too exclusive a dependence on them has been questioned, as if the discipline of the arts was in no sense a moral discipline. We have not to discuss that here. It is enough to have brought poetry and painting into relation as sources of our present conception of reality, without asserting that they are the sole sources, and as supports of a kind of life, which it seems to be worth living, with their support, even if doing so is only a stage in the endless study of an existence, which is the heroic subject of all study.

1951

Paul Gauguin, *Contes barbares*, oil on canvas, 51 x 35 in. Folkwang-Museum, Essen. Photograph Giraudon.

Henri Matisse, *Blue Nude*, oil on canvas, 36 1/4 x 55 1/4 in. The Baltimore Museum of Art: The Cone Collection, formed by Dr. Claribel Cone and Miss Etta Cone of Baltimore, Maryland.

Henri Lebasque, *Paysage avec femme,* oil on canvas, 19 x 23 1/2 in. Formerly
Wallace Stevens's collection. Montgomery Gallery, San Francisco.

René Magritte, *The Light of Coincidences*, oil on canvas, 23 ⁵/₈ x 28 ³/₄ in. Dallas Museum of Art: Gift of Mr. and Mrs. Jake L. Harmon.

Jackson Pollock, *Pasiphaë*, oil on canvas, 56 1/8 x 96 in. The Metropolitan Museum of Art: Purchase, Rogers, Fletcher and Harris Brisbane Dick Funds and Joseph Pulitzer Bequest, 1982.

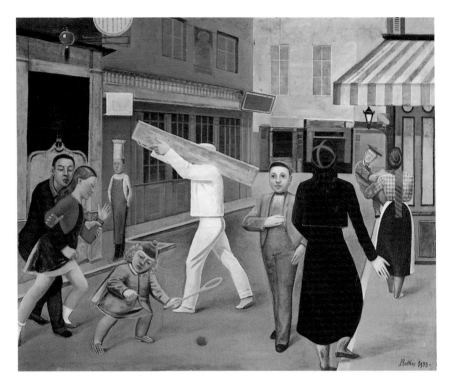

Balthus, *The Street* (1933), oil on canvas, 76 ³/₄ x 94 ¹/₂ in. Collection, The Museum of Modern Art, New York: James Thrall Soby Bequest.

Jane Freilicher, *The Straw Hat*, oil on canvas, 36 x 27 in. Collection of the artist.

Edward Hopper, *House by the Railroad*, oil on canvas, 24 x 29 in. Collection, The Museum of Modern Art, New York: Given anonymously.

Vincent van Gogh, *Self-Portrait,* oil on cardboard, 16 x 12 ³/₄ in.
©1988 by The Art Institute of Chicago: Joseph Winterbotham Collection.

Calm Even in the Catastrophe

W. H. AUDEN

On one wall of Auden's disheveled New York apartment hung Blake's engraving Ancient of Days, *hand-colored by Blake himself. But it has been said that, though possessed of the finest ear among the English poets of this century, Auden had a tin eye. He simply did not care for painting as he did for the "higher" arts of literature and music. And though he wrote the most famous modern poem-about-a-painting, he titled it after a museum (in a city threatened by Hitler) and impatiently compressed several paintings into one moral fable. It was how a painting might instruct us, in the manner of a text or a life, that interested Auden. His poem "The Model" inquires about the past and the prospects of an old woman and concludes:*

> *So the painter may please himself; give her an English park,*
> *Rice-fields in China, or a slum tenement;*
> *Make the sky light or dark;*
> *Put green plush behind her or a red brick wall.*
> *She will compose them all,*
> *Centering the eye on their essential human element.*

"Art's subject is the human clay," Auden insisted in his "Letter to Lord Byron." He even went so far as to claim "All Cézanne's apples I would give away / For one small Goya or a Daumier." It was this same instinct for the "essential human element" that drew him to

Van Gogh as well. Two years after he wrote the following review of
the painter's complete correspondence, Auden edited his own selec-
tion from the letters in a volume called Van Gogh: A Self-Portrait,
meant to highlight "reflections upon the art of painting and the
problems of being a painter." Clearly, though, it was not Van Gogh
the painter but Van Gogh the artist, the man, and perhaps the saint
that intrigued Auden. Van Gogh once contradicted someone who
had praised his work: no, he said, blessed are the poor in spirit,
blessed are the pure of heart. No doubt Auden saw in such a rela-
tionship between an artist and his world and his work a model for
his own ideals.

THE GREAT masters of letter-writing as an art have proba-
bly been more concerned with entertaining their friends
than disclosing their innermost thoughts and feelings; their
epistolary style is characterized by speed, high spirits, wit,
and fantasy. Van Gogh's letters are not art in this sense, but
human documents; what makes them great letters is the ab-
solute self-honesty and nobility of the writer.

The nineteenth century created the myth of the Artist as
Hero, the man who sacrifices his health and happiness to his
art and in compensation claims exemption from all social
responsibilities and norms of behavior.

At first sight Van Gogh seems to fit the myth exactly. He
dresses and lives like a tramp, he expects to be supported by
others, he works at his painting like a fiend, he goes mad.
Yet the more one reads these letters, the less like the myth
he becomes.

He knows he is neurotic and difficult but he does not re-
gard this as a sign of superiority, but as an illness like heart

disease, and hopes that the great painters of the future will be as healthy as the Old Masters.

But this painter who is to come—I can't imagine him living in little cafés, working away with a lot of false teeth, and going to the Zouaves' brothels, as I do.

He sees the age in which he is living as one of transition rather than fulfillment, and is extremely modest about his own achievements.

Giotto and Cimabue, as well as Holbein and Van Dyck, lived in an obeliscal solidly-framed society, architecturally constructed, in which each individual was a stone and all the stones clung together, forming a monumental society. . . . But, you know, we are in the midst of downright *laisser-aller* and anarchy. We artists who love order and symmetry isolate ourselves and are working to define *only one thing*. . . . We *can* paint an atom of the chaos, a horse, a portrait, your grandmother, apples, a landscape. . . .

We do not feel that we are dying, but we do feel the truth that we are of small account, and that we are paying a hard price to be a link in the chain of artists, in health, in youth, in liberty, none of which we enjoy, any more than the cab-horse that hauls a coachful of people out to enjoy the spring.

Furthermore, though he never wavers in his belief that painting is his vocation, he does not claim that painters are superior to other folk.

It was Richepin who said somewhere,

L'amour de l'art fait perdre l'amour vrai.

I think that is terribly true, but on the other hand real love makes you disgusted with art. . . .

The rather superstitious ideas they have here about painting sometimes depress me more than I can tell you, because basically it is really fairly true that a painter as a man is too absorbed in what his eyes see, and is not sufficiently master of the rest of his life.

It is true that Van Gogh did not earn his living but was supported all his life by his brother who was by no means a rich man. But when one compares his attitude towards money with that of say, Wagner, or Baudelaire, how immeasurably more decent and self-respecting Van Gogh appears.

No artist ever asked less of a patron—a laborer's standard of living and enough over to buy paints and canvases. He even worries about his right to the paints and wonders whether he ought not to stick to the cheaper medium of drawing. When, occasionally, he gets angry with his brother, his complaint is not that Theo is stingy but that he is cold; it is more intimacy he craves for, not more cash.

. . . against my person, my manners, clothes, world, you, like so many others, seem to think it necessary to raise so many objections—weighty enough and at the same time obviously without redress—that they have caused our personal brotherly intercourse to wither and die off gradually in the course of the years.

This is the dark side of your character—I think you are mean in this respect—but the bright side is your reliability in money matters.

Ergo conclusion—I acknowledge being under an obligation to you with the greatest pleasure. Only—lacking relations with you, with Teersteg, and with whomever I knew in the past—I want *something else.* . . .

There are people, as you know, who support painters during the time when they do not yet earn anything. But how often doesn't it happen that it ends miserably, wretchedly for both parties, partly because the protector is annoyed about the money, which is or at least seems quite thrown away, whereas, on the other hand, the painter feels entitled to more confidence, more patience and interest than is given him? But in most cases the misunderstandings arise from carelessness on both sides.

Few painters read books and fewer can express in words what they are up to. Van Gogh is a notable exception: he read voraciously and with understanding, he had considerable literary talent of his own, and he loved to talk about what he was doing and why. If I understood the meaning of the word *literary* as a pejorative adjective when applied to painting, those who use it are asserting that the world of pictures and the world of phenomenal nature are totally distinct so that one must never be judged by reference to the other. To ask if a picture is "like" any natural object—it makes no difference whether one means a "photographic" or a platonically "real" likeness—or to ask if one "subject" for a picture is humanly more important than another, is irrelevant. The painter creates his own pictorial world and the value of a painting can only be assessed by comparison with other paintings. If that is indeed what critics mean, then Van Gogh must be classified as a literary painter. Like Millet, whom all his life he acknowledged as his master, and like some of his contemporary French novelists, Flaubert, the Goncourts, Zola, he believed that the truly human subject for art in his day was the life of the poor. Hence his quarrel with the art-schools.

As far as I know there isn't a single academy where one learns to draw and paint a digger, a sower, a woman putting the kettle over the fire or a seamstress. But in every city of some importance there is an academy with a choice of models for historical, Arabic, Louis XV, in short, *all really* non-existent figures. . . . All academic figures are put together in the same way and, let's say, *on ne peut mieux.* Irreproachable, *faultless.* You will guess what I am driving at, they do not reveal anything new. I think that, however correctly academic a figure may be, it will be superfluous, though it were by Ingres himself, when it lacks the essential modern note, the intimate character, the real *action.* Perhaps you will ask: When will a figure not be superfluous? . . . When the digger digs, when the peasant is a peasant and the peasant woman a peasant woman. . . . I ask you, do you know a single digger, a single sower in the old Dutch school? Did they ever try to paint "a labourer"? Did Velasquez try it in his water-carrier or types from the people? No. The figures in the pictures of the old master do not *work.*

It was this same moral preference for the naturally real to the ideally beautiful which led him, during his brief stay at an art-school in Antwerp, when he was set to copy a cast of the Venus de Milo, to make alterations in her figure and roar at the shocked professor: "So you don't know what a young woman is like, God damn you! A woman must have hips and buttocks and a pelvis in which she can hold a child."

Where he differs from most of his French contemporaries is that he never shared their belief that the artist should suppress his own emotions and view his material with clinical detachment. On the contrary, he writes:

. . . whoever wants to do figures must first have what is printed on the Christmas number of *Punch:* "Good Will to all"—and this to a high degree. One must have a warm sympathy with human beings, and go on having it, or the drawings will remain cold and insipid. I consider it very necessary for us to watch ourselves and to take care that we do not become disenchanted in this respect.

and how opposed to any doctrine of "pure" art is this remark written only two months before his death.

Instead of grandiose exhibitions, it would have been better to address oneself to the people and work so that each could have in his home some pictures or reproductions which would be lessons, like the work of Millet.

Here he sounds like Tolstoy, just as he sounds like Dostoevsky when he says:

It always strikes me, and it is very peculiar, that whenever we see the image of indescribable and unutterable desolation—of loneliness, poverty and misery, the end and extreme of all things, the thought of God comes into one's mind.

When he talks of the poor, indeed, Van Gogh sounds more honest and natural than either Tolstoy or Dostoevsky. As a physical and intellectual human being Tolstoy was a king, a superior person; in addition he was a count, a socially superior person. However hard he tried, he could never think of a peasant as an equal; he could only, partly out of a sense of guilt at his own moral shortcomings, admire him as his superior. Dostoevsky was not an aristocrat and he was ugly, but it was with the criminal poor rather than the poor as such that he felt in sympathy. But Van Gogh preferred the life and company of the poor, not in theory but in fact. Tolstoy and Dostoevsky were, as writers, successful in their lifetime with the educated; what the peasants thought of them as men we do not know. Van Gogh was not recognized as an artist in his lifetime; on the other hand, we have records of the personal impression he made upon the coalminers of the Borinage.

> People still talk of the miner whom he went to see after the accident in the Marcasse mine. The man was a habitual drinker, "an unbeliever and blasphemer," according to the people who told me the story. When Vincent entered his house to help and comfort him, he was received with a volley of abuse. He was called especially a *mâcheux d'capelots* (rosary chewer) as if he had been a Roman Catholic priest. But Van Gogh's evangelical tenderness converted the man. . . . People still tell how, at the time of the *tirage au sort,* the drawing of lots for conscription, women begged the holy man to show them a passage in the Holy Scripture which would serve as a talisman for their sons and ensure their drawing a good number and being exempted from service in the barracks. . . . A strike broke out; the mutinous miners would no longer listen to anyone except *"l'pasteur Vincent"* whom they trusted.

Both as a man and as a painter Van Gogh was passionately Christian in feeling though, no doubt, a bit heterodox in doctrine. "Resignation," he declared, "is only for those who *can* be resigned, and religious belief is for those who *can* believe. My friends, let us love what we love. The man who damn well refuses to love what he loves dooms himself." Perhaps the best label for him as a painter would be Religious Realist. A realist because he attached supreme importance to the incessant study of nature and never composed pictures "out of his head"; religious because he regarded nature as the sacramental visible sign of a spiritual grace which it was his aim as a painter to reveal to others. "I want," he said once, "to paint men and women with that something of the eternal which the halo used to symbolise, and which we seek to convey by the actual radiance and vibration of our colouring." He is the first painter, so far as I know, to have consciously attempted to produce a painting which should be religious and yet contain no traditional religious iconography, something which one might call "A Parable for the Eye."

Here is a description of a canvas which is in front of me at the moment. A view of the park of the asylum where I am staying; on the right a grey terrace and a side wall of a house. Some deflowered rose bushes, on the left a stretch of the park—red ochre—the soil scorched by the sun, covered with fallen pine needles. This edge of the park is planted with large pine trees, whose trunks and branches are red-ochre, the foliage green gloomed over by an admixture of black. These high trees stand out against the evening sky with violet stripes on a yellow ground, which higher up turns into pink, into green. A wall—also red-ochre—shuts off the view, and is topped only by a violet and yellow-ochre hill. Now the nearest tree is an enormous trunk, struck by lightning and sawed off. But one side branch shoots up very high and lets fall an avalanche of dark green pine needles. This sombre giant—like a defeated proud man—contrasts, when considered in the nature of a living creature, with the pale smile of a last rose on the fading bush in front of him. Underneath the trees, empty stone benches, sullen box trees; the sky is mirrored—yellow—in a puddle left by the rain. A sunbeam, the last ray of daylight, raises the sombre ochre almost to orange. Here and there small black figures wander among the tree trunks.

You will realise that this combination of red-ochre, of green gloomed over by grey, the black streaks surrounding the contours, produces something of the sensation of anguish, called "rouge-noir," from which certain of my companions in misfortune frequently suffer. Moreover, the motif of the great tree struck by lightning, the sickly green-pink smile of the last flower of autumn serve to confirm this impression.

I am telling you (about this canvas) to remind you that one can try to give an impression of anguish without aiming straight at the historic Garden of Gethsemane.

Evidently, what Van Gogh is trying to do is to substitute for a historic iconography, which has to be learned before it can be recognized, an iconography of color and form relations which reveals itself instantaneously to the senses, and is therefore impossible to misinterpret. The possibility of such an iconography depends upon whether or not color-form relations and their impact upon the human mind are governed by universal laws. Van Gogh certainly believed that they were and that, by study, any painter could discover these laws.

The *laws* of the colours are unutterably beautiful, just because they are not *accidental.* In the same way that people nowadays no longer believe in a God who capriciously and despotically flies from one thing to another, but begin to feel more respect and admiration for faith in nature—in the same way, and for the same reasons, I think that in art, the old-fashioned idea of innate genius, inspiration, etc., I do not say must be put aside, but thoroughly reconsidered, verified—and greatly modified.

In another letter he gives Fatality as another name for God, and defines Him by the image—"Who is the White Ray of Light, He in Whose eyes even the Black Ray will have no plausible meaning."

Van Gogh had very little fun, he never knew the satisfaction of good food, glory, or the love of women, and he ended in the bin, but, after reading his correspondence, it is impossible to think of him as the romantic *artiste maudit,* or even as tragic hero; in spite of everything, the final impression is one of triumph. In his last letter to Theo, found on him after his death, he says, with a grateful satisfaction in which there is no trace of vanity:

I tell you again that I shall always consider you to be something more than a simple dealer in Corots, that through my mediation you have your part in the actual production of some canvases, which will retain their calm even in the catastrophe.

What we mean when we speak of a work of art as "great" has, surely, never been better defined than by the concluding relative clause.

1959

Albrecht Dürer, *Traumgesicht (Dream Vision)*, watercolor. Kunsthistorisches Museum, Vienna.

Painters as Writers

STEPHEN SPENDER

Stephen Spender has best described himself as "an autobiographer restlessly searching for forms in which to express the stages of my development." Those forms have included his work as poet, novelist, critic, playwright, teacher, translator, librettist, editor, and memoirist. As a member of the so-called Oxford Group in the 1930s (with W. H. Auden, Louis MacNeice, and C. Day Lewis) he was active in making a new poetry and in making that poetry responsive to the outsized events of the time. By the end of the thirties, he recorded in his autobiography World within World, *"public events had swamped our personal lives and usurped our personal experience." To help himself regain control over the personal, he turned to psychoanalysis and to painting. He had painted since he was a schoolboy, and at twenty-nine he studied seriously with William Coldstream and others. "I envied the painter's life," he wrote, "the way in which he is surrounded by the material of his art." He gave up, though, convinced "it is possible entirely to lack talent in an art where one believes oneself to have creative feeling." He stopped painting but has continued to write about it, producing books on Botticelli and on Ghika and most recently a collaboration with David Hockney. Despite his disclaimer, it is obvious Spender learned a good deal from his studies, not least the pains over detail that are common to painting and poetry. And he has another memory of 1939: "There may seem to be little connection between psychoanaly-*

sis and my desire to be a painter. But whilst, on the one hand, I wished to plunge deep into the sources of childhood and accept myself, on the other I wished to attach myself to outward things. That summer I looked and looked as I had not done for years at the green of the chestnut trees and the ochre of walls, broken by patches of blue and cold grey. I was fascinated by the contrast between opaque surfaces of light, where sunlight is clotted on leaves or flesh, and the transparent darkness of shadows like brown and green glass pools, through whose coldness I could look deeply on to still darker shadows."

WHEN THEY paint, painters are exercising some of the qualities essential to good writing. Apart from the most obvious of these—the organizing power of the visual imagination—they observe what Blake called "minute particulars." They create images and they store memories. For all these things writers may envy them. Painters are the enemies of generalization, journalism, cliché, and these are the pitfalls that surround every writer in our day of newspapers, television, advertising.

At the beginning of the present century, certain poets, more or less unconsciously, looked to painters for salvation for some of their problems in writing. Apollinaire modeled his style on the images of painters, and the Imagist poets drew up a program for writing poetry which might equally have been a manifesto for painters. They insisted that the image was the be-all and end-all of the poem. Delacroix's *Journals* are full of things that make writers envious. They are notes for painting, but, most remarkably in his records of travels in Algiers, they leap to life as raw material for poetry:

The dispute of the soldier with the groom. Sublime, with his mass of draperies, looking like an old woman and yet with something martial about him.

On our return, superb landscapes to the right, the mountains of Spain in the tenderest tones, the sea a dark greenish blue like a fig, the hedges yellow at the top because of the bamboo, green at the base on account of the aloes.

The hobbled white horse that wanted to jump onto one of ours.

The last line seems pure poetry, but the notes are themselves verbal sketches which might change at any moment into paint.

The meeting place of words and painting is those drawings in which painters have scribbled the names of colors as an *aide-mémoire*. The word "grey" written against olive trees by van Gogh or Cotman obviously means something different to the artist from that which it suggests to the reader. When one looks at a sketch and sees a written word, there is the suggestion of a leap from the word to the miracle of the paint, and this is itself an effect of poetry, which Apollinaire tried to exploit when he arranged the words of a poem in the form of sketches. Moreover, the painters who write most on their sketches themselves seem to be extremely open to the suggestion of words, an extreme example being the painter and humorous poet Edward Lear, who did many such sketches.

The writing of painters suggests indeed a kind of borderland which is a meeting between the arts. The painter may be using language as an extremely abbreviated kind of sketch, but there is also a tendency for the sketch to turn into the writing: for him to be experimenting in a medium which he is tempted to think might be better for his purpose than painting. The titles which Paul Klee wrote under his

141

drawings and watercolors—all too often untranslatable puns or clichés—are the meeting place of his painting with poetry.

There is a relationship of love and envy between the arts which we recognize in ordinary speech when we say, for example, of a composition: *this music almost speaks*—a phrase which is worth thinking about. It throws light on the famous passage in one of van Gogh's letters in which he describes his sensations while painting—sometimes "the strokes come with a sequence and coherence like words in a speech or letter." Sometimes we have the impression, reading Constable's notes on his painting or Gauguin's *Journals,* that the process of painting has found words, makes a speech. This is subtly different from the artist explaining what his art is about, as Picasso, Braque and other moderns do frequently, or from the artist showing that he has a message which he could, if he had chosen, have expressed in words rather than in paint—as happens sometimes with van Gogh. Gauguin discovering the frightened soul of his Tahitian mistress is the poetry of his *The Spirit Watching:*

> We were short of oil for the lamp and when I opened the door the lamp was out and the room was in darkness. I had a sudden feeling of apprehension. I lit the matches quickly and then I saw her quite still and naked, lying on her stomach on the bed; and her eyes immensely large in fear looked at me without seeming to know me. . . . I seemed to see a phosphorescence in the light from those fixed eyes.

A remark that Gombrich quotes from Constable's preface to his published landscapes has precisely this quality of the paintings themselves having found their poetry: "One brief moment caught from fleeting time a lasting and sober existence."

The writing of painters seems to be wrung out of the immediate necessity of expression. This necessity can be of a practical kind—the need to keep records, or to explain their projects. The conditions of their work make painters more productive than other artists. With them the sketch of rapid execution can be as significant as all but their most elaborate masterpieces. For this reason, artists have to be their own cataloguers. In the past, they have had to keep records for themselves, and communicate with patrons; and many of them liked to correspond with friends to whom they could explain what they were trying to do in their art. A letter such as this, written from Nuremberg on March 21, 1509, to a patron, by Albrecht Dürer, must be characteristic of thousands such:

> Dear Herr Jakob Keller, I have carefully read your letter. You must know that I have been constantly and steadily painting at your panel from Easter up till now, and I cannot expect to have it finished before Whitsuntide. . . . Don't be anxious about the colors, for I have painted upon it more than 24 florins worth of them. . . . I would not paint another picture of this kind under 400 florins.

Artists are greatly concerned with explaining their art to themselves and others. Thus Dürer apologizes to a friend that some monkeys he has drawn are unsatisfactory because he has not seen any monkeys for a long time. He sees the aim of his work as an idealized form resulting from the putting together of "minute particulars" of observation: "If the best parts, chosen from many well-formed men, are united in one figure, it will be worthy of praise."

The impression one gets from Dürer's letters is of the artist as an essentially simple man—closer to the artisan than to the writer, who is a "clerk." The artist is primarily occupied with understanding nature, God and himself (in that order).

Although artists have long ceased to be regarded as manual laborers, I do not think that the archetype has changed very greatly, at any rate not until the present century, when the sophisticatedness of some painters—for example, the Surrealists, and Picasso in his Dadaist effusions—shows how very closely the artistic consciousness has grown to the literary.

In the writings of visual artists the struggle of inner vision with intractable exterior material is very evident. The struggle is different from that of the writer with his material, because the writer is changing outer experience into something different—language, which is the world of ideas. The painter is translating one kind of outwardness—the objects he sees—into another kind of outwardness—the work of art, which is also seen. The poet can be regarded as a kind of medium who is turning outside experiences into their own voice. Rimbaud expresses this function of the poet in his famous *"Je est un autre,"* and *"on me pense."* But no one could say that a painting is the thoughts of the visible world dictated into language through the mediumship of the painter. Visual art is not things speaking through the artist, but the artist telling us, by the marks he makes on the material, how he sees that outside world. I think that painters often write out of an envy of writers, because they would prefer to be interpreters of experiences and not commentators on them.

It is significant that the movement in painting in which painters have used painting to realize their inner fantasies, to paint their dreams, is nearest to literature. This is, of course, Surrealism, whose advocates have tried to turn painting into poetry, a calligraphy of images dictated from within by the subconscious mind of the artist. But Surrealism began as a movement in poetry, and when there were Surrealist painters, several of the Surrealist poets protested that there could be no such thing as Surrealist painting, because this would simply be a bastard form of literature. The writings of Surrealist painters are hardly distinguishable from those of the Surrealist poets.

The material on which, or with which, the artist creates his work symbolizes for him the actual material of the outside world, to which he struggles to give form. The paper on which I write my poem does not do this: it is a mere recipient of signs representing my words, which might, perhaps, be better spoken than written.

This symbolism of the material of art for the outsideness of nature is especially true of sculpture, the art in which material is most obtrusively present. *Jacob Wrestling with the Angel,* the subject of one of Jacob Epstein's statues, is really the theme of all sculpture: that, and the *Slaves* of Michelangelo, released by the chisel from the marble in which they are imprisoned. The idea of the artist struggling with his material in order to release a beauty that is already there is expressed by Michelangelo in one of his poems:

> Non ha l'Ottimo artista alcun concetto,
> > Ch'un marmor solo in se non circonscriva
> > Col suo soverchio; e solo a quello arriva
> > La man che ubbidisce all'intelleto—

In J. A. Symonds' version this is: "The best of artist hath no thought to show / Which the rough stone in its superfluous shell / Does not include: to break the marble spell / Is all the hand that serves the brain can do."

Although a storyteller or poet might say that the material on which he was working was the life around him, or the stuff of dreams, even in saying this his dream would already be his inner life. The material of art—walls, or stone or canvas—has an intractable, static outsideness which is different from the writer's already inward feelings or interpretations of life or dreams. The writing of artists shows the preoccupation they have with dealing with the obstinate material of their work in order to discover themselves within it. Painters live midway between the physical object which they paint and the physical object which is their painting.

There arises from this the special concern of the artist with realizing his own identity—a kind of search in which writing about his art, and even directly about himself, may be extremely helpful. A painter writes perhaps out of the same passionate self-concern as he paints a self-portrait. Courbet, passionate self-portraitist, was also passionately in search of himself and his aims in his letters: "I hope always to earn my living by my art without ever having lied to my conscience for a single moment, without painting even as much as can be covered by a hand only to please anyone or sell more easily."

Self-portraits and the writings of artists make me suspect that painters have a greater problem than writers in knowing their identity. A good writer knows himself because verbal self-consciousness is his vocation. Painters, even in their writing, seem groping towards self-knowledge: the bright screen of the external world hides them from themselves. Moreover, painting is the art in which the artist most needs to distinguish his own identity from that of others, because he is peculiarly exposed to the identities of colleagues and rivals. A painting is an "open book" in a way that a book never is. The frame is a poor substitute for the covers of a volume. The painting sets out its creator and his methods, and the painter's criticism or dismissal of the methods of other contemporaries is apparent at a glance.

Thus in self-portraits painters seem to look out of the canvas, searching for that truth about themselves which makes them different from the other painters. There are two remarkable pages facing one another in Gide's anthology on Poussin. On the right-hand page, the painter, holding a folio, looks at the spectator. Opposite it, on the left, Gide has printed extracts from eight letters of Poussin which recommend this painting to patrons. In one of the most striking of these, to Chantelou, he writes (July 3, 1650) that the place which the portrait will occupy in Chantelou's house will be an honor bestowed like that of Virgil's portrait in the museum of Augustus. "This will bestow on me the glory, as if my self-portrait were with those of Leonardo, Michelangelo and Raphael, belonging to the dukes of Tuscany." Thus we see that through his writing Poussin confirms the idea which he secretly held that his self-image belongs to the glorious company of those painters he considered ideal.

Van Gogh is as obsessive a self-teacher in his letters as he is a self-portraitist in his paintings. Indeed his letters search his identity when he was a preacher and social worker, before he became a painter, and sustain this search through his life of neglect and derision:

> To sum up, I want to arrive at that point where people say of my work: this man feels deeply, and this man feels with delicacy. In spite of my so-called boorishness, if you understand what I mean, or precisely on account of it.
>
> What I am in the eyes of most people—a nonentity, or an eccentric or disagreeable person—someone with no position in society, or who will never have any, someone who's less than nothing.
>
> Good, supposing then I am exactly that, then I would like to show through my work what the heart of such an eccentric, such a nonentity, may hold.

147

In recent years, a new theme has cropped up in the writings of painters: explanations of the artist's position in relation to "modern art," made with the public in mind. There is here, I think, not only an immense productivity, but a certain bastardization. As my remarks, earlier on, about Apollinaire may suggest, in the first decade of the present century, in Paris, there occurred a marriage between literature and painting (the whole subject is admirably discussed by Roger Shattuck in his *The Banquet Years*). The marriage resulted in the mongrel painting and poetry of the Surrealists, and a generation later, in high-class journalism, either in the form of direct self-expositions or of interviews, by artists about their art.

I don't count interviews quite as artists' writings. They belong really to a more or less respectable branch of advertising, or self-advertising. What do count, however, are some of the manifestoes made by Expressionists and members of the *Blaue Reiter* Group in Munich. The most important of these writings are distinguished not by the kind of sales talk by artists which today is disconcerting, but by an extreme purity of aim, combined with a naïve faith that art may somehow transform appearances—or at any rate the way of looking at things—and even save the world. The writings of Kandinsky and Paul Klee have an apocalyptic force which one hardly finds in contemporary poetry. Thus Kandinsky, in his marvelous treatise *Concerning the Spiritual in Art*, defines one of the aims of his own painting as "largely unconscious, spontaneous expression of inner character, non-material nature. This I call an 'improvisation.'" And the sense of the artist as being the person, not childish, but with the vision of a child, who might lead boshed and bungled modern adults out of the mechanized jungle of their own creating, back to a world of values as pure as the tonal rela-

tions of certain colors, becomes impassioned in the essay of
Paul Klee *On Modern Art:*

> In the womb of nature, at the source of creation, where
> the secret key to all lies guarded.
>
> But not all can enter. Each should follow where the
> pulse of his own heart leads.
>
> So, in their time, the Impressionists—our opposites of
> yesterday—had every right to dwell within the matted
> undergrowth of every-day vision.
>
> But our pounding heart drives us down, deep down to
> the source of all.
>
> What springs from this source, whatever it may be
> called, dream or idea or fantasy—must be taken seri-
> ously only if it unites with the proper creative means to
> form a work of art.

Klee looks on the thin line of the drawing of the dedi-
cated artist as Ariadne's thread, which may lead out of the
modern maze, at the center of which roars the Minotaur of
final destruction. This seems a long way from Dürer's letters
and journals. And yet the writings of artists throughout the
past five hundred years have something in common. This is
the feeling they communicate of the painter or sculptor as
the most innocent of beings—even among those who are
decidedly creative—the one for whom the external world
remains most "outside," if not most alien, while he regards it
with his detached eye. Perhaps these writings also indicate
that the visual artist is the most naturally and spontaneously,
and the least dogmatically, religious of his colleagues in the
other arts.

1962

Foreword to an Exhibit

E. E. CUMMINGS

As a young man, Cummings moved to Greenwich Village to paint. Of the American poets in this book, he probably had the most skill as a painter. At the easel or the typewriter, he liked to experiment with what he called "presentative" art. He first exhibited his work in 1919 at the New York Society of Independent Artists; he entered two works, one called "Sound," one called "Noise." In 1926 he entered a doormat.

WE ARE living in a time of plague" said Fritz Wittels; when I mentioned something called an atomic era "so,like the story-tellers of the Decameron,we must find salvation in ourselves."

Many unregenerate years ago,before everybody was a little better than everybody else,New York City boasted a phenomenon entitled The Society of Independent Artists;whose yearly exhibitions opened with near riots—partly on account of the fantastic number of exhibitors(for membership fees were moderate)but chiefly because (since no jury existed)an

From the catalogue of a one-man show at the University of Rochester, May 1957. Reprinted with permission of the Estate of E. E. Cummings. Essay appeared in *e. e. cummings: A Miscellany Revised*, by E. E. Cummings (October House, 1963), 319–20. Copyright © 1965 by the Estate of E. E. Cummings.

"Independent show" was sure to comprise every not imagi-
nable variety of artfulness and artlessness;plus occasionally a
work(or play)of art.

I was wrestling some peculiarly jovial mob of sightseers at
possibly the least orthodox of all Independent "openings,"
when out of nowhere the sculptor Lachaise gently material-
ized. "Hello Cumming" his serene voice(addressing me,as
always, in the singular)sang above chaos "have you see one
litel cat?" I shook my head. He beckoned—and shoulder to
shoulder we gradually corkscrewed through several huge
rooms;crammed with eccentricities of inspiration and teem-
ing with miscalled humanity. Eventually we paused. He
pointed. And I found myself face to face with a small canvas
depicting a kitten.

During that distant epoch,pictures which couldn't be la-
belled either "academic" or "experimental" were usually
pronounced "naive." But the healthily spontaneous little
painting opposite me transcended classification. Bombarded
by chromatic atrocities ranging all the way from lifeless non-
representationality to deathful anecdotalism,it remained
completely and charmingly itself.

"Dis ting" Lachaise reverently affirmed(in the course of
what remotely resembled a lull)"is paint with love."

1957

Gregorio Valdes, Untitled. Formerly Elizabeth Bishop's collection.

Gregorio Valdes

ELIZABETH BISHOP

Although there are scarcely more than a hundred poems in Elizabeth Bishop's Complete Poems, 1927–1979, *many readers have come to consider the book the grandest achievement by any of the "middle generation" of American poets. Its precisions of detail and phrase, the variety of its landscapes and heartscapes, the almost eerie evenness of tone, its bright, refined originality—these mark it as a classic. On the dust jacket is a watercolor of Mérida, painted by Bishop on a trip through Mexico in 1942. James Merrill has described the sketch: "Beyond a balustrade flanked on one side by an absurd ornamental urn (so much for Art?) and on the other by flourishing palm fronds, with some little, run-down, brilliantly colored houses. Above these, near and far, quite upstaging the few church-spires lost among them, perhaps fifty windmills crowd the horizon. The picture illustrates at once Bishop's delight in foreign parts, her gratitude for the givens of a scene, and her typical way with systems. These tend to fade beside her faith in natural powers." Her delight in foreign places was a matter of climate and of temperament. Before her long residence in Brazil, she lived in Key West from 1938 until 1946. Some of her best poems—"Little Exercise," "Jerónimo's House," "The Bight," and "Faustina, or Rock Roses"—were written there. It was also in Key West that she encountered Gregorio Valdes. Those who have read her poems ("Large Bad Picture" and "Poem") about her great-uncle's third-rate paintings will understand what may have attracted her to Valdes's primitives. The imperfect was a paradise to her, and it is no wonder she warns that the obscure eccentric or self-taught enthusiast or amateur (her favorite, Robinson Crusoe, was one of these) are "dangerous to imitate." Four of Valdes's paintings (two lent by Bishop) were included in a 1939 exhibition at the Museum of Modern Art in New York entitled "Contemporary Unknown American Painters." Valdes has remained unknown, but the charm of his work has not, as Bishop accounts for it.*

THE FIRST painting I saw by Gregorio Valdes was in the window of a barbershop on Duval Street, the main street of Key West. The shop is in a block of cheap liquor stores, shoeshine parlors and poolrooms, all under a long wooden awning shading the sidewalk. The picture leaned against a cardboard advertisement for Eagle Whiskey, among other window decorations of red-and-green crepe-paper rosettes and streamers left over from Christmas and the announcement of an operetta at the Cuban school—all covered with dust and fly spots and littered with termites' wings.

It was a view, a real View, of a straight road diminishing to a point through green fields, and a row of straight Royal Palms on either side, so carefully painted that one could count seven trees in each row. In the middle of the road was the tiny figure of a man on a donkey, and far away on the right the white speck of a thatched Cuban cabin that seemed to have the same mysterious properties of perspective as the little dog in Rousseau's *The Cariole of M. Juniot.* The sky was blue at the top, then white, then beautiful blush pink, the pink of a hot, mosquito-filled tropical evening. As I went back and forth in front of the barbershop on my way to the restaurant, this picture charmed me, and at last I went in and bought it for three dollars. My landlady had been trained to do "oils" at the Convent. —The house was filled with copies of *The Roman Girl at the Well, Horses in a Thunderstorm*, etc.— She was disgusted and said she would paint the same picture for me, "for fifteen cents."

The barber told me I could see more Valdes pictures in the window of a little cigar factory on Duval Street, one of the few left in Key West. There were six or seven pictures: an ugly *Last Supper* in blue and yellow, a *Guardian Angel* pushing two children along a path at the edge of a cliff, a study of flowers—all copies, and also copies of local postcards. I liked one picture of a homestead in Cuba in the same green fields, with two of the favorite Royal Palms and a banana tree, a chair on the porch, a woman, a donkey, a big white flower, and a Pan-American airplane in the blue sky. A friend bought this one, and then I decided to call on Gregorio.

He lived at 1221 Duval Street, as it said on all his pictures, but he had a "studio" around the corner in a decayed, unrentable little house. There was a palette nailed to one of the posts of the verandah with *G. Valdes, Sign Painter* on it. Inside there were three rooms with holes in the floors and weeds growing up through the holes. Gregorio had covered two sections of the walls with postcards and pictures from the newspapers. One section was animals: baby animals in zoos and wild animals in Africa. The other section was mostly reproductions of Madonnas and other religious subjects from the rotogravures. In one room there was a small plaster Virgin with some half-melted yellow wax roses in a tumbler in front of her. He also had an old cot there, and a row of plants in tin cans. One of these was Sweet Basil, which I was invited to smell every time I came to call.

Gregorio was very small, thin and sickly, with a childish face and tired brown eyes—in fact, he looked a little like the

Self-Portrait of El Greco. He spoke very little English but was so polite that if I took someone with me who spoke Spanish he would almost ignore the Spanish and always answer in English, anyway, which made explanations and even compliments very difficult. He had been born in Key West, but his wife was from Cuba, and Spanish was the household language, as it is in most Key West Cuban families.

I commissioned him to paint a large picture of the house I was living in. When I came to take him to see it he was dressed in new clothes: a new straw hat, a new striped shirt, buttoned up but without a necktie, his old trousers, but a pair of new black-and-white Cuban shoes, elaborately Gothic in design, and with such pointed toes that they must have been very uncomfortable. I gave him an enlarged photograph of the house to paint from and also asked to have more flowers put in, a monkey that lived next door, a parrot, and a certain type of palm tree, called the Traveler's Palm. There is only one of these in Key West, so Gregorio went and made a careful drawing of it to go by. He showed me the drawing later, with the measurements and colors written in along the side, and apologized because the tree really had seven branches on one side and six on the other, but in the painting he had given both sides seven to make it more symmetrical. He put in flowers in profusion, and the parrot, on the perch on the verandah, and painted the monkey, larger than life-size, climbing the trunk of the palm tree.

When he delivered this picture there was no one at home, so he left it on the verandah leaning against the wall. As I came home that evening I saw it there from a long way off down the street—a fair-sized copy of the house, in green and white, leaning against its green-and-white prototype. In the gray twilight they seemed to blur together and I had the feeling that if I came closer I would be able to see another miniature copy of the house leaning on the porch of the painted house, and so on—like the Old Dutch Cleanser advertisements. A few days later when I had hung the picture I asked Gregorio to a vernissage party, and in spite of language difficulties we all had a very nice time. We drank sherry, and from time to time Gregorio would announce, "More wine."

He had never seemed very well, but this winter when I returned to Key West he seemed much more delicate than before. After Christmas I found him at work in his studio only once. He had several commissions for pictures and was very happy. He had changed the little palette that said *Sign Painter* for a much larger one saying *Artist Painter*. But the next time I went to see him he was at the house on Duval Street and one of his daughters told me he was "seek" and in bed. Gregorio came out as she said it, however, pulling on his trousers and apologizing for not having any new pictures to show, but he looked very ill.

His house was a real Cuban house, very bare, very clean, with a bicycle standing in the narrow front hall. The living room had a doorway draped with green chenille Christmas fringe, and six straight chairs around a little table in the middle bearing a bunch of artificial flowers. The bareness of a Cuban house, and the apparent remoteness of every object in it from every other object, gives one the same sensation as the bareness and remoteness of Gregorio's best pictures. The only decorations I remember seeing in the house were the crochet and embroidery work being done by one of the daughters, which was always on the table in the living room, and a few photographs—of Gregorio when he had played the trombone in a band as a young man, a wedding party, etc., and a marriage certificate, hanging on the walls. Also in the hall there was a wonderful clock. The case was a plaster statue, painted bronze, of President Roosevelt manipulating a ship's wheel. On the face there was a picture of a bar-keeper shaking cocktails, and the little tin shaker actually shook up and down with the ticking of the clock. I think this must have been won at one of the bingo tents that are opened at Key West every winter.

Gregorio grew steadily worse during the spring. His own doctor happened to be in Cuba and he refused to have any other come to see him. His daughters said that when they begged him to have a doctor he told them that if one came he would "throw him away."

A friend and I went to see him about the first of May. It was the first time he had failed to get up to see us and we realized that he was dangerously sick. The family took us to a little room next to the kitchen, about six feet wide, where he lay on a low cot-bed. The room was only large enough to hold the bed, a wardrobe, a little stand, and a slop-jar, and the rented house was in such a bad state of repair that light came up through the big holes in the floor. Gregorio, terri-bly emaciated, lay in bed wearing a blue shirt; his head was on a flat pillow, and just above him a little holy picture was tacked to the wall. He looked like one of those Mexican retablo paintings of miraculous cures, only in his case we were afraid no miraculous cure was possible.

That day we bought one of the few pictures he had on hand—a still life of Key West fruits such as a coconut, a mango, sapodillos, a watermelon, and a sugar apple, all stiffly arranged against a blue background. In this picture the paint had cracked slightly, and examining it I discovered one eccentricity of Gregorio's painting. The blue back-ground extended all the way to the tabletop and where the paint had cracked the blue showed through the fruit. Apparently he had felt that since the wall was back of the fruit he should paint it there, before he could go on and paint the fruit in front of it.

The next day we discovered in the Sunday *New York Times* that he had a group of fifteen paintings on exhibition at the Artists' Gallery in New York. We cut out the notice and took it to his house, but he was so sick he could only lie in bed holding out his thin arms and saying "Excuse, excuse." We were relieved, however, when the family told us that he had at last consented to have another doctor come to see him.

On the evening of the ninth of May we were extremely shocked when a Cuban friend we met on the street told us that "Gregorio died at five o'clock." We drove to the house right away. Several people were standing on the verandah in the dark, talking in low voices. One young man came up and said to us, "The old man die at five o'clock." He did not mean to be disrespectful but his English was poor and he said "old man" instead of "father."

The funeral took place the next afternoon. Only relatives and close friends attend the service of a Cuban funeral and only men go to the cemetery, so there were a great many cars drawn up in front of the house filled with the waiting men. Very quickly the coffin was carried out, covered with the pale, loose Rock Roses that the Valdeses grow for sale in their back yard. Afterwards we were invited in, "to see the children."

Gregorio was so small and had such a detached manner that it was always surprising to think of him as a patriarch. He had five daughters and two sons: Jennie, Gregorio, Florencio, Anna Louisa, Carmela, Adela, and Estella. Two of the daughters are married and he had three grandchildren, two boys and a girl.

I had been afraid that when I brought him the clipping from the *Times* he had been too sick to understand it, but the youngest daughter told me that he had looked at it a great deal and had kept telling them all that he was "going to get the first prize for painting in New York."

She told me several other anecdotes about her father— how when the battleships came into Key West harbor during the war he had made a large-scale model of one of them, exact in every detail, and had used it as an ice-cream cart, to peddle Cuban ices through the streets. It attracted the attention of a tourist from the North and he bought it, "for eighty dollars." She said that when the carnivals came to town he would sit up all night by the light of an oil lamp, making little pinwheels to sell. He used to spend many nights at his studio, too, when he wanted to finish a sign or a picture, getting a little sleep on the cot there.

He had learned to paint when he and his wife were "sweethearts," she said, from an old man they call a name that sounds like "Musi"—no one knows how to spell it or remembers his real name. This old man lived in a house belonging to the Valdeses, but he was too poor to pay rent and so he gave Gregorio painting lessons instead.

Gregorio had worked in the cigar factories, been a sign painter, an ice-cream peddler, and for a short time a photographer, in the effort to support his large family. He made several trips to Cuba and twenty years ago worked for a while in the cigar factories in Tampa, returning to Key West because his wife liked it better. While in Tampa he painted signs as well, and also the sides of delivery wagons. There are some of his signs in Key West—a large one for the Sociedad de Cuba and one for a grocery store, especially, have certain of the qualities of his pictures. Just down the street from his house, opposite the Sociedad de Cuba, there used to be a little café for the workers in a nearby cigar factory, the Forget-Me-Not Café, *Café no me Olvidades*. Ten years ago or so Gregorio painted a picture of it on the wall of the café itself, with the blue sky, the telephone pole and wires, and the name, all very exact. Mr. Rafael Rodríguez, the former owner, who showed it to us, seemed to feel rather badly because since the cigar factory and the café have both disappeared, the color of the doors and window frames has been changed from blue to orange, making Gregorio's picture no longer as perfect as it was.

This story is told by Mr. Edwin Denby in his article on Valdes for the Artists' Gallery exhibition: "When he was a young man he lived with an uncle. One day when that uncle was at work, Valdes took down the towel rack that hung next to the washbasin and put up instead a painting of the rack with the towel on it. When the uncle came back at five, he went to the basin, bent over and washed his face hard; and still bent over he reached up for the towel. But he couldn't get hold. With the water streaming into his eyes, he squinted up at it, saw it and clawed at it, but the towel wouldn't come off the wall. 'Me laugh plenty, plenty,' Valdes said . . ."

This classical ideal of verisimilitude did not always succeed so well, fortunately. Gregorio was not a great painter at all, and although he certainly belongs to the class of painters we call "primitive," sometimes he was not even a good "primitive." His pictures are of uneven quality. They are almost all copies of photographs or of reproductions of other pictures. Usually when he copied from such reproductions he succeeded in nothing more than the worst sort of "calendar" painting, and again when he copied, particularly from a photograph, and particularly from a photograph of something he knew and liked, such as palm trees, he managed to make just the right changes in perspective and coloring to give it a peculiar and captivating freshness, flatness, and remoteness. But Gregorio himself did not see any difference between what we think of as his good pictures and his poor pictures, and his painting a good one or a bad one seems to have been entirely a matter of luck.

There are some people whom we envy not because they are rich or handsome or successful, although they may be any or all of these, but because everything they are and do seems to be all of a piece, so that even if they wanted to they could not be or do otherwise. A particular feature of their characters may stand out as more praiseworthy in itself than others—that is almost beside the point. Ancient heroes often have to do penance for and expiate crimes they have committed all unwittingly, and in the same way it seems that some people receive certain "gifts" merely by remaining unwittingly in an undemocratic state of grace. It is a supposition that leaves painting like Gregorio's a partial mystery. But surely anything that is impossible for others to achieve by effort, that is dangerous to imitate, and yet, like natural virtue, must be both admired and imitated, always remains mysterious.

Anyway, who could fail to enjoy and admire those secretive palm trees in their pink skies, the Traveler's Palm, like "the fan-filamented antenna of a certain gigantic moth . . ." or the picture of the church in Cuba copied from a liquor advertisement and labeled with so literal a translation from the Spanish, "Church of St. Mary Rosario 300 Years Constructed in Cuba."

1939

Fernand Léger, *The City*, oil on canvas, 90 ³/₄ x 117 ¹/₄ in. Philadelphia Museum of Art: A. E. Gallatin Collection.

The Heroic Object
and Fernand Léger

KENNETH REXROTH

In a letter to Marianne Moore, William Carlos Williams once wrote about his admiring exasperation with Kenneth Rexroth's poetry: "It is not very subtly made as far as the phrasing, the words, the godliness of words is concerned, but its impelling reason is surprisingly refreshing if one has the hardihood to go on reading—and is not thrown over the horse's head by the exuberance of the beast." Rexroth's manner and ideas elicited the same frustration from nearly everyone. Jack Kerouac turned him into Rheinhold Cacoethes in The Dharma Bums *and portrayed him as a "bowtied wild-haired old anarchist." Rexroth was a "character" in another sense too: the homegrown type of the American original—a polymath, a crank, a solitary singer. At various times he was a poet, painter (with one-man shows in New York, Paris, and other cities), critic, playwright, novelist, labor organizer, logger, and horse wrangler. His friend Lawrence Lipton described him this way: "Think of him, first, as an 11th century figure of a man, scholar, poet, priest, a student from the Latin Quarter out on the town. In his youth, a tramp scholar in the tradition of the goliards, unchurched, unfrocked, unschooled, from whose fingers no book was safe if he needed it, no scholarly discipline too formidable to undertake, no language too arduous to study and master, no way of life too unconventional or too dangerous to sample." In an essay on the painting of Morris Graves,*

165

Rexroth said that the artist's duty is "to keep open the channels of contemplation and to discover new ones," and he himself was as influenced by Charlie Parker as by Tu Fu. He tried in his poems to embody principles derived from both cubism and Zen, and it is perhaps because of these converging lines of influence that he could define poetry as "vision, the pure act of sensual communion and contemplation."

SUPPOSE THE faithful Marmon or Velie, that's been in the family for generations, breaks down in the hills above Figeac, and you coast into town and a helpful *routier* gives you a push into the one garage. Does the mechanic tell you to get rid of that piece of junk? Does he look in vain through his strictly up-to-date Motor Manual? Does he tell you he can't fix it? He does not. He whistles through his teeth, rolls a cigarette, then asks you wistfully for an American cigarette, lights it with profuse thanks, opens the hood, detaches the dodecahedron polymerizer from the reciprocating cam, smiles brightly, says, "Ah, m'sieu, c'est la bonne chance, ce fait rien," and proceeds to make another one, better than the first, using no manuals of any kind and only a pliers and a file.

There are not fifty million mechanics like him, but there are a considerable number, and if it weren't for them France would not be in existence today, and would certainly not have survived the years since 1870. Léger is one of them. He is the man who knows what to do when it breaks, the man who can always make it go.

After the first painting of his apprentice days, he is always completely competent to the task at hand. He knows what he wants to do, and he does it with a machinist's efficiency. It is possible that the tasks he has set himself are not the most complex in the history of painting, but each one is conceived with complete clarity and economy and finished with neatness and dispatch. In fact, it might well be said that Léger's directness has bypassed all those problems of modern painting which are not immediately demonstrable as admitting a simple, rational solution, a manipulative rather than a mentalistic, verbal, expressive solution. It should not be forgotten, in these days when Husserl, Heidegger, and Scheler rule the café *terasses*, that this used to be called the specific French genius. And, for that matter, even the *bagarre* of Saint-Germain is only a formalistic and Tedescan elaboration of attitudes always held in Puteaux or Saint-Denis.

The matter-of-fact competence in the face of life's problems which the French common man has always had, must have or go under, did not need a name from the International Set. Everybody in France who doesn't own five pairs of shoes has always been an existentialist. And so, if they want him, Léger is an existentialist painter. An existentialist of the means at hand. An existentialist without a capital E. Such were the men of the seventeenth century, who made the French spirit out of mathematical models and devices for tracing complex curves, over which the countesses and courtesans swooned in the salons. Such was Racine, expert campanologist of the heart strings, supremely efficient tear-jerker. Such was Rimbaud, the child who applied to decadence the efficiency of a future gunrunner.

We often forget that of the major Cubists, only Braque and Léger are French. Between them they divide the Gallic utterance of Cubism, soft and hard, feminine and masculine, ingenious and manipulative, the *midinette* and the *mécanicien*, the chef and the peasant. The rest of Cubism is international megalopolitan, except for Picasso's Black Spain for blood and sand.

This is not idle impressionist, exhortative criticism. The qualities which I have mentioned literally overwhelm you in Léger's comprehensive—better, definitive —show [the Museum of Modern Art, New York, 1953]. In room after room the vast paintings take possession of you. You feel like a character in science fiction, a spectator at a congress of intelligent outsized instruments of precision. There is nothing abstract about these pictures. They are portraits of things, of a man, and of a people.

A lot of nonsense, very plastic, has been written and said about Léger, not least of all by himself. Nothing illustrates the fortuitous character of most critical "modern" seeing than the way in which he has been invested, and has been able to garb himself, with the whole panoply of the contemporary formal revolution, or revolutions. Léger is one of the few artists left who still talk about *passéistes*, Renaissance servility to Nature, "photographic realism," the Greeks who could only copy anatomy. Actually, he is not a modern painter at all in the formal sense, but a man of the Renaissance, a composer of objects in representational space, and a Greek of the Greeks, or at least a Roman of the Romans, a painter of isolated human archetypes.

It shows in his first paintings: a portrait of his uncle, modeled up from a shallow indeterminate background with broken color, Pissarro applied to Carrière; a hillside in Corsica, ochre houses and *terre verte* trees piled up on a hillside like fruit heaped on a platter and seen from above, a problem and a solution which were to satisfy Waroquier for a lifetime. In both pictures the technique is that of an apprentice, but for all that, Léger is perfectly sure of himself even in his mistakes, and the surfaces are certainly modeled. When the uncle was new and the colors bright, he must have more than popped out of the picture.

The next pictures are in what is usually called the African period of Cubism, and it is at this point only that Léger actually joins Picasso and Braque. *Nudes in the Forest* is a minutely painted large canvas completely filled with cubes, tubes, cylinders, and cones of gunmetal blue. It takes Cézanne's injunction literally. The forms of nature are reduced to their geometrical elements. But the elements are represented literally. There is no ambiguity, no interplay of forms. Compare it with Picabia's *Sacre du Printemps*—probably the best picture any of them produced in this period (the Picassos and Braques are very disagreeable productions)—and you will see immediately what I mean. In the Picabia, a blaze of scarlet planes does define the dancers, but no plane stays in place, all weave back and forth, facets first of one form shaped by the attention, then of another. The Léger begins in Mantegna and ends in Wyndham Lewis, and never touches the world of Cubism at all.

Similarly in the heroic age of Cubism, the analytical period, only the appearance of the paintings of the other Cubists is echoed. The picture surface is completely fragmented into a flicker of values. But the flicker is not the result of the transparencies, interpenetrations, and plastic punning of the *Guitar Players* and portraits of Bass's Ale and *Le Journal;* there is no attempt to create a saturation of space; it is simply filled up with a lot of little sharply rounded objects. Incidentally, the catalog says that the portrait of his uncle is the only representation of an actual person known in Léger's *oeuvre.* If the people in *Three Figures* are not portraits, what are they? One is certainly Carco, the woman might be a caricature of Colette of those days, the other face is a masterpiece of portraiture. The grin, sardonic and jolly, even a little tipsy, is the sort of thing you find in self-portraits, but I think Léger had a mustache then.

All the paintings of the analytical period have the same character. The space is filled up, rather than saturated. The planes all stay in one place, the forms are sharply modeled, the "Cubism" itself is merely a geometrical schematization. This is a kind of popular Cubism, a mechanic's idea of what the problem was. As such, it was far more successful than Picasso, Braque, Metzinger, or Gleizes with the public, at least the public of artists around the world. It spread to Italy to the Cubo-Futurists, to Russia, to Chicago to Rudolf Weisenborn, to England to Wyndham Lewis and Wadsworth and their friends. At its worst it died over the mirrors of a thousand Bar Modernes in the postwar (I) world.

Léger's highly articulate remarks about his intentions in these days are very misleading. Of *Woman in Blue* he says, "I obtained rectangles of pure blue and pure red in painting the *Woman in Blue.*" So? Raphael obtained triangles of the same colors in the *Madonna of the Meadow.* Both painters modeled their forms in the same way, and Léger to the contrary, "*Passéiste*" and Modernist, for the same ends, aesthetically speaking.

It is interesting to note that in the more ambitious analytical paintings Léger does seem to be bothered by the bas-relief, piled-up character of his space, and he does try to open it up and cut into it. But to do this he must paint representations of recessions—carved-out slices and corridors, and the step-like figure which from now on he will use again and again. He carries them over into a field in which no one else used them, the postwar period of plane Cubism, of Picasso's *Red Table Cloth,* Braque's *Still Life with Head,* and the finest work of Gris and Marcoussis, a period dominated by the theories of Gleizes.

The great Léger of these days is *The City*. It is, without doubt, a monumental picture, a landmark if not a milestone, in twentieth-century painting, and it is represented in the show by eight or ten different treatments, including the definitve and semi-definitive oils, and a number of closely related watercolor still lifes. Here at last we can see that Léger is not the Douanier of Cubism, he is not a naïf, a primitive. He knows precisely what he is doing. The earliest watercolors, and the painting, *Composition, 1917–1918*, . . . are perfectly straightforward arrangements of planes in bas-relief, piled up toward the spectator—that is, the center plane is the nearest. There is some illusionist modeling, mostly in the oil, only a cylinder in the watercolors. There is a great deal of spiraling movement of form transversely, in the plane of the picture, and even some advance and retreat of planes, all achieved primarily by centrifugal patterning and color snap, by what were called non-illusionist means. They might have been painted by Gleizes in a lively moment.

But when it comes to the painting itself, the final form, all have been subtly altered. The colors are tied to the forms—local colors—the nearest plane is defined by a sharply modeled mauve column which cuts the picture in extreme and mean ratio; behind it two yellow planes recede in conventional perspective, planes of buildings, all brightly colored "for their own sake," recede like stage sets. In the background is a ship; railed staircases lead back in a narrow corridor through the center of the picture, and down them, to complete the illusion, come two black, sharply modeled figures, relatives of the lay figures of Chirico. This may be Cubism but it is not the Cubism of Léger's colleagues. It is the Cubism of Piero della Francesca, perhaps a little reduced. It is as though Léger had deliberately turned his back on the complexities of Gleizes and Gris as trivial.

Once again we have a rejection of the plastic subtleties of intellectual painters in favor of an approach capable of a wide measure of popularization. Out of the work of this period, especially the still lifes, was to come the Suprematism of Ozenfant, some of the Bauhaus painters, particularly Baumeister, and the whole cult of antiseptic modernity in popular art.

The City has already taken a long step in this direction. What city? Possibly a modernized Delft of Vermeer, certainly never the Faubourg St. Antoine, the Marais, or La Villette. This is the imaginary city of the movies and the urbanists.

For this reason alone I would prefer, of this period, Léger's *The Great Tug*, a vaguely nautical Gleizes-like mass of colored planes which chooches and chugs through a schematized river landscape. Of course it is a complete contradiction. The "Neo-Cubism" of Léger's colleagues set out to analyze exhaustively the picture area in terms of large planes of color, the surfaces of saturated color volumes, optically retreating and advancing in space. Now this is what Léger says he was doing too. But he was doing nothing of the sort. The tug, the central mass of colored planes, is an object, an abstract object, like a Calder, but representationally though simply painted, and it does not depend on the proportions of the frame directly. On the contrary, it floats in a space which differs little from the background of Piero's *Queen of Sheba.*

Now come the mid-Twenties and Léger's own revolution, "the reinstatement of the object." In other words, he decided to admit what he had been doing all along, and stopped trying to make his paintings look even superficially like other people's. For my taste, these are the best Légers until very recent years. They are completely individual. They look like nobody else, though lots of other painters try to look like them. And they achieve what Léger can do best, and achieve it superlatively—a wonderful objective immediacy of realization, a true *neue-Sachlichkeit*—"Neo-realism" maybe, but the French already had a word for it—*clarté*. Boucher had a clear image like this of *La Petite Morphi*, as Chardin had of pots and pans, and Diderot of Louis XV, and Saint-Just of Louis XVI. This is the virtue that has kept France great, as once it made her strong.

This is the period of the heroic human figures, beginning with the *Mechanic* and the *Three Women,* including *Woman with Book* and *The Readers.* They have been called impersonal abstractions. But they are abstractions only in the sense that Hans and Fritz and Mama and the Captain are abstractions. They are perfect idealizations of universal French types. They have been compared to Poussin, but they are certainly very shallow Poussin. To me they look more like Roman funerary bas-relief, and they have the same archetypical character as the best Roman portraiture. After them come the medallion-like pictures of the late Twenties, most of them rather wittily, and certainly very originally, bifurcated. I like best *The Mirror,* and it is certainly typical, in its wit, its polish, its enormous self-confidence. Now the craftsman knows his craft by heart. It is his heart. His highest spiritual experience is the sense of absolute competence in the face of the problems of the conquest of matter. Cubism, and the problems of modern space architecture, are ignored completely. These are not even bas-reliefs, they are cameos.

So, the next period—of "free color," by which Léger does not mean dissociated color moving as color volume, but just free color, applied as it struck his fancy; and "free form," that is, painting built without a base, floating in air. In part, this latter development is a protest against Picasso, whose compositions all depend on their enormous specific gravity. But Léger's forms do not really float in the "free space" of the space cadets and the Baroque ceilings. They revolve around a center, without top or bottom, like medals—still the same approach. Although the besetting bas-relief is attacked by reducing much of the form to purely linear relationships, they are never the linear swoops and plunges of either Sesshu or Tiepolo. They are always exactly there where the painter put them. I think, curiously enough, the most successful is not the famous *The Divers*, but the quite simple *Chinese Juggler*.

During this period, too, Léger was developing his alphabet of human types. It was then he began—to work on it for nineteen years—his *Three Musicians*, three *numeros* from a *bal musette*, the Fourteenth of July on the Boulevard La Chapelle. It is an independently conceived and painted picture, but no one could miss the implied criticism of Picasso's internationalized, *déracinés*, Ballet Russe ogres.

And this brings us to the culmination, paintings of pure human archetypes, very human, very pure, and very localized to a class and a land, as is Léger himself. In a way the accomplishment of Léger's later life is not unlike that of William Butler Yeats, who was able to achieve in his old age a whole heroic mythos, the kind of an endowment only a Heroic Age gives most peoples, for the ungrateful Irish. *Leisure, The Great Julie, The Chinese Juggler*, and the rest are close to being Platonic Ideas of the French common people. If you doubt it, ponder *Adam and Eve*, represented as hero and heroine of the *théâtre de foire*, snake charmers, street performers such as you might see any sultry August, in a neighborhood *place* anywhere in France, the immortal parents of Little Remi, Vitalis, and their dogs and the monkey, Joli-Coeur.

And finally, there is the great picture, *The Builders*, on whose title and subject many philosophical and sociological speculations and reveries might be based. These are the builders of France, after another time, out of so many years of war, disorder, and betrayal. And plastically Léger has moved on a little. The space is deep and open, with interchanging diagonals. One is reminded of Signorelli, but a Signorelli in which all the figures are standing at attention. It may be Egypt applied to the High Renaissance. But neither Egypt nor the High Renaissance produced a great many more profoundly moving pictures of human beings.

1953

René Magritte, *The Light of Coincidences*, oil on canvas, 23 ⁵/₈ x 28 ³/₄ in. Dallas Museum of Art: Gift of Mr. and Mrs. Jake L. Harmon.

On Poetry and Painting, with a Thought on Music

HOWARD NEMEROV

"I'd always liked," writes Nemerov, "and still do, looking idly at paintings and drawings, and admiring idly the mysteriousness of the transcription. But I am no thinker, and books were necessary to open my eyes—Gombrich, Arnheim, Gyorgy Kepes. I still would not claim to have thought much, or to any striking effect, about such things as the problem *of perception, or the mind-body* problem *concerning which Marcel Duchamp soundly said 'if no solution, then maybe no problem?' The motto I give my pupils (and the two meanings of that word are related) is that we moon about what philosophers think about." But as the following essay makes clear, he has thought a good deal about such matters. In fact, Nemerov's sense of the artist—painter or poet —is that he or she helps us "see in a thinking way." The work gathered in Nemerov's* Collected Poems *(1977) does precisely that, in ways witty or brooding. Several poems speculate on the painter's ability "to do these mortal miracles / In silence and solitude, without a word." He has written a superb poem about Paul Klee called "The Painter Dreaming in the Scholar's House," and in 1963 he wrote a long essay titled "The Miraculous Transformations of Maurits Cornelius Escher." "Escher didn't much like my essay about his work," he recalls, "and asked cantankerously enough why I wanted to turn him into a metaphysi-*

*cian (funny, for a man first made famous by a congress of mathe-
maticians), but died without staying for an answer." In a sense,
that answer might have been this essay.*

THERE ARE affinities between poetry and painting, and
perhaps the words 'image' and 'language' will help focus
these as well as the differences. Painters make images, poets
make images; the painter too has language, though not per-
haps in so explicit a sense as the poet does; the palette for a
given landscape, say, acts as a negative kind of syntax, ex-
cluding certain colors from the range of possibility; and as a
positive kind as well, indicating the possibilities of gradation
in getting from earth through river through forest to sky.

Both poet and painter want to reach the silence behind
the language, the silence within the language. Both painter
and poet want their work to shine not only in daylight but
(by whatever illusionist magic) from within; maybe even
more from within than by daylight, for many of their works
in times now past had not the object of being viewed in day-
light but went to do their magic in caves, in tombs, among
the dead, and maybe as a substitute for daylight.

The poet walks through the museum and among so many
and so diverse conceptions and manners of treatment he
sees, he hears, especially two things: silence and light. View-
ing the picture frames as windows, he looks into rooms, out
of rooms into landscapes—what the Chinese call 'mountain-
water pictures'—and knows from the silence that he is see-
ing the past, the dead, the irrevocable; and he knows some-
thing else, that what he sees is not only the past, the dead,
the irrevocable, but something that had the intention of

being these things from the moment of its conception: something that is, so to say, past from the beginning. Hence the great silence common among so many differences of subject and execution; hence, too, the solemnity of the museum, crowded with solitudes; the dignity of painting, that stands in a sort of enchanted space between life and death.

He sees also that the light in these rectangles appears to come from within. In the work of an unknown master he sees the thin veil of a small waterfall in sunlight—amazing! He leans in to look closer, the threads of water become white paint mixed with a little gray on a gray ground— amazing again, not quite in the same way, that crossing-point, that exact distance, within which illusion becomes paint, beyond which paint becomes illusion again. Whereas in the painting of a river by Vlaminck, the thin, pale surface of the water, bearing the thinnest and most shivering of pale reflections, is made by means of the heaviest, thickest, grossest applications of paint, made with a virtuosity that is able to make colored dirt produce effects of light. Amazing again.

His own art, in the comparison, begins to seem the merest pitifullest chatter, compounded of impatience and opinion. On thoughts like this, the poet finds it best to hasten from the museum, that marvelous tomb-temple wherein the living are privileged to look so deeply into what is no more, experiencing their own mortality as a dignified silence not without its effects of grandeur and austerity; though all this *looking deeply*, that so magicks the beholder, is done on a plane surface.

Out in the day again, he thinks about the matter some more. First about some poems of his own time, especially some he cares for, that have a relation with painting or drawing. There is Auden's 'Musée des Beaux Arts,' with its reflections that rely on Brueghel, on *The Fall of Icarus* and on the *Massacre of the Innocents.* There is John Berryman's

'Hunters Returning at Evening,' also referring to Brueghel; there is Randall Jarrell's emblem drawn from Dürer's *Knight, Death, and Devil;* there is even one of his own, composed and called after René Magritte's *The Human Condition (I)*. These things have a relation to painting, and they are not painting. It would be interesting to speculate what that relation might be.

It is not, certainly, that the poems speak about the paintings they refer to; no, for the poems offer relatively bare and selective descriptions; no art student sent to the museum would dare come back with such descriptions, which sometimes hardly serve to identify the paintings. No, the poems speak about the silence of the paintings; and where the poet was lucky his poem will speak the silence of the painting; it too will say nothing more than: It is so, it is as it is. The poem, too, when it works, is a concentrated shape illuminated by an energy from within; its opinions do not matter, but it matters. Here, too, he observes, all that happens happens while the poem, like the painting, lies flat on a plane surface, the surface of the page.

From the other side, he is reassured to think, ever so much of painting comes from poetry, refers to poetry, and is poetical in its own nature as well as in its subject matter. Not only the biblical subjects, for example, but the various conceptions and styles that transfigure the subjects, that poetize upon the Crucifixion, say, with respect to an eternal glory in so many medieval masters, a superhuman grandeur in Michelangelo, a bitter suffering in Grünewald, the light of an ordinary day in Brueghel.

So both painter and poet are makers of images, and traditionally there is a connection between the images they make. And when we say they *make* images, we do not seek to distinguish, for the present, the component of invention from that of discovery.

And both painter and poet write in languages. This seems at first to mark a decisive and unbridgeable difference, the difference in their languages. But it invites a little further thought.

Surely the painter's language has the dignity of being the oldest ever written down. Minerals, plants, the liquids of the body even to blood, all gave up their substance many thousand years ago to the representation by signs of perceptions based upon fear, desire, hunger, dreams, and a certain decorative and geometrizing distance from all these, a certain coldness. Whereas writing came much later. Writing in an alphabet wholly independent of pictorial elements is usually dated not much earlier than the middle of the second millennium B.C.

Perhaps nothing in the alphabet cannot also be seen in nature: O in a hole, W or M in a distant flying bird, Y in the branching of a tree, and so on. But that's not pertinent. What really matters is that no alphabet could exist as long as these signs were seen exclusively as belonging to nature; they had to be got out of nature, so that you could write C without any thought of the curve of the shoreline, S without thinking about snakes, any letter without thinking of it except as a letter—something that had never before been, something in effect literally 'nonsensical' that yet could 'make sense' of the realms to which its immense range of combinations was applied. If the conservative element in society got as mithered as it did at the advent of 'abstract art' at the Armory Show of 1913, imagine its probable resentment at so great an innovation as the alphabet: 'It don't look like anything I ever seen,' 'A child could do stuff like that if he thought it worth the bother,' and so on.

With respect to painting, E. H. Gombrich, who has written so beautifully against the grain of an abstract age about the miraculous thing that is representation, suggests that perhaps painting too arose out of coincidences in nature—as the alphabet did, but in the opposite direction. The earliest cave drawings might have been, he speculates, those in which a peculiar form of the rock itself was first *recognized* as resembling an animal, and then modified by artistic means with a view to increasing the degree of this resemblance; rather as the earliest portrait statuary, too, employed the human skull itself as armature—a thought that even yet retains a depth of sinister magical intent.

And the development of painting might be conceived of as having three main branches. The first would be in the direction of greater fidelity to appearances, ending in the peculiar magic of the waxworks, which so clearly and instantly distinguishes itself from the magic of art. The second would be in the direction of ornament, rhythm, pattern, figuration, of an abstract character. And the third would be in the direction of language, of alphabet and the codifying of signs, ending in the magic of writing; the process is indeed perceptible in the history of Chinese writing; while in Egypt, though writing and painting were clearly distinguishable, yet writing remained a species of representational drawing, though abstract and conditioned by the introduction of specifically linguistic and nonrepresentational signs.

It will be worthwhile to remember here Coomaraswamy's (Ananda Kentish Coomaraswamy, *Christian and Oriental Philosophy of Art* [New York: Dover, 1956], passim) demonstration that in traditions of sacred art, the medieval Christian as much as the Hindu, painting was treated as linguistic; the characters of iconography were dictated at least as much by the codified formulas of priesthoods as by any free observation of the visible world; which offers an answer, and a good one, to the question of how, in a world without photography, the features of gods and saviors become so quickly fixed and invariant.

In both languages, then, of writing and of painting, the shapes and substances of the earth rose up and assumed a mental and a spiritual quality, conferring upon the mind that brought them forth a thrilling if somewhat frightening power of detachment from the world as viewed by the pre-human mind, or at least the mind that was before these things were.

Maybe the comparison has to end there. For push and pull as we may, writing and painting *did* separate off from one another. Might they ever come back together? Ought they ever to come back together? If their very different but immense powers were to fuse into something not really much like either—what then?

We do already have an instance in which this happens: the making of maps, charts, diagrams, blueprints . . . where the representing of the visible, at which painting is supremely capable, is accomplished in parallel with the strict and abstract syntax of writing able without modification of its own nature to transmit an indefinite variety of messages, which is the supreme contribution of written language. Might this somewhat elementary compound of writing and painting have still some way to go in the world?

I should like to make a rather wild leap at such a question, and hope to be going in a forward direction. Writing and painting could come together, though I don't know in the least what their offspring would look like. (Possibly it would not *look* at all.) It is here that I get the vaguest glimmer of a hint from music, or from some thoughts about music. Proust touches the thought, but almost at once lets it go:

And just as certain creatures are the last surviving testimony to a form of life which nature has discarded, I asked myself if music were not the unique example of what might have been—if there had not come the invention of language, the formation of words, the analysis of ideas—the means of communication between one spirit and another. It is like a possibility which has ended in nothing.

Marcel Proust, *The Remembrance of Things Past,*
translated by C. K. Scott-Moncrieff
(New York: Random House, 1934), II, 560

Another writer, François le Lionnais (*The Orion Book of Time,* translated by William D. O'Gorman, Jr. [New York: The Orion Press, 1966], p. 108), also encourages this sort of speculation, also without demonstration, when he says that certain music—his examples are the Elizabethan virginalists, J. S. Bach, Schumann, Anton von Webern—'consists not only of fluctuating sound patterns capable of delighting the ear but also of psychological hieroglyphics not yet decoded.'

The vaguest glimmer of a hint, and one which I am, at least at present, unable to take any further, though perhaps some of my readers may. For this of 'hieroglyphics' and 'decoding' has its charms, because the arts have always had, in addition to their popular side, their deep affinity for mystery and the esoteric, for the secret which is also the sacred.

1978

Against Abstract Expressionism

RANDALL JARRELL

He was the best poet-critic of his generation: a precise surveyor of literary culture; an essayist with high standards and a wry, witty buoyancy; a sympathetic but sometimes caustic reviewer who, in retrospect, seems almost always to have been right. *But not, I think, in what follows, where in order to play the devil's advocate he is uncharacteristically a literalist: all painting from Giotto to Picasso is one thing, abstract expressionism another. He resents what he perceives as its one-dimensional plane of action, its pretentious self-absorption. As he says, painting lives in the distance between an object and its representation, in the echo chamber of distortion and allusion. That statement brings to mind Matisse's sidelong remark, "I don't paint things, I only paint differences between things." It also recalls Jarrell's own poems which seek out "a reality behind the outer reality; it is no more real than the other, both are as real as they can be, but it is different." Robert Lowell has observed that "what Jarrell's inner life really was in all its wonder, variety, and subtlety is best told in his poetry," and in his* Complete Poems *are some wondrously subtle meditations on art: "The Knight, Death, and the Devil," "Jerome," "The Bronze David of Donatello," "In Galleries," and "The Old and the New Masters."*

Some of Jarrell's best writing about art—not so subtle, but wickedly funny—occurs in his satirical, epigrammatic novel Pictures from an Institution *(1954), set on the campus of fictive Benton College, so progressive its students and faculty "would have swallowed a porcupine, if you had dyed its quills and called it Modern Art." During the climactic "Art Night," when the students display their year's work, the narrator comes upon Miss Rasmussen's welded sculpture: "Her statues were—as she would say, smiling— untouched by human hands; and they looked it. You could tell one from another, if you wanted to, but it was hard to want to. You felt, yawning: It's ugly, but is it Art?" Next he wanders among the paintings: "The paintings were paintings of nothing at all. It did not seem possible to you that so many things could have happened to a piece of canvas in vain. You looked at a painting and thought, 'It's an imitation Arshile Gorky; it's casein and aluminum paint on canvasboard, has been scratched all over with a razor blade, and then was glazed—or scrumbled, perhaps—with several transparent oil washes.' And when you had said this there was no more for you to say. If you had given a Benton student a pencil and a piece of paper, and asked her to draw something, she would have looked at you in helpless astonishment: it would have been plain to her that you knew nothing about art." So much for progressive education. Earlier in the novel, Jarrell describes the house of the school's com- poser-in-residence, a genial Viennese serialist for whom he obviously feels affection. When Jarrell catalogues the "many reproductions and few originals" on the composer's walls, I sense he has chosen some of his own favorites:* Vermeer's Girl with the Red Hat *and* Girl with the Flute, the painting of Degas' Father Listening to Pagans, several Cézannes, Delacroix's Portrait of Paganini, a real Vuillard, Kokoschka's The Tempest, two real Klees, Uccello's The Rout of San Romano, and a Persian painting of a battle between owls and crows.*

A DEVIL'S advocate opposes, as logically and forcibly as he can, the canonization of a new saint. What he says is dark, and serves the light. The devil himself, if one can believe Goethe, is only a sort of devil's advocate. Here I wish to act as one for abstract expressionism.

Continued long enough, a quantitative change becomes qualitative. The latest tradition of painting, abstract expressionism, seems to me revolutionary. It is not, I think, what it is sometimes called: the purified essence of that earlier tradition which has found a temporary conclusion in painters like Bonnard, Picasso, Matisse, Klee, Kokoschka. It is the specialized, intensive exploitation of one part of such painting, and the rejection of other parts and of the whole.

Earlier painting is a kind of metaphor: the world of the painting itself, of the oil-and-canvas objects and their oil-and-canvas relations, is one that stands for—that has come into being because of—the world of flesh-and-blood objects and their flesh-and-blood relations, the "very world, which is the world / Of all of us,—the place where, in the end, / We find our happiness or not at all." The relation between the representing and the represented world sometimes is a direct, mimetic one; but often it is an indirect, farfetched, surprising relation, so that it is the difference between the subject and the painting of it that is insisted upon, and is a principal source of our pleasure. In the metaphors of painting, as in those of poetry, we are awed or dazed to find things superficially so unlike, fundamentally so like; superficially so like, fundamentally so unlike. Solemn things are painted gaily; overwhelmingly expressive things—the Flagellation, for instance—painted inexpressively; Vollard is painted like an apple, and an apple like the Fall; the female is made male or sexless (as in Michelangelo's *Night*), and a dreaming, acquiescent femininity is made to transfigure a body factually masculine (as in so many of the nude youths on the ceiling

of the Sistine Chapel). Between the object and its represen-
tation there is an immense distance: within this distance
much of painting lives.

All this sums itself up for me in one image. In Georges de
La Tour's *St. Sebastian Mourned by St. Irene* there is, in the
middle of a dark passage, a light one: four parallel cylinders
diagonally intersected by four parallel cylinders; they look
like a certain sort of wooden fence, as a certain sort of cubist
painter would have painted it; they are the hands, put to-
gether in prayer, of one of St. Irene's companions. As one
looks at what has been put into— withheld from—the hands,
one is conscious of a mixture of emotion and empathy and
contemplation; one is moved, and is unmoved, and is some-
thing else one has no name for, that transcends either affect
or affectlessness. The hands are truly like hands, yet they are
almost more truly unlike hands; they resemble (as so much
of art resembles) the symptomatic gestures of psychoanalysis,
half the expression of a wish and half the defense against the
wish. But these parallel cylinders of La Tour's—these hands
at once oil-and-canvas and flesh-and-blood; at once dynamic
processes in the virtual space of the painting, and spiritual
gestures in the "very world" in which men are martyred, are
mourned, and paint the mourning and the martyrdom—
these parallel cylinders are only, in an abstract expressionist
painting, four parallel cylinders: they are what they are.

You may say, more cruelly: "If they are part of such a
painting, by what miracle have they remained either cylin-
drical or parallel? In this world bursting with action and ac-
cident—the world, that is, of abstract expressionism—are
they anything more than four homologous strokes of the
paintbrush, inclinations of the paint bucket; the memory of
four gestures, and of the four convulsions of the Uncon-
scious that accompanied them? . . . We need not ask—they

are what they are: four oil-and-canvas processes in an oil-and-canvas continuum; and if, greatly daring, we venture beyond this world of the painting itself, we end only in the painter himself. A universe has been narrowed into what lies at each end of a paintbrush."

But ordinarily such painting—a specialized, puritanical reduction of earlier painting—is presented to us as its final evolution, what it always ought to have been and therefore "really" was. When we are told (or, worse still, shown) that painting "really" is "nothing but" this, we are being given one of those definitions which explain out of existence what they appear to define, and put a simpler entity in its place. If this is all that painting is, why, what painting was was hardly painting. Everyone has met some of the rigorously minded people who carry this process of reasoning to its conclusion, and value Piero della Francesca and Goya and Cézanne only in so far as their paintings are, in adulterated essence, the paintings of Jackson Pollock. Similarly, a few centuries ago, one of those mannerist paintings in which a Virgin's face is setting after having swallowed alum must have seemed, to a contemporary, what a Donatello Virgin was "really" intended to be, "essentially" was.

The painting before abstract expressionism might be compared to projective geometry: a large three-dimensional world of objects and their relations, of lives, emotions, significances, is represented by a small cross section of the rays from this world, as they intersect a plane. Everything in the cross section has two different kinds of relations: a direct relation to the other things in the cross section, and an indirect—so to speak, transcendental— relation to what it represents in the larger world. And there are also in the small world of the picture process many absences or impossible presences, things which ought to be there but are not, things which could not possibly be there but are. The painter changes and distorts, simplifies or elaborates the cross section; and the things in the larger world resist, and are changed by, everything he does, just as what he has done is changed by their resistance. Earlier painters, from Giotto to Picasso, have dealt with two worlds and the relations between the two: their painting is a heterogeneous, partly indirect, many-leveled, extraordinarily complicated process. Abstract expressionism has kept one part of this process, but has rejected as completely as it could the other part and all the relations that depend on the existence of this other part; it has substituted for a heterogeneous, polyphonic process a homogeneous, homophonic process. One sees in abstract expressionism the terrible aesthetic disadvantages of directness and consistency. Perhaps painting can do without the necessity of imitation; can it do without the possibility of distortion?

As I considered some of the phrases that have been applied to abstract expressionism—revolutionary; highly non-communicative; non-representational; uncritical; personal; maximizing randomness; without connection with literature and the other arts; spontaneous; exploiting chance or unintended effects; based on gesture; seeking a direct connection with the Unconscious; affirming the individual; rejecting the external world; emphasizing action and the process of making the picture—it occurred to me that each of them applied to the work of a painter about whom I had just been reading. She has been painting only a little while, yet most of her paintings have already found buyers, and her friends hope, soon, to use the money to purchase a husband for the painter. She is a chimpanzee at the Baltimore Zoo. Why should I have said to myself, as I did say: "I am living in the first age that has ever bought a chimpanzee's paintings"? It would not have occurred to me to buy her pictures—it would not have occurred to me even to get her to paint them; yet in the case of action painting, is it anything but unreasoning prejudice which demands that the painter be a man? Hath not an ape hands? Hath not an animal an Unconscious, and quite a lot less Ego and Superego to interfere with its operations?

I reminded myself of this as, one Saturday, I watched on Channel 9 a chimpanzee painting; I did not even say to myself, "I am living in the first age that has ever televised a chimpanzee painting." I watched him (since he was dressed in a jumper, and named Jeff, I judged that he was a male) dispassionately. His painting, I confess, did not interest me; I had seen it too many times before. But the way in which he painted it! He was, truly, magistral. He did not look at his model once; indeed, he hardly looked even at the canvas. Sometimes his brush ran out of paint and he went on with the dry brush—they had to remind him that the palette was there. He was the most active, the most truly sincere, painter that I have ever seen; and yet, what did it all produce?— nothing but that same old abstract expressionist painting . . .

I am joking. But I hope it is possible to say of this joke what Goethe said of Lichtenberg's: "Under each of his jokes there is a problem." There is an immense distance between my poor chimpanzee's dutiful, joyful paintings and those of Jackson Pollock. The elegance, force, and command of Pollock's best paintings are apparent at a glance—are, indeed, far more quickly and obviously apparent than the qualities of a painter like Chardin. But there is an immense distance, too, between Pollock's paintings and Picasso's; and this not entirely the result of a difference of native genius. If Picasso had limited himself to painting the pictures of Jackson Pollock—limited himself, that is, to the part of his own work that might be called abstract expressionism—could he have been as great a painter as he is? I ask this as a typical, general question; if I spoke particularly I should of course say: If Picasso limited himself in anything he would not be Picasso: he loves the world so much he wants to steal it and eat it. Pollock's anger at things is greater than Picasso's, but his appetite for them is small; is neurotically restricted. Much of the world—much, too, of the complication and contradiction, the size and depth of the essential process of earlier painting—is inaccessible to Pollock. It has been made inaccessible by the provincialism that is one of the marks of our age.

As I go about the world I see things (people; their looks and feelings and thoughts; the things their thoughts have made, and the things that neither they nor their thoughts had anything to do with making: the whole range of the world) that, I cannot help feeling, Piero della Francesca or Brueghel or Goya or Cézanne would paint if they were here now—could not resist painting. Then I say to my wife, sadly: "What a pity we didn't live in an age when painters were still interested in the world!" This is an exaggeration, of course; even in the recent past many painters have looked at the things of this world and seen them as marvelously as we could wish. But ordinarily, except for photographers and illustrators—and they aren't at all the same—the things of our world go unseen, unsung. All that the poet must do, Rilke said, is praise: to look at what is, and to see that it is good, and to make out of it what is at once the same and better, is to praise. Doesn't the world need the painter's praise any more?

Malraux, drunk with our age, can say about Cézanne: "It is not the mountain he wants to realize but the picture." All that Cézanne said and did was not enough to make Malraux understand what no earlier age could have failed to understand: that to Cézanne the realization of the picture necessarily involved the realization of the mountain. And whether we like it or not, notice it or not, the mountain is still there to be realized. Man and the world are all that they ever were—their attractions are, in the end, irresistible; the painter will not hold out against them long.

1957

Jackson Pollock, *Pasiphaë*, oil on canvas, 56 1/8 x 96 in. The Metropolitan Museum of Art: Purchase, Rogers, Fletcher and Harris Brisbane Dick Funds and Joseph Pulitzer Bequest, 1982.

Jackson Pollock

FRANK O'HARA

*Frank O'Hara was the quintessential Poet among Painters. The
group that came to be known as the New York School of poets—a
misleading term meant to designate not a school's fixed idea but a
network of poet-friends whose work took off, in several different
directions, from that of painters—owes everything to his example
and energies. He not only moved in the circle of the liveliest artists of
his day, but seemed their epicenter. They liked to paint him, his
Napoleonic nose and widow's peak, his figure "hipless as a snake."
Willem de Kooning, Fairfield Porter, Larry Rivers, Jane Freilicher,
John Button, Grace Hartigan, Philip Guston, Alice Neel, Elaine de
Kooning, and Alex Katz are among those for whom he sat. He col-
laborated on paintings, lithographs, collages, and films with Rivers,
Norman Bluhm, Joe Brainard, and Alfred Leslie. He wrote a great
deal of art criticism, was an editorial associate of* Art News *from
1953 through 1955, and from 1952 until his death in 1966 he
worked in various capacities for the Museum of Modern Art, first as
a special assistant in the International Program, finally as associate
curator. He directed many exhibitions for the museum and at the
time of his death was organizing a major retrospective of Jackson
Pollock. "Frank was so sure of his own reactions towards works of
art that he did not need to be aggressive. He had absolute integrity,"
wrote René d'Harnoncourt. "Many of us, because of Frank's pres-*

Reprinted with permission of Maureen Granville-Smith for the Frank O'Hara Estate.
Essay first appeared in *Jackson Pollock* (Braziller, 1959), 12–39. Copyright © 1975 by
Frank O'Hara.

ence, learned to see better, to communicate our experiences in clearer forms." During all this time, and often in his office at the museum, he was writing poems—hundreds of breezy, cloudstruck, experimental, ebullient poems, the urban vernacular.

Art is full of things that everyone knows about, of generally acknowledged truths. Although everyone is free to use them, the generally accepted principles have to wait a long time before they find an application. A generally acknowledged truth must wait for a rare piece of luck, a piece of luck that smiles upon it only once in a hundred years, before it can find application. Such a piece of luck was Scriabin. Just as Dostoievsky is not only a novelist and just as Blok is not only a poet, so Scriabin is not only a composer, but an occasion for perpetual congratulations, a personified festival and triumph of Russian culture.

Pasternak, *I Remember*
(Essai d'Autobiographie)

AND SO IS Jackson Pollock such an occasion for American culture. Like the Russian artists Pasternak mentions, his work was nourished by international roots, but it was created in a nation and in a society which knew, but refused to acknowledge, the truths of which Pasternak speaks.

We note that Pasternak puts these general truths in the plural, for culture is capable of entertaining more than one truth simultaneously in a given era. Few artists, however, are capable of sustaining more than one in the span of their activity, and if they are capable they often are met with the accusation of "no coherent, unifying style," rather than a celebration. Even Picasso has not escaped from this kind of criticism. Such criticism is panoramic and nonspecific. It tends to sum up, not divulge. This is a very useful method if the truth is one, but where there is a multiplicity of truths it is delimiting and misleading, most often involving a preference for one truth above another, and thus contributing to the avoidance of cultural acknowledgment.

If there is unity in the total oeuvre of Pollock, it is formed by a drastic self-knowledge which permeates each of his periods and underlies each change of interest, each search. In considering his work as a whole one finds the ego totally absorbed in the work. By being "in" the specific painting, as he himself put it, he gave himself over to cultural necessities which, in turn, freed him from the external encumbrances which surround art as an occasion of extreme cultural concern, encumbrances external to the act of applying a specific truth to the specific cultural event for which it has been waiting in order to be fully revealed. This is not automatism or self-expression, but insight. Insight, if it is occasional, functions critically; if it is causal, insight functions creatively. It is the latter which is characteristic of Pollock, who was its agent, and whose work is its evidence. This creative insight is the greatest gift an artist can have, and the greatest burden a man can sustain. . . .

Surrealism

The influence of Surrealism, though as a movement it provoked few masterpieces, has been considerable and seldom has been given its just due. It is true that the Surrealist periods of Picasso, Miró, and others produced great works, but the powerful personalities of these artists, the broad sweep of their creativity, tends to minimize their debt to Surrealism. For American painters, I think, the importance of Surrealism's influence lay in a less direct stimulation. For instance the whole basis of art-consciousness and art-confidence in America was changed by Surrealism, and even if more literary than painterly works influenced American life, the basic findings of the Surrealist struggle toward subliminal meaning has not failed to affect all modern art which is not commercial, and much that is ("the hidden persuaders," for instance).

The basic theory of Surrealism is a far greater liberation from the restrictions of preconceived form than any amount of idiosyncratic experimentation, and it finally destroyed the post-Renaissance vision of visual structure supported by the rationalizations and syllogisms of semi-popular science. That the principles of Surrealism were often expounded in painting by means perversely counter to the genuine accomplishment of Cubism does not negate the fact that Surrealism destroyed, where Cubism only undermined on the same rationalistic basis as before. Cubism was an innovation, Surrealism an evolution. The former dealt with technique, the latter with content. The truths implicit in Surrealism were touched upon and hinted at by Picasso (who did not need them) and Masson (who did), but they had to wait for the works of Pollock, and of such other American artists as Mark Rothko and Clyfford Still, to be acknowledged, to come to life, to speak, to apply. Surrealism enjoined the duty, along with the liberation, of saying what you mean and meaning what you say, above and beyond any fondness for saying or meaning. Max Ernst is to me a "fond" painter. As with those images of the American Indian, of sand-painting, that most natural and fragile of arts, those images of the Western reaches, all of which seem to have haunted his subconscious from time to time, recurring by allusion, the many "influences" which can be traced are less interesting as influences than as materials for Pollock's spirited revaluation. Now that Pollock has touched and clarified them, it is hard to see these materials as he found them. In their quality, which he created by his work and which we find by relating them to him, not by his analogy to them, he has given them reality for us outside his work, as a cultural by-product of his own achievement. This goes, too, for Miró, whose work has been enhanced for us by Pollock.

Arshile Gorky

Gorky, that magnificent painter, provides us with a case of artistic revaluation which contrasts with that of Pollock. For in Gorky pertinent developments of much European art, not only recent, were assimilated for American painting. But it was at the expense of Europe. Gorky, by his peculiar genius for something-of-value, is able to make a certain aspect of Picasso boorish, Miró frivolous, Masson leaden; and even a master like David may seem overexplicit when compared to *The Orators* (now destroyed) or *Diary of a Seducer*. Not so Pollock, who did not appropriate (as an artist has every right to do—I am simply making a distinction) what was beautiful, frenzied, ugly or candid in others, but enriched it and flung it back to their work, as if it were a reinterpretation for the benefit of all, a clarification and apotheosis which do not destroy the thing seen, whether of nature or art, but preserve it in a pure regard. Very few things, it seems, were assimilated or absorbed by Pollock. They were left intact, and given back. Paint is paint, shells and wire are shells and wire, glass is glass, canvas is canvas. You do not find, in his work, a typewriter becoming a stomach, a sponge becoming a brain.

Male and Female, 1942

His first masterpiece, *Male and Female*, was painted when Pollock was thirty and sums up the interests of the preceding

years, fluent in imagery, strong in stance; the two protago-
nists face each other in a welter of cabalistic signs and num-
bers and emotional flurries. They are in search of a unifying
symbol. This unity is found by Pollock through the confu-
sion of their aims and choices, in the unity of their search,
which is mutual. Like Picasso's famous *Girl before a Mirror,* the
images reflect each other's sexual characteristics, but now
the emphasis is on the love which has occasioned their
search. The sexual imagery is extraordinarily complex in
that it seems to be the result of the superimposition of the
protagonists at different stages of their relationship. They
are not double-images in the routine Surrealist sense, but
have a multiplicity of attitudes. At different times one sees
them facing each other, then both facing in the same direc-
tion (to the left), then with their backs to each other but the
memory of the confrontation vivid in their appearance.
Suggestions of eyes (upper and middle right, left-of-center
and lower left) peer at the viewer, as if to guard the lovers
without veiling them. Their youth and ambivalence are car-
ried by the brilliance of the color and its almost brutal rele-
vance to the subject.

Since several of the paintings of this period have mytho-
logical titles, it may not be idle to wonder if perhaps this
male and female do not have some allegorical significance.
Certainly the painting is not "about" Surrealist or Freudian
sexual motivations. It is an expression of classical, resolved
violence; one is present at the problem and at the solution
simultaneously. The imagery is not privately sensual, but cat-
egorically sexual, forensically expounded. The obscurity of
the relationship is made utterly clear. The occasion is im-
portant and public.

In *The She-Wolf* of the following year, one of six works
which bear on the probability of allegory, Lupa, the saving
nurse of Romulus and Remus, is advancing with full dugs

toward a child whose face appears in the lower left. This is undoubtedly Romulus, for though the wolf nursed both brothers, Romulus later killed Remus. She is not yet giving suck, and Romulus, the stronger, would be first to feed.

That Pollock was deeply interested in the mythology surrounding Romulus and Remus seems fairly certain. To cite only a few instances, we may remember that when Romulus and Remus came to vie for the rule of what was to be Rome, precedence was decided by omens and flights of birds. Remus saw only six vultures, Romulus twelve; therefore Romulus ruled. This may be the subject of *Bird Effort*, 1946. Later Romulus, after killing his brother, was shunned by his neighbors. By establishing a sacred grove as sanctuary, he surrounded himself with a number of criminals, fugitives, and foreigners (the future citizens of Rome). Deprived of the possibility of intermarriage with the neighboring inhabitants, Romulus established games and feasts in honor of the god Consus, held in great secrecy, to which were borne kidnapped virgins. It is these festivities, perhaps, that *Guardians of the Secret* is celebrating, a painting which is a marvel of spatial confinement and passionate formalism, formalism brought to the point of Expressionistic defensiveness. If so, the *Wounded Animal* is one of the sacrifices at these Consualia. We are told that during one of these celebrations the rape of the Sabine women took place. As we all know, the Sabines were defeated, but a major disaster was averted by the intervention of the Sabine women, who entreated their parents and husbands to lay down arms. All the Sabines then came to live in Rome, and their king ruled jointly with Romulus. It seems to me that the strange love and ambivalence of *Male and Female* reflects this embracing of the Romans and the Sabines, which we are told had such "salutary consequences." The *Mural* must be the bacchanalian festival attending this resolution, imbued as it is with the abstract ardor of the images in the other paintings of this group.

Pasiphaë and Others

All this may be pushing interpretation to a rather fancy point, but if it is wrong it at least brings one to look closer at the works, either to prove or disprove it. Nor are we finished with mythology quite yet. It is amazing how thoroughly Pollock investigated the derivations of Surrealism which were especially pertinent to his temperament without deviation into facility or mystification. The greatness of *Pasiphaë* lies in the candor of its richness and licentiousness. Its varied palette produces an aura of vigorous decadence, like the pearly, *cerné* eyelids of Catherine the Great, vigorous to the point of ennui. It is not just a glamorous painting, it is glamor in painting. Far from the sterile liberalism of a Gide, Pollock encompasses the amorous nature of bestiality (which most of the Surrealists were ambitious to do, but were either precocious or queasy about accepting) and gives it credit for originality of impulse and action. In this painting, mythological still, we move away from the area of allegory into the human disaster of desire—fatal, imaginative, willful. It is the ritual of an original human act, and therefore noble—where the mythology comes in, is that the artist sees it in all its legendary splendor, not as a tale told by a tart in a Melbourne bar (as T. S. Eliot or Francis Bacon might do). The stark, staring, and foreboding figure of Pasiphaë is present, with her foreknowledge of the Minotaur and her lust, as are the other figures of her fancy or necessity; a rectangle at left containing the signature of the artist is like a calendar of her doom. This is a recognition of the ritual which he is renewing. For in Pollock it is not a god in the form of a bull who seduces Pasiphaë. It is the bull.

If *There Were Seven in Eight*, a remarkable work of 1945, is based as I believe on the *Seven Against Thebes*, it also bears a strong relationship to the *Mural* of 1953. The iconography is less discernible than in *Pasiphaë*, which is almost its companion painting, yet it is still strongly involved in the ritualistic discovery of a recognizable event. Glowing and subdued, its double-figures are dominated by an equally double single-figure, that of Eteocles-Polynices, the brothers who agreed to share on alternate years the kingdom of their dead father, Oedipus. When they disagreed, Eteocles being unwilling to give up the throne in his turn to Polynices, they marshaled seven generals against each other. The battle at a stalemate, the "eighth" of each side agreed to decide the issue in personal combat, and the two brothers slew each other. If the cool ardor and concern with linear power of this painting is related to this myth, the myth is also germane to an understanding of its complicated juxtapositions, and its mysterious unity of forms.

Added

Thanks to the special interpretation his temperament put upon Surrealism, Pollock, alone in our time, was able to express mythical meanings with the conviction and completion of the past. Whatever qualities he saw in these myths, they were not the stereotyped, useful-to-the-present ones, which have made so many playwrights into dons, so many painters into academicians.

Gothic, 1944

Here is the efflux of the soul,
The efflux of the soul comes from within through
    embower'd gates, ever provoking questions,

> These yearnings why are they? these thoughts in the
> darkness why are they?
>
> —Whitman

Totemism

The use of totemic figures in varying degrees of ab-
stractness occurs in several periods of Pollock's work. They
are the household gods, so to speak, of his interest in
American Indian art and they seem always to present a pro-
tective influence in the painting. We see this figure in the
early *Birth* of 1937 in all its complicated life-renewal; in
Guardians of the Secret, 1943, the two totemic guardians stand
to right and left of the central rectangle which contains the
hieroglyphic secret, while underneath crouches the Anubis-
like dog with one eye open and ears alert. Or are these fig-
ures Romulus and Remus themselves, guarding their young
city from its hostile neighbors with the help of the She-Wolf?
All these interpretations may be pertinent, for *Guardians of
the Secret* is a meeting of Near East and Far West, a painting
of superb unity created from the fusion of elements of
Egyptian, Roman, and American Indian art. That the mean-
ing of these totemic figures is evocative rather than denota-
tive, is true to the nature of totemic art.

After exploring these figures with great authority and fi-
nality in the two beautiful paintings of 1944 and 1945, *Totem
I* and *Totem II*, Pollock in the following year seems to move
directly into the "secret." It appears that the central rectan-
gle of *Guardians of the Secret* had become the painting-subject
not only of the two prophetic works of this year, *The Blue
Unconscious* and *The Key*, but also of much of the nonobjec-
tive work which followed and which solved the hieroglyphic
secret and dissolved its signs in a lyricism of immediate im-
pact and spiritual clarity.

Action Painting

In the state of spiritual clarity there are no secrets. The effort to achieve such a state is monumental and agonizing, and once achieved it is a harrowing state to maintain. In this state all becomes clear, and Pollock declared the meanings he had found with astonishing fluency, generosity, and expansiveness. This is not a mystical state, but the accumulation of decisions along the way and the eradication of conflicting beliefs toward the total engagement of the spirit in the expression of meaning. So difficult is the attainment that, when the state has finally been reached, it seems that a maximum of decisions has already been made in the process, that the artist has reached a limitless space of air and light in which the spirit can act freely and with unpremeditated knowledge. His action is immediately art, not through will, not through esthetic posture, but through a singleness of purpose which is the result of all the rejected qualifications and found convictions forced upon him by his strange ascent.

But how much clarity can a human being bear? This state may be the ultimate goal of the artist, yet for the man it is most arduous. Only the artist who has reached this state should be indicated by Harold Rosenberg's well-known designation Action Painter, for only when he is in this state is the artist's "action" significant purely and simply of itself. Works of this nature are new in the history of Western civilization, and the spiritual state of their creation is as different from that of previous artists as is the look of the paintings different from that of previous paintings. Action Painting did not emerge miraculously from the void, and it is interesting and even comforting to make not-too-farfetched analogies with the works of predecessors because art is, after all, the visual treasury of man's world, as well as of individual men. Nevertheless this new painting does have qualities of passion and lyrical desperation, unmasked and uninhibited, not found in other recorded eras; it is not surprising that faced with universal destruction, as we are told, our art should at last speak with unimpeded force and unveiled honesty to a future which well may be nonexistent, in a last effort of recognition which is the justification of being.

Pollock's works of this nature, which appeared from 1947 to 1950 and again in 1952–53, culminating in the heroic *Blue Poles*, are painfully beautiful celebrations of what will disappear, or has disappeared already, from his world, of what may be destroyed at any moment. The urgency of his joy in the major works of this period is as great, and as pertinent to our time, as the urgency of *Guernica*, not with the latter masterpiece's obviousness.

1947 to 1950

Not that the nonobjective paintings of Pollock are devoted entirely to this joy. With means continually more inventive and radical, he pushed a wide range of expressive utterances to remarkably personal lengths. Despite his intense activity, the works never became categorical or doctrinaire. Each is an individual, a single experience. *Full Fathom Five* is full of nostalgia, its dominant color a green that is like a reminiscence of blue, with linear trailings of black, flowery-white and aluminum, with exclamations of orange, and a number of extraneous objects imbedded in the surface, like souvenirs of accident: a cigarette, half its paper torn off to expose the tobacco, two keys, nails, a cluster of tacks, and paint-tube tops making little blind eyes here and there. Earlier the "eyes" were painted to a more Expressionistic effect in *Eyes in the Heat*, and they also are hinted at in the heavy impasto of *Shimmering Substance*. *Cathedral* is brilliant, clear, incisive, public—its brightness and its linear speed protect and signify, like the façade of a religious edifice, or, in another context, the mirror in the belly of an African fetish, the mysterious importance of its interior meaning (as anticipated in *Magic Mirror*, another "white" painting of 1941). *Eyes in the Heat II*, on the other hand, is a maelstrom of fiery silver; it is one of those works of Pollock, like *Shimmering Substance*, 1946, and the *White Light*, which has a blazing, acrid, and dangerous glamor of a legendary kind, not unlike those volcanoes which are said to lure the native to the lip of the crater and, by the beauty of their writhings and the strength of their fumes, cause him to fall in. These smaller paintings are the *femmes fatales* of his work.

Digression on "Number 1," 1948

I am ill today but I am not
too ill. I am not ill at all.
It is a perfect day, warm
for winter, cold for fall.

A fine day for seeing. I see
ceramics, during lunch hour by
Miró and I see the sea by Léger;
Light, complicated Metzingers
and a rude awakening by Brauner,
a little table by Picasso, pink.

I am tired today but I am not
too tired. I am not tired at all.
There is the Pollock, white, harm
will not fall, his perfect hand

and the many short voyages. They'll
never fence the silver range.
Stars are out and there is sea
enough beneath the glistening earth
to bear me toward the future
which is not so dark. I see.

This is the classical period of Pollock, classical in all its comprehensive, masterful, and pristine use of his own passions, classical in its cool, ultimate beauty, classical in that it is "characterized especially by attention to form with the general effect of regularity, simplicity, balance, proportion, and controlled emotion," to quote the dictionary. In the sense of this definition Pollock is the Ingres, and de Kooning the Delacroix, of Action Painting. Their greatness is equal, but antithetical. Because of this, to deny one would be to deny the other.

During this period Pollock made several friezes, including the *Number 24*, 1948, with its drenched pools of white in black let into an ocher ground punctuated with red; *Summertime*, a strange, serpentine flourish with colored-in areas bounded with black, as in a stained-glass window, and pointillist strokes here and there, denoting warm air; *White Cockatoo*, a lavish iconography of color and charm, perhaps his most amiable painting—and several others, each distinctive and original in their exploration of format and possibility. In these works we see a Pollock relaxed and grand, in the opposite mood from his earlier (and later) Gothic aspiration, not building, but writing out his marvellous inspirations in a full lyric hand.

The friezes seem soft and luxurious compared to the great paintings of this period, several of them masterpieces of twentieth-century art. *Number 1*, 1948, has an ecstatic, irritable, demanding force, an incredible speed and nervous legibility in its draftsmanship; and the seemingly bloodstained hands of the painter, proceeding across the top just beyond the main area of drawing, are like a postscript to a terrible experience. *Number 5*, 1948, reveals the opposite kind of mastery, a structure of vigor and fullness, which seems to present the respite of accomplishment. In *Number 1*, 1949, one of the most perfect works of his life or anyone else's, viewer or artist, Pollock gives us a world of draftsmanship, color, and tactile profundity which relates him to Watteau and Velasquez. It is a work of purity, modesty, and completion. At one time it was thought that the "all-over" paintings of Pollock represented an infinitely extensible field of force which could continue out into all four areas of space surrounding its boundaries. This is true of sight, but his work is not about sight. It is about what we see, about what we *can* see. In the works of this period we are not concerned with possibility, but actuality. *Number 1* could not but *have* exactly what it *has*. It is perfection.

There has never been enough said about Pollock's draftsmanship, that amazing ability to quicken a line by thinning it, to slow it by flooding, to elaborate that simplest of elements, the line—to change, to reinvigorate, to extend, to build up an embarrassment of riches in the mass by drawing alone. And each change in the individual line is what every draftsman has always dreamed of: color. The quick, instinctive rightness of line in a work like the *Drawing* of 1950 is present in profusion in the major works of this period, whether it takes on the cool Baroque quality of *Number 2*, 1949, or fuses in a passionate exhalation, as in *Lavender Mist*. That it could be heroic (*One*, 1950), ritualistic (*Autumn Rhythm*), and dramatic (*Number 32*, 1950) is not so much a credit to technical flexibility as to purpose. It was Pollock's vision that was infinitely extensible. *Number 28*, 1950, belongs in this company, and *Convergence*. With *Number 12*, 1952, we are in a different area. Following the burgeoning sensitivity of *Convergence*, it is a big, brassy gigolo of a painting; for the first time the aluminum paint looks like money, and the color is that of the sunset in a technicolor Western. But its peculiar quality is its natural vulgarity: it is not beautiful, but it *is* real. And it may be arbitrary. Yet, the arbitrary was already conquered in *Out of the Web* which, despite its gouged-out forms, has the subtle luminosity of a pearl.

Perhaps the most remarkable work of 1950, from a technical standpoint, is the *Number 29*. A painting-collage of oil, wire-mesh, pebbles, and shells composed on glass, it is majestic and does not depend on novelty for its effect. It is unique in that it is a masterpiece seen front or back, and even more extraordinary in that it is the same masterpiece from opposite sides of viewing. What an amazing identity *Number 29* must have!—like that of a human being. More than any other work of Pollock, it points to a new and as yet imponderable esthetic. It points to a world a young experimentalist like Allan Kaprow, who has written on Pollock in another vein, is searching for, and it is the world where the recent works of Robert Rauschenberg must find their emotional comfort. Other paintings of Pollock contain time, our own era with valuable elements of other eras revalued, but *Number 29* is a work of the future; it is waiting. Its reversible textures, the brilliant clarity of the drawing, the tragedy of a linear violence which, in recognizing itself in its own mirror-self, sees elegance, the open nostalgia for brutality expressed in embracing the sharp edges and banal forms of wire and shells, the cruel acknowledgment of pebbles as elements of the dream, the drama of black mastering sensuality and color, the apparition of these forms in open space as if in air, all these qualities united in one work present the crisis of Pollock's originality and concomitant anguish full-blown. Next to *Number 29*, Marcel Duchamp's famous work with glass seems mere conjecture, a chess-game of the non-spirit. This is one of the works of Pollock which it is most necessary to ponder deeply, and it is unfortunate for the art of the future that it is not permanently (because of its fragility) installed in a public collection.

Scale, Size and Violence

Pollock has done paintings of enormous size, as have most of the recent abstract painters in America. In Europe there seems to be a general belief that if a painting is 7' x 10' or over, it naturally must have been painted by an American. And the size of the painterly projection *is* a significant characteristic of Action Painting or Abstract Expressionism.

As the critic Clement Greenberg pointed out almost a decade ago, the New York School was early involved in the conception of the "wall" as opposed to that of the "easel." This may have come from the participation of so many of these artists in the Federal Arts Project which, in basic accord with the aims, if not the ideology, expressed in Rivera's remark . . . [that art should express "the new order of things . . . and that the logical place for this art, . . . belonging to the populace, was on the walls of public buildings"] had undertaken a large program of murals for public buildings. The theory behind this was, I imagine, less spiritual than that of Rivera: if the taxpayer is paying for the art it should be available to the taxpayer, physically at the very least. Clement Greenberg has noted that Pollock worked as an easel painter on the Federal Arts Project, but many other painters, among them Arshile Gorky and Willem de Kooning, worked on the mural projects, and undoubtedly this experience had an effect on the pictorial ambitions of the New York School. Certainly the great 9' x 17' paintings of Pollock done in 1950 have the effect of murals, whether installed in a private or public collection.

Scale, that mysterious and ambiguous quality in art which elsewhere is a simple designation, has a particular significance in Pollock's work, but it has nothing to do with perspectival relationships in the traditional sense or with the relationship of the size of the object painted to the size of the object in reality. It has to do, rather, with the emotional effect of the painting upon the spectator. His explorations of this quality lead to the strange grandeur of that modestly sized, 2 1/2' x 2' painting, *Shimmering Substance*, whose dispersed strokes of impasto create a majestic, passionate celebration of matter, purely by their relation to the plane and format of the picture's surface. Another use of scale is seen in *Easter and the Totem*, whose seven feet of thinly-painted, large-scale arabesques have the intimacy and lyricism of a watercolor. When we approach the all-over, "drip" paintings of 1948–50, however, a different aspect of scale is apparent.

It is, of course, Pollock's passion as an artist that kept his works from ever being decorative, but this passion was expressed through scale as one of his important means. In the past, an artist by means of scale could create a vast panorama on a few feet of canvas or wall, relating this scale both to the visual reality of known images (the size of a man's body) and to the setting (the building it would enhance). Pollock, choosing to use no images with real visual equivalents and having no building in mind, struck upon a use of scale which was to have a revolutionary effect on contemporary painting and sculpture. The scale of the painting became that of the painter's body, not the image of a body, and the setting for the scale, which would include all referents, would be the canvas surface itself. Upon this field the physical energies of the artist operate in actual detail, in full scale; the action of inspiration traces its marks of Apelles with no reference to exterior image or environment. It is scale, and no-scale. It is the physical reality of the artist and his activity of expressing it, united to the spiritual reality of the artist in a oneness which has no need for the mediation of metaphor or symbol. It is Action Painting.

This is a drastic innovation hitherto unanticipated, even in the mural-size works of Picasso and Matisse. No wonder, then, that when these paintings were first shown in the Betty Parsons Gallery the impression was one of inexplicable violence and savagery. They seemed about to engulf one. This violence, however, was not an intrinsic quality of the paintings, but a response to Pollock's violation of our ingrained assumptions regarding scale. So impressively had Pollock expounded his insight into the qualities dormant in the use of scale that when seen only a few years later at the Janis Gallery or in The Museum of Modern Art the violence had been transmuted into a powerful personal lyricism. The paintings had not changed, but the world around them had.

Nor is the meaning of these paintings ambiguous. Each is a direct statement of the spiritual life of the artist. Each is its own subject and the occasion for its expression. There is no need for titles. This was, in fact, the "spiritual climate" of the New York School in those years, and most of the painters involved in it simply used numbers for identification of canvases, though many had previously used titles and would return to them again, as did Pollock.

Black and White

Pollock, Franz Kline, and Willem de Kooning have completely changed the concept of color in contemporary art, not by a concerted program, but by adamant individuality of interest. To generalize hastily, but I hope not unprovocatively: de Kooning, in the late 1940s and early 1950s, loved white as all-color with black as negative; Kline had an equal passion for black and for white in the works exhibited between 1951 and 1957; Pollock, following the triumphant blacks of *Number 29* and *Number 32*, both of 1950, restricted himself almost exclusively to black on unsized canvas in the 1951–52 pictures. Giving up all that he had conquered in the previous period, Pollock reconfronted himself with the crisis of figuration and achieved remarkable things. The only color that is allowed to intrude on the black stain of these figurative works is a sepia, like dried blood (*Number 11*, 1951, a monumental, moon-struck landscape) and the strange *maquillage* on the face to the right of *Portrait and a Dream*, dated 1953, but properly belonging to this group.

The wonderful draftsmanship of the early drawings and the "drip" periods is here brought to bear on heads and figures of nightmarish variety and semblance. *Echo*, that effulgence of sensory indulgence, the two "heads," *Number 3* and *Number 26*, the reclining figure of *Number 14*—who makes one wonder if she is not Cassandra waiting at night in the temple of Apollo for the gift of prophecy, as does the figure in *Sleeping Effort*—the savagely (as opposed to brilliantly) virtuoso handling of spatial negation in *Number 6*, 1952, each brings an aspect of the early Pollock up-to-date, half Dionysius, half Cyclops. They are disturbing, tragic works. They cry out. What this must have meant to him after the Apollonian order of *Autumn Rhythm* is unimaginable.

The Last Period

Much has been written about Pollock's difficulties in the last three years of his life, and more has been spoken. The works accomplished in these years, if created by anyone else, would have been astonishing. But for Pollock, who had incited in himself, and won, a revolution in three years (1947–50), it was not enough. This attitude has continued to obscure the qualities of some of these works, for in *Blue Poles* he gave us one of the great masterpieces of Western art, and in *The Deep* a work which contemporary esthetic conjecture had cried out for. *Blue Poles* is our *Raft of the Medusa* and our *Embarkation for Cytherea* in one. I say *our*, because it is the drama of an American conscience, lavish, bountiful, and rigid. It contains everything within itself, begging no quarter: a world of sentiment implied, but denied; a map of sensual freedom, fenced; a careening licentiousness, guarded by eight totems native to its origins (*There Were Seven in Eight*). What is expressed here is not only basic to his work as a whole, but it is final.

The Deep is the coda to this triumph. It is a scornful, technical masterpiece, like the *Olympia* of Manet. And it is one of the most provocative images of our time, an abyss of glamor encroached upon by a flood of innocence. In this innocence, which ambiguously dominates the last works, Pollock painted his final homage to those whose art he loved and thought of in his need: the American Indian (*Ritual*), Matisse (*Easter and the Totem*), and Soutine (*Scent*). Though *Search*, for us a difficult, for him an agonizing work, was prepared to reveal again a classical level of objectivity, a new air, a new light, the causal insight mentioned earlier was stopped by accident—that accident which had so often been his strength and his companion in the past was fatal.

As Alfonso Ossorio, his friend, fellow-painter, and collector, wrote of his paintings in 1951: "We are presented with a visualization of that remorseless consolation—in the end is the beginning.

"New visions demand new techniques: Pollock's use of unexpected materials and scales is the direct result of his concepts and of the organic intensity with which he works, an intensity that involves, in its complete identification of the artist with his work, a denial of the accident."

And his work does deny accident. It is as alive today as when, in 1947, Pollock wrote:

> My painting does not come from the easel. I hardly ever stretch my canvas before painting. I prefer to tack the unstretched canvas to the hard wall or the floor. I need the resistance of a hard surface. On the floor I am more at ease. I feel nearer, more a part of the painting, since this way I can walk around it, work from the four sides and literally be *in* the painting. This is akin to the method of the Indian sand painters of the West.
>
> I continue to get further away from the usual painter's tools such as easel, palette, brushes, etc. I prefer sticks, trowels, knives and dripping fluid paint or a heavy impasto with sand, broken glass and other foreign matter added.
>
> When I am *in* my painting, I'm not aware of what I'm doing. It is only after a sort of "get acquainted" period that I see what I have been about. I have no fears about making changes, destroying the image, etc., because the painting has a life of its own. I try to let it come through. It is only when I lose contact with the painting that the result is a mess. Otherwise there is pure harmony, an easy give and take, and the painting comes out well.[1]

This is the affirmation of an artist who was totally conscious of risk, defeat, and triumph. He lived the first, defied the second, and achieved the last.

1959

[1]From *Possibilities I*, 1947–8, "Problems of Contemporary Art," v. 4, New York, George Wittenborn, Inc.

Franz Kline, *New York, N.Y.,* oil on canvas, 79 x 51 in. Albright-Knox Art Gallery, Buffalo, New York: Gift of Seymour H. Knox, 1956.

A Note on Franz Kline

ROBERT CREELEY

This note originally appeared in a 1954 issue of the Black
Mountain Review, *which Creeley then edited. Both he and Kline
taught at Black Mountain College, though not at the same time,
and it was primarily at the Cedar Bar in New York City (the closest
America ever came to an artists' café) that he came to know Kline.
But it was through Black Mountain connections that Creeley formed
close relationships with elders like Pollock, Guston, Tworkov, de
Kooning, and Vicente and with peers like John Chamberlain, Dan
Rice, and John Altoon. Analogous methods and a common ferment,
brewed at Black Mountain, drew together in later cultural histories
the work of the abstract expressionists and those poets (including
Creeley) who wrote under the influence of Charles Olson's theories of
"projective verse." From the start of his career Creeley collaborated
with artists (among them Marisol, R. B. Kitaj and Jim Dine), and
has written catalogue notes and reviews of their work—trying, as he
puts it, to "avoid the extraordinary rhetoric that becomes increas-
ingly the case after Clement Greenberg. As a friend said, now even
the artist being discussed can't read it." He also claims he prefers the
company of painters to that of poets: the former "have nothing (of a
literary order at least) up their sleeve, they are often exceptionally
bright, very articulate, explicit, and often read more than their liter-*

Reprinted with permission of the Four Seasons Foundation from *A Quick Graph*, ed.
Donald Allen (Four Seasons Foundation, 1970), 341–42. Copyright © 1954 by Robert
Creeley.

ary counterparts." But one senses from the following brief essay that it is precisely because they don't "know," and need not "articulate," that Creeley envies the painters. It was Franz Kline himself—a brilliant talker—who once remarked, *"You don't paint the way someone, by observing your life, thinks you* have *to paint, you paint the way you have to in order to* give, *that's life itself, and someone will look and say it is the product of knowing, but it has nothing to do with knowing, it has to do with giving."*

THERE ARE women who will undress only in the dark, and men who will only surprise them there. One imagines such a context uneasily, having no wish either to be rude or presumptuous. Darkness, in effect, is the ground for light, which seems an old and also sturdy principle. Think of the masses of misunderstanding that come from a betrayal of this. Make a list. Picasso? Much a way of being *about* something, minus night, etc. There are some men for whom it seems never to get dark. As, for example, for Klee it never quite seems to be sun, etc.

But, more interesting, think of it, a woman undressing in broad sunlight, black. What if light were black—is there black light? If there is black light, what is black. In other words, argue to the next man you meet that we are living in a place where everything has the quality of a photographic negative. Take hold of his coat, point to anything. See what happens.

With Kline's work, if the blacks were white, and vice versa, it would make a difference, certainly. It has to be black on white, because there he is, New York, etc. He has no wish to fight senses and all. But he is a savagely exact laugher, call it. I don't know if he depends on argument for a means to cohabitation, but I would myself argue that he is a lonely man. Men rarely laugh this precisely, without such a thing for a control. What is 'funnier' than forms which will not go away. If you say this to someone, they will laugh at you, but all the time, right behind them, there is a skyscraper! It's incredible how they can notice it, if they do, and still talk to anyone.

So what is form, if it comes to that. That question I once tried to answer in relation (as they say) to the theater. I was convinced that a man, formally, is no more and certainly no less than a chair. Fool that I was, I took two chairs, placed them either side of me, and sat down on the floor. The answer was, from these friends: Who would go to the theater to see a man be a chair? What would Kline have said, if anything. Is this thing on the page opposite looking at you too? Why do you think that's an eye. Does any round enclosed shape seem to you an eye.

There is no 'answer' to anything. A painter (possibly a musician) can assert this more effectually, more relevantly, than any other 'artist.' He can be present all at one time, which no writer can quite be—because he has to 'go on.' If no one sees a painter, or, rather, what he is doing—finally, not 'doing'—doesn't he still have *things*. At least no man can point at a painting and say it's nothing, he'll be lucky if it doesn't come down off the wall and club him to death for such an impertinence.

God knows we finally enjoy, deeply *enjoy*, wit, the grace, the care, of any thing—how it is. Kline's audience (no doubt in Paradise) will be a group of finely laughing women, plus what men won't be jealous.

1954

Jess, *Seventy XXth Success Story*, collage, 59 x 42 ³/₄ in. University Art Museum, University of California, Berkeley: Purchase with funds from NEA, the UAM Council, and the Turnbull Foundation funded by William D. Turnbull and Paule Anglim.

An Art of Wondering

ROBERT DUNCAN

In Art as Experience *John Dewey distinguishes between "the art product (statue, painting or whatever), and the* work *of art." It is that work, those workings of art that have preoccupied Robert Duncan: the "scales of the marvelous," fictions to arrive at wisdom. His has been the wisdom of the Romantics. As an infant he was adopted by theosophical foster parents on the basis of his astrological chart, and he grew up steeped in hermetic myths and "sacred presences." He claims to "receive" his hieratic poems, each of them at once a "permission" or access to magic and a copy or visible idea of the artist's original vision. Since 1951 Duncan and Jess Collins (known professionally by his first name) have lived together and have been crucial to the so-called Berkeley Renaissance. Together they have pursued their occult studies, especially the relationships between written words and visual images. Jess's paste-ups (he calls them "assemblies of images"), which owe a good deal to the example of Max Ernst's collages, might allude to Plato and Dick Tracy, cabbalistic lore or bubble-gum cards. In his poem "Passages 31 The Concert," Duncan wrote of them:*

> Yet the quality of the stars
> reigneth *in the spirit; tho the spirit can*
> *and may raise or drown itself*

Reprinted with permission of Robert Duncan. Essay first appeared in a catalogue for *Translations, Salvages, Paste-Ups,* an exhibition by Jess (Dallas Museum of Fine Arts, 1977).

in its own qualities, or take its life
in the influence of the stars, as it pleaseth.
For it is free. It has got for its own
the qualities it has in itself, its own

plot or myth, its feel
of what belongs to it

The following essay was written for the catalogue of an exhibition of Jess's work, called "Translations, Salvages, Paste-Ups," organized by the Dallas Museum of Fine Arts in April 1977. Six years earlier in a similar essay, entitled "Iconographical Extensions," Duncan wrote: "Blake speaks in the tradition of poetry's mysteries of a four-fold vision of reading; and we may likewise speak of a four-fold 'reading' of the visual world. The experience of 'meaning' is the experience of interrelationships. The 'language' of painting in which we read the meaning of the process of art itself, analogous to the meaning of the oral/aural processes of literary poetry, presents itself in the way of painting, and it is important in Jess's work that this 'way' is itself a goal of the artist. The 'language' of picture arises, as if there were a tongue in the mouth of what we see, and the eye were an ear, in which visual elements—light and dark, opacity and translucence, color and mass, and, then, lines and rhythms—lead into boundaries and the syntax of a world and the lexicon of its things and beings."

IF WE THINK of Vision as instant and given, as an immediate insight into the divine world, self-evident in its presentation, that saints, clairvoyants, shamans in ecstatic intoxication, and dreamers, have known and sought then to communicate—the instant transport of seeing in itself—then Jess's art is not primarily a visionary art, for, though vision is there, it is the ground of a searching and researching work. Whatever his initial perception or impression is—whether it be the recognition of a picture to be translated or of a painting to be salvaged or of the ground and the contributing members of a paste-up work—it is experienced as a call to undertake a work, as an impending quest, in which first sight leads on into research and imagination toward second sight, where at last first sight is to be founded, and in the working out of the picture-to-be the artist seeks the realization of an order in which there is a visible co-inherence of all the elements in one presence. Painting, for Jess, is a realization of what is going on in Vision; and an in-dwelling in that realization. In the development of his way of painting he has sought to prolong and deepen the time and Mind of his involvement in each painting. "Mind," I would capitalize, because I mean to call to mind the complex of elements we have separated in our language into feeling and thought— Jess's art means to be profoundly senti-mental—and into mind and spirit—the French word *Esprit* keeps the integrity of the concept we tend to lose. In the division into "mind" and "spirit" in our common speech, we have allowed "mind" to spiritless businesses of professional interest only, and yet we keep alive another sense of mind, for we speak of minding what we do. "I do mind," we say when we are deeply concerned. And the assemblage of the meaning of "spirit" includes for us the lively tone of a spirited horse, the verve of a Sargent water colour, the surge of alcohol, the aweful presentation of a spook or the presiding command of the Sanctus Spiritus.

In the design of the title page of *Translations by Jess* (Odyssia Gallery, New York, 1971), superimposed upon an Hermetic emblem from the seventeenth century, showing the formation of the macrocosm, the artist has projected an acrostic, a version of the popular game *Scrabble* in which we

are given terms that may illustrate in their assemblage some-
thing of what Jess thinks to be at work in his art:

```
                        Q           M  A  Y  B  E
                     B  U  D         A     E     M  U  M
               A  S     I     L  I  G  H  T     B        I
                  P     E     I     I        F  L  E  X
            P  A  I  N  T     F  A  C  T        A              E
      F     L     R        P  E  N     E        Z     W  I  T
   W  A  K  E     I     L        A     S     N  O  D  E     C
   I  N     A     T  R  A  N  S  L  A  T  I  O  N     B  Y
   S  E  T           N        O     I     N        H
   H     R     I  M  A  G  E        G     M  Y  S  T  E  R  Y
      S  E  L  F     S  U  N              O     E     R     O
         M        S  H  A  D  E        A  N  O  N  Y  M  O  U  S
   E  M  B  R  Y  O     G        L     Y     S     I     N
         L        N     E  C  H  O        S  E  N  T     G
         E     A  G  O     R     V  E  I  L     E
               L        L  Y  R  E     S  E  R  V  E
         L  O  S  T     O     O     D  I  E     E
               O     C  O  L  O  R     S  P  A  R  K
               K        T  O           I
                        D  R  E  A  M
```

Wondering what this all means, if we start with the imme-
diate recall of the game *Scrabble,* we are struck with the mes-
sages the game conveys. As the poet plays with the letters to
build an emerging structure of words, he is also, it seems, the
medium of an emerging message, playing into the hands of a
spirit who means to speak to him and to us. The game is first
cousin then to the ouija board where messages are spelled
out from another world. And paintings too, for Jess, have
something of their own to say. Each day he works with the
canvas, addresses himself to the canvas, the painting speaks
to him, Jess feels, calling for the color that must be mixed:
the colors present call for a color to be found in the inven-
tion of a color; and the images present in the work call forth
the need for missing images belonging to the picture. In this
colloquy, the picture is picturing itself in the artist's "Mind"

as he works. His work is also a ground of consultation and his seeing is a listening to a voice or governing tone of the painting seeking its materialization. What Jess keeps alive in his sense of his art is the secret in childhood of playing house, playing worlds, playing with blocks, in which both a conversation with and an exploration of play things goes on.

But this projection of a figure out of a game of *Scrabble* may also be related to the Hermetic magic squares that in Renaissance practice were related to demonic theurgy, to calling up and consulting with demonic and angelic powers, and that continue to our day as intellectual entertainments and puzzles. Among his texts for one of the Translation series (24, "Fig. 8—De Macrocosmi Fabrica"), Jess includes a word square found in *Scientific American*, where it was quoted from *Notes & Queries*, July 21, 1895:

```
C  I  R  C  L  E
I  C  A  R  U  S
R  A  R  E  S  T
C  R  E  A  T  E
L  U  S  T  R  E
E  S  T  E  E  M
```

Clearly the painter feels that a process of communion and communication is going on throughout the created world, that things speak to him, and that a spiritual message is spelling itself out in his work and his life. It is all the more remarkable that Jess specifically projects here neither the relation of the devotees dictated to by the ouija board nor the Faustian relation of the magician commanding by a closed and systematic formularization the service of his informant, but the open invention of a popular game, a play with letters in which the words lead us on to a gathering meaning. These paintings are direct descendants of the hieroglyphics of earlier mystery cults and alchemical theaters, but they belong now (as do the hieroglyphics and alchemical scenes) to a theater of our mind's free election and entertaining of ideas, wherein a play of associations is going on.

The paste-ups are assemblages, as the present world assembles itself in the congress of all its events and persons and things. What the artist celebrates and performs in the "collage" of various elements is the mystery of tenor: the charge of each element exists not for itself alone but for the sake of the meaning of the whole. It is a sense of the world as a potentiality throughout of "world." In his sense of the redemptive (as he indicates in the title of the set "Salvages") and generative order of his art, Jess is close in spirit indeed to Dante's sense of what he calls "the potential intellect"— the mind's work leading ever to its belonging to Mind. "There must be a multiplicity of things generable," Dante proposes—striking here where we would be thinking of the multiplicity of elements that are assembled to illustrate the oneness of a work, "in order that the whole potentiality of first matter may always be in act." In the novels and religious essays of Charles Williams, which we read together in the early 1950s, Jess found the term "co-inherence": in the truth of a fiction or created world, each element of creation becomes true to itself as it becomes true to its meaning or its way of belonging to the meaning of the whole. The communion of individualities in the redemption of the community of the "world" underlies his feeling of the composition of the painting and of the relation of the individual painting to his life work in painting. Within the complex society of each individual canvas, this particular red has the truth and vividness of its "self" in the life of the color-community; this particular turn of line or weight of mass has its uniqueness in its relation to the community of events that line and mass belong to. Each individual factor has its highest individualization not alone but in the company of individualizations it contributes to in its co-existence, its co-operation, its co-inherence toward the fabric of factors. The work is "there" for Jess (what we commonly call "finished"—but how strange to call it "finished" just when it has reached that wholeness in which it is the beginning or the threshold of the life of the painting itself in the world) when it presents such a co-inherence of its elements—painting, color, line, mass, texture, figure, picture.

The *Scrabble* figure projected by Jess is charged with meaning throughout by the magic tenor of language as such. A spirit speaks to us in the game we are in the depths of playing. "M-A-Y-B-E", the player spells out in the first horizontal line from the initial "M" of the vertical word "M-A-G-I-C", and, once the word appears (in our reading, being at the top of the figure, read as a leading sign), the word *Maybe* is most haunting. It is the germinal term of our wondering. Dante imagines, he does not wonder—certainly not in the sense of the "I wonder?" or "I wonder if . . ." which comes into the word for us, though he does posit that Man's true mode of thought is speculation. Hans Vaihinger's "system of the theoretical, practical and religious fictions of mankind", as presented in his *Philosophy of 'As If '*, played an important role in the early formation of Jess's thought; and in the *Scrabble* figure, sure enough, the word "A-S" in the third horizontal line leads into the initial "S" of "S-P-I-R-I-T" which descends into the initial "T" of "T-R-A-N-S-L-A-T-I-O-N-S", and the initial "I" of "I-M-A-G-E" in the ninth horizontal line descends thru the word "I-F" to form the terminal letter of "S-E-L-F" in the line below.

These assemblies, these salvages or redemptions, these translations or transubstantiations, belong to the orders of a personal mystery, paintings for a hall of the mysteries. In the revealing *Scrabble* construct, the appearance of the pointers

"S-P-I-R-I-T", "F-A-N-E", "M-Y-S-T-E-R-Y", "S-H-A-D-E", and "V-E-I-L", as well as the name of "I-S-I-S", the goddess of the phenomenal world, hint in such a direction, and, if they so existed in themselves in a closed system, they would substantiate the suspicion of a specific cult; but they do not exist in themselves but in the company of "A-S", "I-F", "N-O-N-S-E-N-S-E", "W-I-T", "Y-E-T", and "A-L-S-O", in whose light their meaning must be redeemed. Even the meaning of "M-A-Y-B-E" must be saved, translated to come true in the co-inherence of the company it belongs to. In the terms of the co-inherence, *nonsense* redeems the sense of *paint* and *light*, even as *paint* and *light* as they enter the weave translate the meaning of *as* and *if*.

Each painting, each paste-up proposes a world "in itself", that has its own life, its own glowing presentation of a world; but that we find, in turn, in its association with other paintings in the artist's work—either in the order of the particular sets designated by the artist in his project—"Salvages" or "Translations"—or in an order of a set freely forming in our own imagination's creation—has a more resonant life in the company of the assemblage of sets. But everywhere in his work he proposes that the true life of these works belongs to the company of painting itself, that Imaginary Museum, as Malraux has described it, that gathers in the Mind, in which the paintings of Lascaux convene with the works of great Egyptian art, of the Renaissance master Titian, and of George Herriman, the master of *Krazy Kat.* Just as Jess does not present his translation of Egyptian mysteries as such, so he does not present *Krazy Kat* as a token of popular culture. What he proposes is an art whose identity is not realized in itself and whose vitality does not arise from signature or style but in an intensifying recognition of spiritual affinities and in the quest of new correspondences.

1977

Balthus, *The Street* (1933), oil on canvas, 76 ³/₄ x 94 ¹/₂ in. Collection, The
Museum of Modern Art, New York: James Thrall Soby Bequest.

Balthus

GUY DAVENPORT

"I'm a left-handed poet," says Davenport, "and a right-handed prose-writer." He continues to publish poems, and translations in verse, and actually began as a poet—his book-length Flowers and Leaves *appeared in 1966. "Its failure to attract any notice whatsoever convinced me that I should try prose." His stories have since brought him to prominence. They are not conventional stories but what he calls "assemblages of history and necessary fiction." Some of the history is art history; some of the "necessary fiction" is—and neatly defines—interpretation. Several of Davenport's stories, such as "Tatlin!," "Au Tombeau de Charles Fourier," and "The Death of Picasso," are in part fanciful commentaries on painters, with asides like: "Cézanne comes from Virgil. Picasso takes up the Classical just when it was most anaemic, academic, and bleached of its eroticism. . . . Traverse Picasso with two vectors: the long tradition of the still life (eating, manners, ritual, household) and the pastoral (herds, pasturage, horse, cavalier, campsite)." Or this: "Matisse began to include the edges especially of women as they are seen more to the left than you would see if the right is there and a little more to the right than you would see if the left is here, a primitive and intelligent way of looking." Among the subjects of Davenport's brilliant, eclectic essays are Pavel Tchelitchew and Grant Wood (whom he wants to see as the American Memling). In writing about*

Reprinted with permission of Guy Davenport. The essay first appeared in *Antaeus* 39 (1980): 80–89. Copyright © 1984 by Guy Davenport.

233

Balthus, Davenport is writing about the painter who has most attracted—by his secret erotic grammar and allegorical literalism—contemporary poets, and he is thereby offering an oblique look at poetry too. Asked to name the art criticism he himself likes best, he lists "les frères Goncourt on Hokusai and Hiroshige, Malraux's Goya, Adrian Stokes on Duccio, Gertrude Stein on Raoul Dufy (also on Picasso), Hugh Kenner on Wyndham Lewis, Marilyn Aronberg Lavin on Piero della Francesca's The Flagellation.*"*

SENSUOUS clarity, children in the old-fashioned smocks of a France only recently folded into history forever, high-ceilinged rooms, Parisian streets, chateaux: Balthus' accomplished realism turns out on inspection to be both lyric vision and a complex enigma.

Like his childhood mentor Rilke in the Fifth Duino Elegy he is asking who we are in our cycle of budding, blossoming, falling to seed again *in diesem mühsamen Nirgends.* Our "never-contented will" pitches us like acrobats even in boredom and contemplative repose.

Rilke was meditating on Picasso's *Les Saltimbanques,* and Picasso's gesture in buying and leaving to the Louvre Balthus' *The Children* (1937) seems a deliberate return of Rilke's *hommage,* defining the kinship of three symbols of *Dastehns,* the Existential *thereness.*

Balthus' adolescents are Rilke's "bees of the invisible," taking in from books, from daydreaming, from as yet ambiguous longing, from staring out windows at trees, sustenances that will be available in time as Proustian ripenesses, necessities of the heart.

Ultimately it is Balthus' sensibility that gives his canvases their distinction, the quality of his attention, the unlikely subtlety and boldness of his sensuality, the harmony he creates of tensions, inarticulatenesses, ambiguities, volume, light, elusive moments.

Where in Greek writing you always find a running account of all the senses in intimate contact with the world, in Latin you find instead a pedantry accustomed to substituting some rhetorical convention for honest and immediate perception. Balthus has Greek wholeness.

He has the immediacy of a naive painter. Picasso's people are all actors, wearers of masks, mediators, like Picasso himself, between reality and illusion. Pierrot, woman as artist's model, the Ballet Russe, the Commedia dell' Arte dominate his entire *oeuvre.*

Nowhere in Balthus does this theme of actor and theatre appear. There is great integrity in his resisting it. His tradition stands apart from that of Rouault, Braque, Picasso, Klee, Ensor, many another for whom acting has been a metaphor and art a stage.

Nor do we find in Balthus any of the enlistments of mythology characteristic of the century. No Venuses, no Danaës, among all those girls. Even his cats and gnomes do not derive from folklore or myth. He is not part of any renaissance. His work is an invention.

Each painting is an invention, not the application of a technique. Each painting holds an imaginary conversation with some other painter, *The Window* with Bonnard, *The Farmyard* with Cézanne, *The Living Room* with Courbet, *The Dream* with Chardin.

The Mountain (in which the girl in the foreground stretches with the feline inflection of Gregor Samsa's healthy sister at the end of "The Metamorphosis") is a dialogue with the Courbet of *Les rochers de Mouthiers* and *La falaise d'Etretat après l'orage.*

The term "modern artist" has never had a strictly temporal sense; from the beginning it has designated a totemistic clan to which one belongs according to a structure of rules with tribal overtones yet to be described. Balthus is a provisionally kin country cousin.

Sir Herbert Read, for instance, decreed that Stanley Spencer was not a modern artist. We remember that Brancusi, to please a committee, had to redraw a portrait of Joyce because it wasn't modern enough for their taste. This is like asking Shakespeare to be more Renaissance.

Balthus, I suspect, has been excluded from the clan for reasons of awesome primitiveness, and has thus remained in the distinguished category of the unclassifiable like Wyndham Lewis, Stanley Spencer, and Lord knows who else. Modernity ended by trivializing its revolt.

Balthus and Spencer illuminate each other. Spencer's intrepid religious grounding (eccentric, Blakean, British, Bunyanesque, the naive inextricably in harmony with the sophisticated elements) is like Balthus' privileged, undisclosed, but articulate psychology.

Both painters express a sensual delight in the material world that is openly hedonistic, an accomplishment of the imagination beyond the sensitivity of criticism: the way light rakes a brick wall in Spencer, the respect for carpentry and architecture in Balthus.

Both Balthus and Spencer give us the surface of the canvas as a mimesis of natural textures, not paint. In Picasso, van Gogh, on out to the *reductio ad absurdum* of Pollock, it is paint. The difference is a philosophical one, perhaps even a religious one.

Spencer's iconography of saws, ironwork, human flesh reseen without the authority of neoclassical conventions, kettles, drying laundry, the location of shadows in naked light, parallels Balthus' return to a realism of an accomplished eye that demands accuracy of detail.

We have yet to study in modern painting the choice of *motif* after the break between patron and artist in the early nineteenth century. Not even the portrait as document or landscape as a sentiment for a room's decoration survives this new context for the visual arts.

This change was also a metamorphosis in taste. Malraux has his theory: that art became an absolute, that from Goya forward painting had only its authority as a witness to proceed with, alienated in one sense (from church and palace) but liberated in another to its own destiny.

Balthus' adolescents have a history. The Enlightenment, removing encrustations of convention from human nature, discovered the *durée* of childhood as the most passionate and beautiful part of a lifetime. Rousseau, Blake, Joshua Reynolds, Gainsborough, Wordsworth.

By the Belle Époque children (in a pervasive, invisible revolution) had come into a world of their own for the first time in Western civilization since late antiquity, and we begin to have (in Proust, in Joyce) dramatic accounts of their world as never before.

Henry James' "The Turn of the Screw" (which now that we have Balthus seems Balthusian) is a skirmish on the border between the inner worlds of child and adult. James follows with symbols the serious misunderstanding between the interiority of the two realms.

It is significant that anthropologists around this time, inspecting other cultures, thought of themselves as studying "the childhood of mankind." Balthus is a contemporary of Gide and Henry de Montherlant who, like Fourier and Wordsworth, were trying to *place* the child's random vitality.

Balthus' adolescents in an endless afternoon of reading, playing cards, and daydreaming seem to have come, we are told, as a subject for inexhaustible meditation from *Wuthering Heights* (which he has illustrated), a dismal and hysterical novel that he reads in his own way.

What caught Balthus' imagination in it was the way in which children create a subsidiary world, an emotional island which they have the talent to *robinsoner*, to fill all the contours of. This subworld has its own time, its own weather, its own customs and morals.

The only clock I can find in Balthus is on the mantel of *The Golden Days* of the Hirshhorn, and its dial is out of the picture. Balthus' children have no past (childhood resorbs a memory that cannot yet be consulted) and no future (as a concern). They are outside time.

Modern French writing has been interested in childhood and adolescence in a way that American and English writing has not. The French see not an innocent but an experienced mind in the child. Montherlant treats children as an endangered species needing protection from parents.

Gide's understanding runs parallel, except that he makes allowance for the transformation to maturity. The child in Alain-Fournier, Proust, Colette, Cocteau inhabits a realm imaginatively animated with a genius very like that of the artist. Children live in their minds.

Baudelaire saw genius as childhood sustained and perfected. There is a sense among the French that adulthood is a falling away from the intelligence of children. We in the United States contrast child and adult as we contrast ignorance and knowledge, innocence and experience.

We do not give our children credit for having arrived at anything. They have no driver's license, no money, no sexual emotions (and are forbidden them), no real sports they can play, no power. Balthus' children are as complacent as cats and as accomplished in stillness.

We have postponed fulfillment of heart and mind far too late, so that the spiritual rhythm, or bad habit, of American children is perpetual procrastination. American writing and art make the child an actor in an adult world (Mark Twain, Salinger), not a real being in its own.

Of the autistically interior, dreaming, reading, erotic, self-sufficient child in Balthus' painting we have practically no image at all. Balthus' children are not being driven to succeed where their parents failed, or to be popular, adjusted, or a somebody.

Children are the creatures of their culture. The nakedness of human nature is clothed so soon by every culture that we are at wide variance, within and among cultures, as to what human nature might be. It was one of the hopes of our century to find out, a hope wholly dashed.

In France this question was thoroughly and originally debated during the Enlightenment and Revolution. The building facing us in *The Passage du Commerce Saint-André* was Marat's newspaper office, and the neighborhood once saw the movements of David and Diderot.

Charles Fourier concocted an elaborate philosophy to discover human nature and invented a utopian society to accommodate it, a society of children organized into hives and roving bands. Adults were, so to speak, to be recruited from the ranks of this aristocracy.

Proust's "little band" of adolescent girls at Balbec derives from Fourier, and the narrator's male presence among them is according to Fourier's plan of organization. St-Loup and his circle constitute a Little Horde, the complement "of Spartans" to the Athenian bands.

Balthus' erotic sense disarms because of its literalness, explicitness, and evasion of vulgarity or cheapness of any sort. He brings the taste of Fragonard and Watteau into our century where it is unlikely to survive except in Balthus' careful, protective sensibility.

Watteau's ladies and milkmaids know that we are looking at them, and are forever beyond us in an imaginary world. Balthus' girls with bared crotches are usually looking at themselves, in a brown study or revery, provocative, vulnerable, neither innocent nor naive.

The girl in *The Golden Days* is looking at her fetching self in a hand mirror and is sitting so that the young man starting the fire will see her underwear, if any, when he turns. We see instead slim and charming adolescence trying on an expression for effect.

Balthus' treatment of the human figure ranges from a *gaucherie* thoroughly primitive (crones, the boy with pigeons, that cat) to a sensuality and accuracy that puts him among the master draughtsmen. He paints from inside the figure outward, as if the figure painted itself.

The psychological acumen of the portraits of Derain and Miró is Shakespearean: speaking portraits in the common lore of what a portrait should be. They are, in a disturbing sense, too lifelike. And they are not here as painters primarily, but as the fathers of daughters.

(Chagall around the time of the Derain and Miró portraits had himself photographed with his deliciously sexy twelve-year-old daughter wholly naked, achieving an *hommage* to and subtle parody of Balthus, but recognizing his authority of innovation and iconology.)

The portrait of the Vicomtesse de Noailles (1936), curiously like Wyndham Lewis' portrait of Edith Sitwell, is beguiling because of its honest, unflattering likeness and unconventionality of pose: a third-grade schoolteacher, surely, resting between classes.

This portrait illustrates as well as any of Balthus' his ability to take the bare minimum of a subject and bring it to the highest pitch of clarity, of presence. This rich spareness contrasts with the century's aesthetic of merging figure and ground in a dazzle.

The Passage du Commerce Saint-André, Balthus' masterwork, has the spaciousness and presence of a Renaissance wall painting (it is eleven feet long, ten feet high) and invites and defies a reading of its meaning as vigorously as Piero della Francesca's *The Flagellation*.

Reproductions of it trick one into believing that it is an intimist canvas, fairly small. I was unprepared for its size when I saw it first at the Centre Pompidou in an afternoon of surprises. I had just seen my first Tatlin and some late Malevitches unknown until then.

I had seen an abstraction by Ivan Puni that made me feel for the moment that western design still had everything to learn all over again from the Russians. The surprise of suddenly turning and gazing into (not *at*) Balthus' great painting was a splendid and complex emotion.

For the first time I remembered how familiar the street was to me, a locale I crossed time and again when I first knew Paris just after the war. The painting did not exist then, though Balthus must have been making studies for it, a picture to epitomize all his work.

Inside the painting's fetching mysteriousness there had been all along a familiarity that I had not isolated until I stood before the canvas itself. A more wonderful way of seeing Proust's theory of the redemption of time in triumphant proof I cannot imagine.

Another surprise was to notice that for all the resonances in this most Balthusian of all Balthus' work (the Rilkean question, as of the *Saltimbanques*, "Who are these people?", its kinship to Beckett and Sartre) it belongs with a rightness to the Paris of Simenon.

There's the same flatness and ordinariness, as if to say: Look, the world is not really a mystery at all. It appears to be, but look again. These eight people, a dog, and a doll are the very essence of a Left Bank backstreet. The fine strangeness of it all is in our minds.

The old woman with her cane, a concierge nipping out briefly to do her shopping, can tell you all about these people. She is the kind of spiteful old soul who gives Maigret and Janvier their best information. Seeing the painting is very like Maigret learning a neighborhood.

The figure we see from the back (a self-portrait, Jean Leymarie says in his introduction to the Skira *Balthus*), who is coming from the baker's, is a standard type in the *quartier*. Maigret would suspect him of all manner of irresponsibility, Bohemian attitudes, and cosmopolitan vice.

The man at the left, resettling his trousers, and the aging dwarf on the right, are standard Simenon characters. They also belong to Beckett, a denizen of this street, whose *Molloy* and *En attendant Godot* are contemporary with the painting in the Spenglerian and literal sense.

These gnomish creatures, the most accessible of Balthus' enigmas, are not satiric, symbolic, or archetypal. They are simply misshapen bodies for which Balthus makes a place in order to chasten his voluptuous taste for the world. Apollo is dull without Hobgoblin.

Balthus' earlier cityscape *The Street* of 1933 (there are several versions) states with more theatricality the theme of *The Passage du Commerce Saint-André:* that pedestrians on a street are preoccupied, sealed within themselves, without cognizance of each other.

Each painting, *The Street* and *The Passage,* insists that the eye that's awake in all this sleep of attention is the artist's, making a basic definition, sweetly obvious but extraordinarily important, of what a painting is in the most archaic meaning of image, the *seen.*

We have adequate, if not accurate, reasons for the visual fields of all the epochs of graphic mimesis except the earliest and the latest. We feel confident that a Hogarth or a Goya exists in a history, an iconographic tradition, an anthropology which we can successfully examine.

We do not have this confidence with prehistoric murals or with Balthus. We are as uncertain of Archilochos' exact meaning as of Beckett and Joyce. One pattern of meaning is lost, the other has chosen to move outside our received structure of references to enlarge it.

In the two street paintings there is first of all a sense of absurd tragedy in the discreteness of the characters. Two adolescents struggle playfully in *The Street*, unaware that they look like a rape, perhaps wholly unaware of the emotional forces disguised in their play.

They are like the adolescents in the roomscapes who take poses that are erotically suggestive, ambiguous, tentative of symbolism. There's the same vagueness of purposelessness in Cocteau and Proust: the love scenes between Marcel and Albertine are all purest Balthus.

These adolescents are like kittens enjoying themselves immensely at a game of disembowelling each other. Their claws are retracted; we are fairly certain that they don't know what they are doing, though nature does. What does nature know about Balthus' pedestrians on a street?

Adolescents play at sex, a cook strolls on the sidewalk, a little girl plays with a racquet and ball, a carpenter carries a plank across the street, a boy walks with a gesture like a bandleader at the head of a parade, his face rapt with inner attention and Whittingtonian aspiration.

A well-dressed woman steps onto the curb, seemingly in a revery; a mother in an apron carries a child in a sailor suit reading a handbill, as awkwardly posed as a ventriloquist's dummy. There is something of Oskar Schlemmer's lay-figure poise and plumb-line balance to them.

Indeed, if we were told that we are looking at puppets, our eye immediately supplies the strings and notices all the perpendicular lines directly above heads, wrists, and ankles that might be puppet strings visible for sections of their length: a metaphysical idea.

We remember Rilke's symbolism of puppet and angel in the *Duino Elegies*, the empty and the full, the fated and fate itself, and remember the iconography of doll, straw man, puppet in de Chirico, Eliot, Pound, Yeats, *Petroushka*, Karel Čapek, Jarry, Carrá, Ensor, Wyndham Lewis.

These sentient puppets inhabit two simultaneous worlds: they yearn (inchoate yearning applies as subject to a good half of Balthus' work) and they are "tossed and wrung" (Rilke's words in the Fifth Elegy) by fate, like the figures in Picasso's blue and rose periods.

If Balthus' figure paintings are all purgatorial in the sense that brooding, looking inward, abiding patiently for things to come are modes of existential suffering, his landscapes are his visions of paradise. Where they have figures, they are active and jubilant.

What is Balthus? The blue and rose period in color and translated from Montmartre to the Faubourgs St-Germain and St-Honoré? Courbet in the age of Rilke and Cocteau? He is, most certainly, the artist whose vision of the French spirit will increase in subtlety and radiance.

1980

Fairfield Porter, *The Harbor Thru the Trees*, oil on canvas, 25 ^{1}/$_2$ x 25 ^{1}/$_2$ in. The Chase Manhattan Bank Collection. Photograph Jan Jachniewicz.

Respect for Things as They Are

JOHN ASHBERY

"I feel basically disinterested—not uninterested—in art," John
Ashbery *once told an interviewer. This disinterest has kept him a
close observer. He backed into his career of art critic. In 1960, he
says,* "a friend of mine, leaving her job as art critic at the Paris
Herald Tribune, *asked me if I would like it. I had no job in Paris,
and I said yes."* He stayed on, writing weekly articles, for five years.
When Thomas Hess took over as editor of Art News *and turned to
the poets as critics, it was because he felt they had a fresh eye and no
preconceived notions about brand-new art and they could take notes
on everything that happened around them.* "And because they were
cheaper," *adds Ashbery, who joined Hess at the magazine as execu-
tive editor (until 1972) and coedited with him several collections of
art criticism. From 1963 until 1966 Ashbery was joint editor of Art
and Literature, *and from 1980 until 1985 he served as senior art
critic for Newsweek. *But that is merely the professional or "disin-
terested" profile of things. He has also dabbled in art; as long ago as
1948 one of his collages appeared on the cover of the *Harvard Ad-
vocate. *He has been the subject of many artworks (by Andy Warhol,
Larry Rivers, Jane Freilicher, Alex Katz, Philip Pearlstein, and
others) and a close friend to several artists. Fairfield Porter was one.
The following essay about Porter, as much memoir as appreciation,*

Reprinted with permission of the Boston Museum of Fine Arts from *Fairfield Porter
(1970–1975): Realist Painter in an Age of Abstraction* (New York Graphics Society, 1982),
7–13. Copyright © 1982 by John Ashbery.

*testifies to their warm intimacy. Ashbery once praised Anne Ryan's
"secret language of around-the-house," a quality he admires in
Joseph Cornell, Charles Ives, Marianne Moore—and in Porter too.
There is something of an American tradition in this homespun sub-
lime, one that Ashbery has described and is himself part of: "In our
art we want to get beyond 'mysteries of construction,' to quote Miss
Moore's useful phrase, into mysteries of being which, it turns out,
have their own laws of construction." Porter not only painted Ash-
bery's portrait, he wrote about Ashbery's poetry. (Porter was a feisty,
perceptive critic and an occasional poet.) Here is what he said in
1961 about "early Ashbery": "Ashbery's language is opaque; you
cannot see through it any more than you can look through a fresco.
And as the most interesting thing about abstract painting is its
subject matter, so one is held by the sibylline clarity of Ashbery's
simple sentences, in which words have more objective reality than
reality of meaning. One is back in first grade, about to learn to
read." Now, Ashbery on Porter's paintings, whose surfaces are
inflected with a light one is about to learn to see.*

IN HIS introduction to Fairfield Porter's posthumous col-
lection of art criticism, *Art in Its Own Terms,* Rackstraw
Downes quotes a remark Fairfield Porter made during what
must have been one of the more Byzantine discussions at the
Artists' Club on Eighth Street, around 1952. The members
were arguing about whether or not it was vain to sign your
paintings. With the flustered lucidity of Alice in the court-
room, Porter sliced this particular Gordian knot once and
for all: "If you are vain it is vain to sign your pictures and vain
not to sign them. If you are not vain it is not vain to sign

them and not vain not to sign them."[1] We do not know the reaction of his colleagues; quite possibly this *mise au net* fell on the same deaf ears that ignored the urgent but plain and unpalatable truths that Porter voiced again and again in his writings on art, at a time of particularly hysterical factionalism. No one likes to be reminded of the obvious, when half-truths are so much richer and more provocative; thus it was Porter's fate both as critic and as painter to play the role of a Molière gadfly, an Alceste or a Clitandre in a society of stentorian *précieuses ridicules*. And to a certain extent, his reputation as an eccentric remains, though it stemmed from a single-minded determination to speak the truth. Handsome is as handsome does; actions speak louder than words: who, in the course of the Artists' Club's tumultuous sessions, could pause to listen to such drivel?

I hadn't known this statement of Porter's before reading Downes's preface, but somehow it caused all my memories of the man I knew well for more than twenty years (without, alas, pausing very often to look or listen well) to fall into place. Porter was, of course, only the latest of a series of brilliant know-nothings who at intervals have embodied the American genius, from Emerson and Thoreau to Whitman and Dickinson down to Wallace Stevens and Marianne Moore. Her title "In Distrust of Merits" could stand for all of them and her preference for winter over summer reminds me of Porter's saying in a letter to a friend: ". . . November after the leaves have fallen may be one of the best times of year on Long Island. That is, I like the way the trees don't block the light any more."[2] And I realized after such a long acquaintanceship that his paintings, which most people like

[1]Fairfield Porter, *Art In Its Own Terms*, ed. Rackstraw Downes (New York: Taplinger, 1979), pp. 21–22.

[2]Fairfield Porter, "Letters to Claire and Robert White," *Parenthèse*, no. 4 (1975), p. 209.

but have difficulty talking about (Are they modern enough?
Too French? Too pleasant? Hasn't this been done before?),
are part of the intellectual fabric that underlay his opinions,
his conversation, his poetry, his way of being. They are intel-
lectual in the classic American tradition of the writers men-
tioned above because they have no ideas in them, that is, no
ideas that can be separated from the rest. They *are* idea, or
consciousness, or light, or whatever. Ideas surround them,
but do not and cannot extrude themselves into the being of
the art, just as the wilderness surrounds Stevens's jar in
Tennessee: an artifact, yet paradoxically more natural than
the "slovenly" wilderness that approaches it, and from which
it takes "dominion."[3] Porter wrote of de Kooning: "His
meaning is not that the paintings have Meaning. . . . The
vacuum they leave behind them is a vacuum in accomplish-
ment, in significance, and in genuineness,"[4] and, as so often,
the critic's words apply to his own art as well.

Porter had a horror of "art as sociology," of the artist who
"treats art as though it were raw material for a factory that
produces a commodity called understanding."[5] For art and
that commodity are one, and art that illustrates an idea,
however remotely or tangentially, has forfeited its claim to be
considered art by introducing a fatal divisiveness into what
can only be whole. "I can't be distracted from paying the
closest possible attention to what I am doing by evaluating it
ahead of time," he wrote in a letter to the critic Claire
Nicolas White. "What one pays attention to is what is real (I
mean reality calls for one's attention) and reality is every-
thing. It is not only the best part. It is not an essence.
Everything includes the pigment as much as the canvas as

[3]Wallace Stevens, *The Collected Poems of Wallace Stevens* (New York: Alfred
Knopf, 1955), "The Anecdote of the Jar."
[4]Porter, *Art In Its Own Terms*, p. 38.
[5]*Ibid.*

much as the subject."[6] Although Porter's work is in some ways the product of an idea—the idea that ideas have no place in art, or at any rate that they have no separate life of their own in art, no autonomy that might siphon off part of the "reality" of the ensemble—it is in accord, appearances to the contrary, with the seemingly more "advanced" work of the contemporaries he admired: de Kooning, Johns, Lichtenstein, Brice Marden, the music of Cage and Feldman—artists whose work at first seems worlds apart from the backyards and breakfast tables that were Porter's subjects but were only a part of "everything." Even today there are admirers of Porter's painting who are bemused by his apparently wayward tastes in art, just as there are those who can't understand how Cage and Virgil Thomson can see anything in each other's music, forgetting how art submerges categories. "You can only buck generalities by attention to fact," Porter continued. "So aesthetics is what connects one to matters of fact. It is anti-ideal, it is materialistic. It implies no approval, but *respect* for things as they are." This last point seems hardest to digest for artists who believe that art is "raw material for a factory that produces a commodity called understanding." Thus, politically "concerned" artists continue to make pictures that illustrate the horrors of war, of man's inhumanity to man; feminist artists produce art in which woman is exalted, and imagine that they have accomplished a useful act; and no doubt there are a number of spectators who find it helpful to be reminded that there is room for improvement in the existing order of things. Yet beyond the narrow confines of the "subject" (only one of a number of equally important elements in the work of art, as Porter points out) the secret business of art gets done according to mysterious rules of its own. In this larger context

[6]*Parenthèse*, no. 4, p. 212.

ideology simply doesn't function as it is supposed to, when indeed it isn't directly threatening the work of art by trivializing it, and trivializing as well the importance of the ideas it seeks to dramatize.

For Porter, the enemy was "idealism," which was very close to something called "technology." As a citizen he was preoccupied—almost obsessed, in fact—with questions of ecology and politics, and politics of a most peculiar sort; he had been something of a Marxist in the thirties but in later life his political pronouncements could veer from far left to extreme right without any apparent transition. And in conversation he could become almost violent on subjects like pesticides or fluoridation, to the extent that his friends would sometimes stifle giggles or groans, though one almost always had to agree with him, and the years since his death in 1975 have proved him even righter than he knew. Nevertheless, this passionately idealistic man felt threatened by idealism. "Technology . . . has only to do with evaluation and usefulness. Technology is what threatens all life on this planet. It is idealism put into practice."[7] If I understand him, it is not idealism that is dangerous, far from it, but idealism perverted and destroyed by being made "useful." Its uselessness is something holy, just like Porter's pictures, barren of messages and swept clean, in many cases, by the clean bare light of November, no longer masked by the romantic foliage.

In an earlier letter to Mrs. White, Porter complained about several sentences in an article she had written about him and submitted to him before publication. One was: "Since he does not like the white, misty summer light of the Hamptons he goes to an island in Maine in the summer." This nettled him because: "the fact is, we go to Maine in the summer because I have since I was six. It is my home more

[7] *Ibid.*

than any other place, and I belong there. . . . The white misty light would never be a reason for my doing anything."[8] And no doubt the suggestion that he would travel to paint in a place where the light was better was inconceivable, since the whole point was to put down what was there wherever he happened to be, not with approval but with respect. "Subject matter must be normal in the sense that it does not appear sought after so much as simply happening to one," writes Louis Finkelstein in what is the best discussion I have ever seen of the technique and content of Porter's paintings.[9] (Finkelstein is not giving a prescription here, merely characterizing Porter's "naturalness.")

Another sentence that Porter objected to in Mrs. White's article was this: "The Porters are quiet, intense and rather fey and seem to live on an enchanted planet of their own."[10] He did not give a reason for his objection, and perhaps none was necessary. But Mrs. White could not really be blamed for her assessment; there was an element of truth in it despite the discomfort it caused Porter. His house in Southampton was an enchanting place: large and gracious but always a little messy and charmingly dilapidated. One of the bathrooms was more than that, while in an upstairs hall the wallpaper hung in festoons and no one seemed to mind. The children were strangely beautiful, wide-eyed, and withdrawn, and they spoke like adults. There were idiosyncratically chosen paintings by de Kooning, Larry Rivers, and Leon Hartl (a little-known artist whom Porter admired enormously) on the walls, along with Audubon and *Ukiyo-e* prints and a strange Turner drawing; there was a lovely smell in the house, made up of good cooking, oil paint, books, and fresh air from the

[8]*Ibid.*, p. 210.

[9]Louis Finkelstein, "The Naturalness of Fairfield Porter," *Arts*, May 1976, p. 102.

[10]*Parenthèse*, no. 4, p. 210.

sea. All of which might lead one to see Porter as a homespun Intimist, a view that his trumpeted admiration for Vuillard would seem to reinforce. (Characteristically, he tended to prefer the late woolly Vuillards to the early ones everyone likes.) And it may be that Porter's unexplained objection to Mrs. White's "enchanted planet" line was prompted by his unwillingness to have his work thus construed and thereby diminished.

For, the more one looks at them, the less the paintings seem celebrations of atmosphere and moments but, rather, strong, contentious, and thorny. He painted his surroundings as they looked, and they happened to look cozy. But the coziness is deceiving. It reverberates in time the way the fumbled parlor-piano tunes in the "Alcotts" section of Ives's "Concord" Sonata do. The local color is transparent and porous, letting the dark light of space show through. The painting has the vehemence of abstraction, though it speaks another language.

In the same letter Porter quoted from memory a line of Wittgenstein that he felt central to his own view of aesthetics: "Every sentence is in order as it is." And he went on astonishingly to elaborate: "Order seems to come from searching for disorder, and awkwardness from searching for harmony or likeness, or the following of a system. The truest order is what you already find there, or that will be given if you don't try for it. When you arrange, you fail."[11] I think it is in the light of statements like these that we must now look at Porter's painting, prepared to find the order that is already there, not the one that should be but the one that is.

1982

[11] *Ibid.*, p. 211.

Jane Freilicher, *The Straw Hat*, oil on canvas, 36 x 27 in. Collection of the artist.

The Painting of Jane Freilicher

JAMES SCHUYLER

The pairing of James Schuyler and Jane Freilicher is a natural. His is a plein-air *style: open, scoured, genial, flush—as he says Freilicher's is—with "the unexpectedness of nature." Schuyler has been closely associated with painters, both in the studio and in the galleries. For many years he lived with Fairfield Porter and his family in Southampton, and he was painted by Porter, as a member of the family, on several occasions. Schuyler was once on the staff of the Museum of Modern Art and for two decades served as an associate editor of* Art News. *He has only this to say about his career as an art critic: "The first painting that I remember seeing is* The Helping Hand *at the Corcoran Gallery in Washington, D.C. I don't remember who painted it. The first painter I ever knew was my stepfather. We didn't get along. My favorite painter is Fairfield Porter, with whom I did get along. I first wrote about painters and paintings for* Art News *in 1955; I liked it then because I liked describing things. I stopped in 1975 because by that time I had pretty much exhausted my interest in that particular line of work."*

SOME OF the best painting in New York is done by painters who are unaffiliated, either by themselves or by critics and reviewers, with any school. Figurative is a better word for what they have in common than realist, though neither is satisfactory. Most, like Fairfield Porter, Alex Katz, Jane Wilson, John Button, Robert Dash and Paul Georges, have a wide range of subjects: figure, interior, landscape. Others, like Philip Pearlstein, concern themselves only with the figure. There are also those who work on a small, rather intimate scale: Elias Goldberg, Lawrence Campbell, Ina Garsoian. And there is the rather chilling Andrew Wyeth and the glazed chintzes of John Koch: but then, fool-the-eye has found its public since antiquity, nor is much of Op and Pop lacking in its particular appeal. Among the best of these, the most personal and the most persuasive colorist is Jane Freilicher.

If one were to look for antecedents of her paintings, two would be Rubens and Bonnard. In her first show (spring, 1952, at the Tibor de Nagy Gallery, where she still exhibits), a *Leda and the Swan* and a then vast-seeming *Football Game* had a Rubens looseness, as though the energy of action in the latter and of repose in the former, caused the forms to fly apart a little, making the lines and strokes that defined them also include the air disturbed by gesture, as Rubens often did in his sketches.

The Bonnard connection is more elusive: she has never borrowed his "little touch" (as a lot of New York painters did in the 'fifties, usually getting the effect of a sweater knit by loving hands at home) nor his affectionately smudged contiguity of shapes across the canvas. Nevertheless, it is an affectionate alertness that her work shares with his: that alertness to the witty subjects constantly presented to the eye, along with the means and will to make something out of them. And like him, she has always celebrated the Impressionists' legacy, to see fully all the color there is to be seen. Some painters' eyes are more sensitive than others, they see more color, just as a dog detects more subtle and distant scents.

Another painting in Jane Freilicher's first show was of a clump of palm trees. A few weeks earlier this had been an ape sitting under some banana leaves. It was done from a postcard (as a number of her pictures have been over the years) of a very real looking beast. But in the casual imaginativeness of painting it, it became what it was like, rather than what it was. The solipsism was the painting's, not the painter's.

For a few years after that show, her studio was a small fifth-floor apartment whose views and interior she began to paint. The windows were framed in clumsy neo-classic tenement woodwork and the view to the northeast, beyond patchy brick apartment houses, took in huge gasometers and the towering, belching smoke-stacks of a power station near the East River. This view she painted several times, usually in the violet light of early evening.

In addressing herself to the actual, her paintings in part became much tighter: within one of these views some objects seemed more sharply seen than others: a length of window frame caught the eye, as though slightly magnified. This inconsistency within the picture creates exactly New York as it is: out of the visually deafening plethora the eye is forced to abstract detail in varying sequences. Another kind of inconsistency was the differing perspectives within an interior. Floor boards might be more of a rising wedge than a recession, while a chunky chest parallel to them turned its front flatly at right angles to the canvas. This delicate adjustment of perspective was not derived—as has been suggested—from Cézanne; it was arrived at by accepting and putting down the small shifts the eyes make in moving the gaze from object to object to undiscriminated distance.

This inconsistency, begun within individual paintings, soon created paintings apparently not consistent one to the other. The courage to experiment had the effect of making a good part of the gallery-going public wary. A Jane Freilicher show signally lacked that authoritarian look, public-spirited and public-addressed, stamped on so much post-war work like a purple "OK to Eat" on a rump of beef. The big, cold, dramatic gesture may be welcome, but can't tell us much about the distinctions and nuances that most delight and sharpen apprehension.

The reward of not painting shows was learning to paint her own solutions.

The most time-consuming pictures of this period were a series of portraits. Going after both the voluptuousness of flesh and anatomical fact, her native and extreme spontaneity was driven into detail. The way the rattan of a chair was painted was what most caught the attention; or the fall of a piece of cloth seemed more at ease than the sitter. Is that bad? I doubt it: most sitters do seem rather stunned at finding themselves there.

But it seems only natural that subjects which, so to speak, flowed more easily off her brush should at the same time have attracted her. Among them were some superb paintings of flowers, such as a small runny one that got the rich mashed look of bunched violets, and the way their darkness ignites whatever is around them. (She has always an uninsistent respect for the character of what she paints; not its thingness, but its own aliveness.)

And she continued to paint invented and found subjects —a group of figures based on her own reflection, or a chunk lopped off Mexico, or an aspect of Torcello, from a postcard, that embeds it in the everyday rather than the monumental past.

In the 'fifties she and her husband began to spend their summers on the South Fork of Long Island, near the village of Water Mill and nearer still to the ocean: a flat landscape bound off by dunes, under a high and often blazing sky.

This landscape moved her, in the first years, to a kind of painting that developed away from the thing seen. *From a Volkswagen* spread around the pendent shape of a Volkswagen window a disarray of big, open brushing of ag-glomerated color, like the nearby fields where goldenrod and wild mallows mix in the sharp grass. Or, in others, what form the picture had was in the placing of a thick line, painted at a stroke, as though the horizon could be picked up like a stick and placed where she wished: high, low, or sometimes running from top to bottom (*The Green Stripe*).

Further acquaintance bred greater reserve, as though the effort was to deliver as much extent of land and sky as thinly and brilliantly as possible. These pictures were almost alto-gether abstract: there were landscape references, but often only in the kinetic twist of, say, the place where a road hits a distant tilted field that lifts up to bulky clouds of greater sub-stance than what lies under them. These abstract paintings, whose "nature references" partook not at all of the blurry disguises of socalled Abstract-Impressionism, seemed almost empty. They left a visual after-taste of high thin color, the palest yellow and a lot of white; and the sense of a big space vivified with the least and most effective means.

The landscapes painted subsequently have followed on the abstractions as naturally as a change of focus.

Her color now is built up from white: "There did seem to be a change," she says, "when I really got started painting landscapes. I think I began thinking of color as, 'How much light does a picture hold?' Alex Katz and Fairfield Porter think this way, and it can make a picture very luminous. A lot of painters seem to think of it as a matter of weight. This works okay, I guess, but I'm more interested in light."

Succulence and bigness are qualities of her latest work. A still-life is set up as far from the easel as it can get. But in-stead of reducing it to a point of emphasis in the interior the eye comprehends, it is brought up close, right on top of the canvas, right on top of you. This not only eliminates niggling, but gives the color of the flowers—hot and cold peonies, flushed mallows—its breadth, so they appear as prismatic hunks within the light-returning, arbitrary prism of the painting.

The scale of objects goes unadjusted (mediocrity in painting is often merely an inability to leave things as they are). If a bowl is too big, that is how big it is; if stems are floppy, then let them slump. It is as they are that they caught her attention, so why fiddle?

The duality in her work, the imagined and the real, has turned out a mutual enhancement. A landscape is translated to canvas with the ease of the imagined, an invention has the casual presence of reality. In a large nude, seated, seen from the back, the buttocks are not squashed and spread to give an impression of sitting-downness; rather, we are given the curving fullness, verisimilitude sacrificed to a more convincing truth. The gain is great.

In her latest paintings, a still life is often combined with an interior and a landscape, a wide view seen through a glass wall divided by studs into panels. What might seem a progression of planes is dealt with only as color: a stud is related by its brightness to what is next to it, field or flowers. In a black-and-white photograph a bowl of flowers may seem a silhouetted mass, but in fact it is not. Only the light-absorbency of deep reds and orange is described, and the same with a burnt-over potato field in August: a great distance is brought up to the surface of the picture so that a play of light moves over it at different speeds, flashing, sauntering and standing still. Detail is minimal, nor is the brushwork onomatopoeic. An arabesque of paint is a stroke securely attached to a thin scrubbing it abuts on. Illusion is replaced by paint, and everything seems bigger, more itself. Seductiveness is not an aim.

While abstract painting has, in large part, gone toward a calculated placement, the best figurative painters have availed themselves of the unexpectedness of nature, where the right place for a thing is where you find it. In Jane Freilicher's pictures the emotional force of an object is allowed its compositional weight. There may be more to a bowl of cosmos than there is to a wide and rather empty view, although the emptiness can be subject and constructing force. Structure is an improvisation, composed as painted, not a skeleton to be fleshed out. The result is freshness, like that of ocean air and constantly changing light.

"Usually," she says, "I tip the horizon up, which makes the picture more two-dimensional." And, "I don't think I 'frame' a picture in the old-fashioned way. Usually it's a color or something in the landscape—an expansiveness —that gets me started. Of course a landscape goes on forever but a picture doesn't. So very soon it has a composition or a form of its own."

And, "I'm interested in landscape, but there's a paradox: it's depressing to get that realistic look, 'Why, that's just the way it looks!' or, 'I know that time of day.' At the same time I don't want really to lose the place. It's like the difference between Andrew Wyeth and Bonnard."

1966

Paul Cézanne, *Skull and Fruit,* oil on canvas, 21 $^1/_4$ x 25 $^5/_8$ in. Photograph
©1988 by The Barnes Foundation, Merion Station, Pennsylvania.

The Poet as Painter

CHARLES TOMLINSON

*Charles Tomlinson, who was born at Stoke-on-Trent in 1927, first
set out to be a painter, not a poet. But the poems took over, and the
appropriately titled* Seeing Is Believing *appeared in 1960. Actu-
ally, a slightly different version of the book was first published in
America in 1958. Tomlinson has had an abiding interest in matters
American, especially the culture of the Southwest, as his collection*
American Scenes *(1960) and his memoir* Some Americans
*(1980) both testify. There are other divided loyalties too, for he con-
tinued to work at drawings and collages: they bore the marks of in-
fluence as various as that of Max Ernst, Georgia O'Keeffe, and
Hercules Seghers. "The 18th of June 1970 was a day of discovery for
me," he has written. Long fascinated with Oscar Dominguez's
decalcomania and with his memory of the architectural arabesques of
the dining-room windows in Gaudí's Casa Batlló, Tomlinson fash-
ioned a mask of the windows and a moonscape of the decalcomania,
and so began a series of imaginary "visions." Many of them are in-
cluded in* In Black and White: The Graphics of Charles
Tomlinson *(1976), for which Octavio Paz has written an essay on
the poet at work in both mediums. Thinking of the writing by one
sort of artist about another, Tomlinson remarks: "It is the crisis in
these paintings that I recognized because I had reached it in my own*

Reprinted with permission of Charles Tomlinson. Essay first appeared in *Essays by
Divers Hands: Innovation in Contemporary Literature,* ed. Vincent Cronin, vol. XL
(Transactions of the Royal Society of Literature, 1979), 147–62. Copyright © 1975 by
Charles Tomlinson.

work,' says Rilke of Cézanne. The relation of certain poets to certain painters arises out of a similar feeling of challenge and identification. They may be exact or they may be passionately partial in their response, as is Blake on Reynolds, Nietzsche on Delacroix, Rosenberg on the vorticists. But the exactness and the partiality are both witnesses to the wholly unique sense of necessity: they are upon oath to respond and to interpret now *and history will not wait.*"

'THE POET as Painter' is not an altogether adequate title for what I want to talk about this evening. Although I can read to you from my poems, I shall not be able to show you my pictures. All I can do there, is to mention the appearance of a book of my graphic work, *In Black and White*, introduced by Octavio Paz and published by Carcanet Press. Perhaps some of you were even present earlier this year at my exhibition at the Cambridge Poetry Festival. What I shall be speaking of is chiefly the *materia* the poet and painter have in common. 'We live in the centre of a physical poetry,' says Wallace Stevens. This is surely the basic fact which would make a poet want to paint or, if he couldn't do that, to comprehend the painter's way of regarding the physical poetry they both share. It is because of this same basic fact of '[living] in the centre of a physical poetry' that Samuel Palmer's follower, Edward Calvert, could write of 'a good poem whether written or painted'. 'To a large extent,' says Stevens, 'the problems of poets are the problems of painters, and poets must often turn to the literature of painting for a discussion of their own problems.' One could add to this remark of Stevens that they not only turn to the literature of painting, but help create that literature. Stevens' *Opus Posthumous* has for its epigraph a passage by Graham Bell on the integrity of Cézanne, a painter Stevens has commented on memorably more than once. Besides Stevens, Rainer Maria Rilke, D. H. Lawrence, William Carlos Williams are all poets who have written penetratingly about Cézanne. All found in him a reflection of their own problems as writers as they fought preconception and subjectivity in their art. 'It is the crisis in these paintings that I recognized,' says Rilke, 'because I had reached it in my own work.' And D. H. Lawrence: 'Cézanne felt it in paint, when he felt for the apple. Suddenly he felt the tyranny of mind, the enclosed ego in its sky-blue heaven self-painted.' And Williams: 'Cézanne—The only realism in art is of the imagination. It is only thus that the work escapes plagiarism after nature and becomes a creation.' So Cézanne looms gigantically over literature as well as over painting, as the forerunner of a new sensibility and a new inventiveness. Indeed, Cézanne—to traverse the common ground between poet and painter in the other direction—composed many poems of his own. As a young man, he wrote:

> A tree, shaken by raging winds,
> Waves in the air, like a gigantic corpse,
> Its naked branches which the mistral sways.

As an old man, he made good this vision in an astonishing water colour that acquired the title 'Bare Trees in the Fury of the Wind'. Whatever the final product, the point of departure was the same: 'We live in the centre of a physical poetry.'

To Cézanne and his meaning for poetry I shall return. But, first, let me add to the title of my lecture, a subtitle, which will permit me to explore the centre of that physical poetry in which Stevens says we live. My subtitle is 'The Four Elements' and the place of my exploration, the Potteries where I was born. The element that touched most persistently on the imagination there of the child as a growing artist, was water. For that region of smoke and blackened houses, of slag-heaps, cinder-paths, pitheads, steelworks, had for its arterial system a network of canals. The canals brought back the baptismal element to a landscape by day purgatorial and by night infernal. The canals were not the only bringers of water into that place whose atmosphere, according to Arnold Bennett, was as black as its mud. One must not forget the great pools that formed in the pits where marl was dug for tile-making: as the pits were gradually abandoned, nature re-invaded, greenness appeared beside the water and fish in it. Fish! It was their existence, not just in the marl pools, but in the canals, that helped bring back contemplation into lives lived-out in the clatter of mines and factories. The fishing-club, the Sunday matches, long hours watching the rufflings and changes of water, something both sane and mysterious came from all this. Why mysterious? Because the fisherman, if he is to be more than a random dabbler, must acquire an intuitive knowledge of the ways of fish and water, and within his stillness, at the centre of his capacity to wait and to contemplate, there is a sense that is ready to strike at the exact moment, that even knows, perhaps, how to lure into its own mental orbit creatures that he cannot even see under that surface on which his whole attention is concentrated. Piscator is an artist, as Walton knew. His discipline, looking out from himself but with his inner faculties deeply roused, might make a poet or a painter of him if he had the latent powers within.

So much for water. What of earth and fire in this same Midland childhood? 'The district'—the Potteries, that is—says Bennett, 'comprehends the mysterious habits of fire and pure, sterile earth'. He means, of course, the action of fire on the potting clay. My own most remembered and most dwelt on experience of the physical poetry of fire concerns the making of steel rather than the making of pots. And it was an experience, principally, of fire by night. When the furnaces were tapped by night, or when molten metal was poured in the great open sheds of the steel works, immense dazzling shafts of fire flared outwards to be reflected in the waters of the nearby canal. Thus the remembered experience was also of fire associated with water, of fire not as the opposite of water, but mingling with it, kindling reflections in that element and also in the onlooker. To see was also to see *within.*

You gained this experience by following the canal beyond the factory established by Josiah Wedgwood in the eighteenth century, in the place named by him Etruria. You went on until the canal cut through the centre of the Shelton Bar-Iron and Steel Works. And you went by night, so as not to be seen, because children were not particularly welcome there. Etruria—Etruria Vale to give it its full name—had long since lost the nymphs one might associate with the name. But the red jets and glarings from molten steel, and from the furnaces seen in the canal, confronted one with a sense of the primal and the elemental such as nymphs themselves were once thought to symbolize in relation to landscape. And, after all, a dryad would only be a veil between yourself and a tree once your eyes had been opened by this other intenser nakedness. For, with the soot drifting down through the darkness on to your hair, you had experienced fire as the interior of water.

Earth, like air, fared badly in the district. 'Its atmosphere as black as its mud': Bennett's verdict. Earth, like air, took on the tinge of blackness. Earth was close to the sterile earth not only of pots but of slag-heaps and cinderpaths. For all that, gardeners coaxed miracles out of the sooty allotments that crowned the slopes where Etruria Woods had once flourished. As for air—air was something of a joke. There were local post-cards showing bottle-ovens and factory chimneys all smoking at once with dark hints of houses and perhaps a drab church-tower. These cards carried stoical titles like, 'Fresh Air from the Potteries'. At school, when the potteries 'stoked-up', it was sometimes difficult to see over to the far side of the playground. A familiar image returns from that time, of black smoke mounting from a factory chimney and, caught by the wind, fraying out across and into the air. Air was an element that yet had to be created there. It was, in part, the search for air, as well as water, that drew the fishing clubs out to the surrounding countryside, still along those canals, that seemed to lead back to Eden.

So of the four elements it was water that held the imagination of the child as growing artist—water fire-tinged, water promising a cleansing, an imaginative baptism, rocking, eddying, full of metamorphoses.

I left the district in my early twenties and subsequently lived among many landscapes both urban and rural—London, Italy, New Mexico, the northern United States, the Cotswolds. I think it was Liguria and Tuscany and then Gloucestershire taught me the way men could be at home in a landscape. And how necessary this different view of things was, in order to place those earlier experiences of streets that threatened to enclose you, to shut you off from a wider and more luminous world, from intuitions of what Ezra Pound calls 'the radiant world where one thought cuts through another with clear edge, a world of moving energies, magnetisms that take form . . .' I wanted to recover that 'radiant world' in poems, and by doing so I seemed to have lost touch with the Midlands. But the Midlands were always present as one term in a dialectic, as a demand for completeness subconsciously impelling the forms of one's art, even demanding *two* arts where the paradisal aspect of the visual could perhaps be rescued and celebrated.

Coming back to the Potteries almost thirty years later, I saw how much the world of my poems depended on the place, despite and because of the fact that they were an attempt to find a world of clarities, a world of unhazed senses, an intuition of Edenic freshnesses and clear perceptions. I tried to concentrate the history of all that into a short poem called

The Marl Pits

It was a language of water, light and air
    I sought—to speak myself free of a world
Whose stoic lethargy seemed the one reply
    To horizons and to streets that blocked them back
In a monotone fume, a bloom of grey.
    I found my speech. The years return me
To tell of all that seasoned and imprisoned:
    I breathe familiar, sedimented air
From a landscape of disembowellings, underworlds
    Unearthed among the clay. Digging
The marl, they dug a second nature
    And water, seeping up to fill their pits,
Sheeted them to lakes that wink and shine
    Between tips and steeples, streets and waste
In slow reclaimings, shimmers, balancings,
    As if kindling Eden rescinded its own loss
And words and water came of the same source.

Can my 'psychoanalysis of water', to appropriate a term of Gaston Bachelard, point to any single prompting insight, any happy combination of perception and intuition that unifies the attitudes of poet and painter? Pondering this question, I remembered an early poem, 'Sea Change', formally quite simple in that it seeks to catch the nature of water—this time, the sea—in a series of images, 'uneasy marble', 'green

silk', 'blue mud', then is forced to concede their inadequacy:
they are like

> white wine
> Floating in a saucer of ground glass
> On a pedestal of cut glass:

> A static instance, therefore untrue.

Much later—the better part of twenty years later—in a
formally much more complex poem, 'Swimming Chenango
Lake', I watch a swimmer watching water. Here is an extract
from the opening:

> Winter will bar the swimmer soon.
> He reads the water's autumnal hesitations
> A wealth of ways: it is jarred,
> It is astir already despite its steadiness,
> Where the first leaves at the first
> Tremor of the morning air have dropped
> Anticipating him, launching their imprints
> Outwards in eccentric, overlapping circles.
> There is a geometry of water, for this
> Squares off the clouds' redundances
> And sets them floating in a nether atmosphere
> All angles and elongations: every tree
> Appears a cypress as it stretches there
> And every bush that shows the season,
> A shaft of fire. It is a geometry and not
> A fantasia of distorting forms, but each
> Liquid variation answerable to the theme
> It makes away from, plays before:
> It is a consistency, the grain of the pulsating flow . . .

I pondered this passage, along with that earlier poem 'Sea
Change', to find out the constant that governed my attitude

as poet and painter. Poems based like this—as are the many landscape poems I have written—on exposure to and observation of the fleeting moments of visual sensation; poems that endeavour to catch this fleeting freshness and unite it to a stable form where others may share in it; poems such as these look away from the merely personal. And so does painting where the presence of the external world is strongly felt, where the painter is concerned—I quote Rilke on Cézanne—with 'the incarnation of the world *as a thing carrying conviction,* the portrayal of a reality become imperishable through his experiencing of the object'. To make the reality of water imperishable! The painter must acquire great formal power to achieve that: because he who looks into water, and into the changing world of perception which water represents, looks into the heart of time.

Cézanne himself was very conscious of this problem for the painter—how to reconcile sensation and form without bullying your picture into a wilful unity, a triumph of personality at the expense of a truth to relationship: 'There mustn't be a single link too loose,' Joachim Gasquet reports him as saying, 'not a crevice through which may escape the emotion, the light, the truth . . . All that we see disperses, vanishes; is it not so? Nature is always the same, but nothing remains of it, nothing of what comes to our sight. Our art ought to give the shimmer of duration with the elements, the appearance of all its changes. It ought to make us taste it eternally . . . My canvas joins hands . . . But if I feel the least distraction, the least weakness, above all if I interpret too much one day . . . if I intervene, why then everything is gone.'

Long before I read that conversation with Gasquet, I wrote a poem called 'Cézanne at Aix,' a kind of manifesto poem where I wanted my poetry to take its ethic of perception from Cézanne, an ethic distrustful of the drama of personality of which Romantic art had made so much, an ethic where, by trusting to sensation, we enter being, and experience its primal fulness on terms other than those we dictate:

Cézanne at Aix

And the mountain: each day
Immobile like fruit. Unlike, also
—Because irreducible, because
Neither a component of the delicious
And therefore questionable,
Nor distracted (as the sitter)
By his own pose and, therefore,
Doubly to be questioned: it is not
Posed. It is. Untaught
Unalterable, a stone bridgehead
To that which is tangible
Because unfelt before. There
In its weathered weight
Its silence silences, a presence
Which does not present itself.

What impressed me about Cézanne, and what on my own humbler level I wanted for poetry, was the entire absence of self-regard. 'Cézanne's apples,' says D. H. Lawrence, 'are a real attempt to let the apple exist in its own separate entity, without transfusing it with personal emotion.' Cézanne must surely have felt the narrowing lure of what Lawrence calls 'personal emotion' here. Cézanne *in himself* was threatened by misunderstanding, neglect, ill-health and prone to deep melancholy. Had he chosen to ignore nature or merely to dramatise that self and impose it on nature, his pictures would have wanted the liberating Mediterranean radiance that we find there. Even his self-portraits lack introspection. Rilke, once more, supplies the classic comment. He writes to his wife: '. . . how great and incorruptible this objectivity of his gaze was, is confirmed in an almost touching manner by the circumstance that, without analysing or in the remotest degree regarding his expression from a superior standpoint, he made a replica of himself with so much humble objectiveness, with the credulity and extrinsic interest and attention of a dog which sees itself in the mirror and thinks: there is another dog.'

In speaking of Cézanne's incorruptible objectivity, it is clear that Rilke was not thinking of the purely imaginary and outmoded objectivity of nineteenth-century positivistic science—the objectivity which supposed a complete division between the observer and the observed. The objectivity with which Rilke credits Cézanne implied an outward gaze that would draw the sensuous world closer to the inner man and that would narrow the gap between abstraction and sensation, between intellect and things. As Merleau-Ponty reflects in his great essay, 'Eye and Mind'—an essay that begins by quoting Gasquet's book on Cézanne: 'Quality, light, colour, depth which are there before us, are there only because they awaken an echo in our body and because the body welcomes them . . . Things have an internal equivalent in me; they arouse in me a carnal formula of their presence.'

So much for Merleau-Ponty. I wanted to earn the right to use the artistic ethic of Cézanne as a basis for poetry, and I believe it made possible to me a range from natural landscape to civic landscape. It seemed to me a sort of religion, a bringing of things to stand in the light of origin, a way, even, of measuring the tragic fall from plenitude in our own urban universe. But let me make a confession. As a painter, I could find no direct way of using this inheritance. I confronted the four elements, but the only way I could resolve them in paint was to will their cohesion, to intervene, to put personal pressure on my forms in the shape of an anxious black outline.

Time and again, I would approach the expression of some realization, only to disfigure it with black. I could find no way of letting the given suggest to me forms that could elude the preconceptions of the too conscious mind and the too conscious hand, blackening nature as surely as the factory chimneys of my boyhood had blackened it. Black became an obsession. Although I continued to draw, little by little I lapsed from painting, partly under pressure from this insoluble dilemma, partly because the time that might have gone to finding an answer went into earning a living. For fifteen years, almost nothing except the poems; then, in 1970, after a renewed, intensive spell of drawing, a solution appeared almost casually.

I think, once more, of Wallace Stevens, and that entry in his *Adagia* which reads: 'The aspects of earth of interest to a poet are the casual ones, as light or colour, images.' By 'casual', I take it that he refers to the fortuitous nature of art—the way one may find its deepest meanings on a dull street corner, in an old pair of shoes, in the chance conjunction of the totally unforeseen and the apparently unrelated. Suddenly things knit up—the canvas joins hands, in Cézanne's words. You cease to impose and you discover, to rephrase another aphorism of Stevens. And you discover apparently by chance. But what is chance? And if one accepts it, does it not cease to be chance?

The element of chance that helped resolve my problems as a painter was the surrealist device known as decalcomania. Briefly, the recipe for this is the one drawn up by Oscar Dominguez in 1936: 'By means of a thick brush, spread out black gouache more or less diluted in places, upon a sheet of glossy white paper, and cover at once with a second sheet, upon which exert an even pressure. Lift off the second sheet without haste.' Well, the result of this process, as the pigment separates out into random patterns, can be a lot of wasted paper, occasionally a very beautiful entire image, sometimes interesting fragments that prompt and defy the imagination to compose them into a picture. You can alter what is given with a brush, or you can both alter and recombine your images by going to work with scissors and paste and making a collage. The weakness of this technique is that it can lead to a flaccid fantasy of imaginary animals, or of lions turning into bicycles. Its strength lies in its challenge to mental sets, in the very impersonality of the material offered you and that you must respond to. A very unCézannian undertaking, and yet what I have called the ethic of Cézanne—submission to the given, the desire to break with preconceived images of the given, the desire to seize on and stabilize momentary appearances—this ethic, once applied, can lead your decalcomania away from the arbitrariness of fantasy towards the threshold of new perceptions.

I had followed Dominguez very literally: 'Spread out black gouache,' he says. Max Ernst, using this technique for the basis of some of his best pictures, clearly employs several colours. Almost blindly, I reached for my old enemy, black. I continued to use it and to use that colour only. The first move was to paint the black on to a wet surface and the first thing you saw was the strokes of pigment fraying out into the water just as the smoke of your childhood had frayed out into the air. There seemed an odd rhyme here between the one experience and the other. And as I covered sheet after sheet, altered, blotted, painted with brush, finger-tips, pieces of string, and then cut up and recombined, I saw black become dazzling: I saw the shimmer of water, light and air take over from the merely fortuitous: I saw that I was working now as poet *and* painter once more.

The 'merely' fortuitous! *There* is a theme for them both: the fact that 'chance' rhymes with 'dance' is a nutrifying thought for either poet or painter. As is that other fortuity, that in the south of England, they are pronounced 'darnce' and 'charnce', a source of wonder to the Midlander, as no doubt *his* pronunciation is to the southerner. There seems no intrinsic reason why these two words should have much to do with each other. And there seems no intrinsic reason, either, why the strokes of a brush covered in pigment, the dabbing of a paint-covered finger, the dashes, slashes or dots a painter makes, should have much to do with a face, a landscape, a stone or a skull. Turner grew an immensely long eagle's talon of a thumb-nail in order to scratch out lights in his water-colours. It seems oddly fortuitous that these jabbings into the surface of water-colour paper should come to represent luminosity.

'Chance' undoubtedly rhymes with 'dance' and meditation on this fact feeds the mind: chance occurrences, chance meetings invade what we do every day and yet they are drawn into a sort of pattern, as they criss-cross with our feeling of what we are, as they remind us of other happenings, or strengthen our sense of future possibility. Poetry is rather like this, also. Something seemingly fortuitous sets it off—a title, say, out of the blue, asking for a poem to go with it, a title like 'The Chances of Rhyme' and you find yourself writing on the back of an envelope:

> The chances of rhyme are like the chances of meeting—
> In the finding fortuitous, but once found binding . . .

Already, you have started to knit up those chances, with 'finding' and 'binding' reinforcing the pattern and before long the chances of rhyme are becoming the continuities of thought, and you continue writing:

> To take chances, as to make rhymes
> Is human, but between chance and impenitence

(A half rhyme) come dance, vigilance
And circumstance . . .

Yes, that makes sense. It seems to be getting somewhere: a
pattern in the words, a pattern in the thought, a pattern in
the way the line settles mostly for four main stresses, some-
times stretches to five, mostly dances back to four. To handle
measure thus seems a human thing to do: your recurrences
are never so pat as to seem simply mechanical, your out-
growths never so rambling or brambled as to spread to mere
vegetation. A human measure, surrounded by surprises, im-
penetrable and unknowable, but always reasserting itself, this
could be a salutary aim—one in which rhythm and tone are
both allies—faced as we always are by the temptation to
exaggerate and to overvalue the claims of self:

The Chances of Rhyme

The chances of rhyme are like the chances of meeting—
    In the finding fortuitous, but once found, binding:
They say, they signify and they succeed, where to succeed
    Means not success, but a way forward
If unmapped, a literal, not a royal succession;
    Though royal (it may be) is the adjective or region
That we, nature's royalty, are led into.
    Yes. We are led, though we seem to lead
Through a fair forest, an Arden (a rhyme
    For Eden)—breeding ground for beasts
Not bestial, but loyal and legendary, which is more
    Than nature's are. Yet why should we speak
Of art, of life, as if the one were all form
    And the other all Sturm-und-Drang? And I think
Too, we should confine to Crewe or to Mow
    Cop, all those who confuse the fortuitousness
Of art with something to be met with only

At extremity's brink, reducing thus
Rhyme to a kind of rope's end, a glimpsed grass
    To be snatched at as we plunge past it—
Nostalgic, after all, for a hope deferred.
    To take chances, as to make rhymes
Is human, but between chance and impenitence
    (A half-rhyme) come dance, vigilance
And circumstance (meaning all that is there
    Besides you, when you are there). And between
Rest-in-peace and precipice,
    Inertia and perversion, come the varieties
Increase, lease, re-lease (in both
    Senses); and immersion, conversion—of inert
Mass, that is, into energies to combat confusion.
    Let rhyme be my conclusion.

Painting wakes up the hand, draws-in your sense of muscular coordination, your sense of the body, if you like. Poetry also, as it pivots on its stresses, as it rides forward over the line-endings, or comes to rest at pauses *in* the line, poetry also brings the whole man into play and his bodily sense of himself. But there is no near, actual equivalent in painting for tone and rhythm adjusted by line lengths and by pauses within and at the ends of lines. There is no near equivalent because the medium is so very different. You may write with a pencil, but once you come to draw with it, what a diverse end those marks serve. But the fortuitous element is still there—the element of meeting something you didn't expect, something that isn't yourself. And once you attend to it, whatever you are starts to see an interesting challenge to its own relaxed complacency. Quite by accident you find, on a beach, the skull of a sea bird, for instance. You could put it in a cabinet or forget it in a safe place, but instead you draw it. You begin to know far more about the structure of that particular skull, as eye and pencil try to keep up with each other.

There is a lot, though, you can't know about—the mysterious darkness of its interior, the intriguing and impenetrable holes and slots where something or other has now rotted away and left a clean emptiness. The cleanliness, the natural geometry of the skull suggest the idea of surrounding it in a geometry of your own—carefully ruled lines that set off the skull, that extend it, that bed it in a universe of contrasting lines of force. Just as rhyme dancing with thought led you through to a world of human values, so skull and line build up and outwards into a containing universe.

Now, there is something very resistant about this skull. You feel you could etch a very tiny poem on it called, perhaps, 'To be Engraved on the Skull of a Cormorant'. To do so you would have to be both tough and careful with it—

> . . . as searching as the sea
> that picked and pared
> this head yet spared
> its frail acuity.

And so you go on to write a whole poem:

> To be Engraved on the Skull
> of a Cormorant
>
> across the thin
> façade, the galleried-
> with-membrane head:
> narrowing, to take
> the eye-dividing
> declivity where
> the beginning beak
> prepares for flight

in a still-
perfect salience:
here, your glass
needs must stay
steady and your gross
needle re-tip
itself with reticence
but be
as searching as the sea
that picked and pared
this head yet spared
its frail acuity.

And so a poem comes out of this find, as well as drawings. But that interior darkness goes on bothering you. How could I relate it, you think, to the little universe my lines netted together around it?

This particular problem was solved by forgetting about it. Or by seeming to forget and doing something else. Three years after making a drawing, 'Long-beaked Skull', I did a decalcomania-collage called 'The Sleep of Animals': here two skulls are filled by a dream of the landscapes the bird and animal presences have been moving through. The dream articulates the darkness. I try to suggest a whole world in each head. There is the hint that this sleep is, perhaps, death in which both the head and nature are now one.

In writing poetry, you sometimes run aground on silence, and it takes months or sometimes years to learn what it is you wish to say. In the meantime, you are half-consciously turning the problem over, while, at the same time, furthering the knowledge of your medium. Among the techniques I had worked with between 'Long-beaked Skull' and 'The Sleep of Animals' were those I have described—collage and decalcomania. I had suddenly seen something rather like—though

not yet *much* like—two skulls merged in the landscape of my
decalcomania, my chaos of crushed pigment floating in wa-
ter. Instead of continuing to paint, once the sheet had dried,
I cut out the skulls with scissors, glued new shapes on to
them, then fitted them into a quite rigorous design held to-
gether by ruled lines and called it 'The Sleep of Animals'. I
realized I had discovered a response to the dark, unenter-
able interior of that first bird's skull. My response seemed to
have arrived instantaneously, but—again like poetry—the
formal pattern had taken up chance elements, had been the
result of conscious and sub-conscious processes and of that
strange, unifying movement of recognition when, reaching
for the scissors, what I'd found became what I'd chosen.
'Chance' rhymed with 'dance' once more.

Why, as an artist, should one return so obsessively to the
shape of the skull, whether animal or human? I do not be-
lieve that one comes back to it merely as a *memento mori*—
though *that* element is present too. What seems equally im-
portant is the skull seen as a piece of architecture. It resem-
bles a house with lit façade and shadowy interior. However
much it possesses of bleak finality, it always involves one in
the fascination of inside and outside, that primary lure of the
human mind seeking to go beyond itself, taking purchase on
the welcoming or threatening surfaces of the world, and
both anxious and enriched because of the sense of what lies
behind or beneath those surfaces. I tried to make this
knowledge present to myself in many drawings, particularly
of animal skulls. I tried, also, to articulate this knowledge
with words, in the form of a poem-in-prose called 'Skull-
shapes.'

Skulls. Finalities. They emerge towards new beginnings
from undergrowth. Along with stones, fossils, flint keel-
scrapers and spoke-shaves, along with bowls of clay

pipes heel-stamped with their makers' marks, comes the rural detritus of cattle skulls brought home by children. They are moss-stained, filthy with soil. Washing them of their mottlings, the hand grows conscious of weight, weight sharp with jaggednesses. Suspend them from a nail and one feels the bone-clumsiness go out of them: there is weight still in their vertical pull downwards from the nail, but there is also a hanging fragility. The two qualities fuse and the brush translates this fusion as wit, where leg-like appendages conclude the skulls' dangling mass.

Shadow explores them. It sockets the eye-holes with black. It reaches like fingers into the places one cannot see. Skulls are a keen instance of this duality of the visible: it borders what the eye cannot make out, it transcends itself with the suggestion of all that is there beside what lies within the eyes' possession: it cannot be possessed. Flooded with light, the skull is at once manifest surface and labyrinth of recesses. Shadow reaches down out of this world of helmeted cavities and declares it.

One sees. But not merely the passive mirrorings of the retinal mosaic—nor, like Ruskin's blind man struck suddenly by vision, without memory or conception. The senses, reminded by other seeings, bring to bear on the act of vision their pattern of images; they give point and place to an otherwise naked and homeless impression. It is the mind sees. But what it sees consists not solely of that by which it is confronted grasped in the light of that which it remembers. It sees possibility.

The skulls of birds, hard to the touch, are delicate to the eye. Egg-like in the round of the skull itself and as if the spherical shape were the result of an act like glass-blowing, they resist the eyes' imaginings with the blade of the beak which no lyrical admiration can attenuate to frailty.

The skull of nature is recess and volume. The skull of art—of possibility—is recess, volume and also lines—lines of containment, lines of extension. In seeing, one already extends the retinal impression, searchingly and instantaneously. Brush and pen extend the search beyond the instant, touch discloses a future. Volume, knived across by the challenge of a line, the raggedness of flaking bone countered by ruled, triangular facets, a cowskull opens a visionary field, a play of universals.

In both graphic and poetic art, I like something lucid surrounded by something mysterious. I see poems and pictures as the place where the civilized, discriminating faculties and the sense of the elemental, of origins, reinforce each other. I go back, time and again, to the idea of a seascape

> with illegible depths
> and lucid passages,
> bestiary of stones,
> book without pages . . .

and a poem seems to be composing itself that could well be a picture, or several pictures:

On Water
'Furrow' is inexact:
no ship could be
converted to a plough
travelling this vitreous ebony:

seal it in sea-caves and
you cannot still it:
image on image bends
where half-lights fill it

with illegible depths
and lucid passages,
bestiary of stones,
book without pages:

and yet it confers
as much as it denies:
we are orphaned and fathered
by such solid vacancies:

When words seem too abstract, then I find myself painting
the sea with the very thing it is composed of—water, and al-
lowing its thinning and separation of the pigment to reveal
an image of its own nature. I spoke earlier of bringing things
to stand in the light of origin. When you paint with water
and are painting the image of water, you return to it, as to all
primal things, with a sense of recognition—water! we came
from this. 'Human tears,' says the scientist, 'are a re-creation
of the primordial ocean which, in the first stages of evolu-
tion, bathed the first eyes.' Perhaps the carnal echo that the
contemplation of water awakens in us sounds over those im-
mense distances of time. Or if that thought is too fanciful,
when from the ruck and chaos of black paint I find myself
paradoxically creating a world of water, light and air, per-
haps that same chance is somewhere present in the deed,
which led a boy by night along a dark canal in a blackened
city and showed him fire unquenchably burning within
water.

I conclude with a final poem:

At Stoke

I have lived in a single landscape. Every tone
    And turn have had for their ground
These beginnings in grey-black: a land
    Too handled to be primary—all the same,
The first in feeling. I thought it once
    Too desolate, diminished and too tame
To be the foundation for anything. It straggles
    A haggard valley and lets through
Discouraged greennesses, lights from a pond or two.
    By ash-tips, or where the streets give out
In cindery in-betweens, the hills
    Swell up and free of it to where, behind
The whole vapoury, patched battlefield,
    The cows stand steaming in an acrid wind.
This place, the first to seize on my heart and eye,
    Has been their hornbook and their history.

1975

Leonard Baskin, *Hanged Man*, woodcut, 67 x 23 in. University of
Nebraska-Lincoln Art Gallery: F. M. Hall Collection.

The Hanged Man and
the Dragonfly

TED HUGHES

*Leonard Baskin and Ted Hughes first met in 1958 when Hughes
and his first wife, Sylvia Plath, were living in Northampton,
Massachusetts. They became close friends, and four years later
Hughes wrote a catalogue essay for a London exhibition of Baskin's
woodcuts and wood engravings. In that essay he had already singled
out* The Hanged Man *as the ambivalent center of Baskin's world,
a symbol charged with cosmic cycles and human history. Hughes was
haunted too by Baskin's image of a dead crow: "Every feather of the
crow," he wrote, "is there and perfect, and the crow is dead, yet this
bird again is the immortal Angel of Life. In the aspect of the Angel of
Death." In 1966 Baskin asked Hughes to write poems to accompany
an edition of his crow engravings. The invitation resulted in* Crow
*(1971), a totemic sequence that gives voice—the voice of a figure
"hairy and slobbery, glossy and raw"—to a macabre anticreation
myth. The celebrity of that book has distracted many readers from the
deeper rhythms of Hughes's poetry, its pulsing, ritualistic intelligence
and its descriptive precision. His abiding theme, emphasized in the
following essay, is* transformation: *the economy of creation,
molecular to global, as it crosses and is changed by the plane of vi-
sion, bestial or sacramental. When he speaks of Baskin's preoccupa-
tion with "the horror within the created glory," with a "startling,*

Reprinted with permission of the New York Graphic Society from *The Complete Prints of
Leonard Baskin: A Catalogue Raisonné 1948–1983,* ed. Alan Fern and Judith O'Sullivan
(New York Graphic Society, 1984), 20–23. Copyright © 1983 by Ted Hughes.

sinister beauty," with the "glamour of deadliness" and a "dark radiance," he is not trading in easy paradox, but elucidating the fable at the heart of his own poems as well: the transforming power of nature and of the imagination, the human form divine and demonic.

The Sibyl, with raving mouth, uttering her unlaughing, unadorned words, reaches us over a thousand years with her voice—through the inspiration of the god.

Heraclitus

The notion of some infinitely gentle
Infinitely suffering thing.

T. S. Eliot

ARTISTIC FORM is, by definition, a lens, but Leonard Baskin's graphic images seem particularly lens-like. The typically rounded glass-blob outline, and the internal lattice of refracted, converging intensities, which lie there on the paper as a superbly achieved solidity of form and texture, in fact compose a web—a transparency, something to be looked through. The depths are focussed right there at the surface—which directs our attention straight into the depths. And that deeper life, in all Baskin's work, is of a peculiar kind.

These images also resemble stained glass windows—not only physically (though they do that too, obviously enough, with their starkly subdivided interiors, their palimpsest of mapped inner regions opening behind and within each other), but in the way they process our attention. They place us within a sacred building, as if we were looking out through these icons and seeing the world's common light changed by them. Or else they place us outside looking in. Then we see through their symbols still further mysterious business going on round an altar. That deeper life, in other words, is not just deeper than ordinary life, or just more universal. It is elect and consecrated. I hesitate to call it religious. It is rather something that survives in the afterglow of collapsed religion.

This rich inwardness of Baskin's art has many components. Some of the more accessible of these, maybe, can be seen in his graphic style itself, which is so like a signature, so unique to him and so consistent, that it might well interest a graphologist. But the oddities of it hint at other sources. As if a calligraphy had been improvised from the knotted sigils and clavicles used for conjuring spirits, those bizarre scratchmarks of the arcane powers, such as we can find in practical grimoires. This element in his draughtsmanship is no more than a trace, but it peers from every interstice, and suggests a natural psychic proclivity, enough to attune his operation, perhaps, to certain freedoms familiar in Jewish mysticism. A passport between worlds usually kept closed to each other. It is one of the essentials of his work's power to disturb, and of its weird beauty too.

At the same time more identifiably, his style springs from Hebrew script itself—all those Alephs, Bets, Lameds, Yods, crammed in a basketry of nerves, growing heads, tails, feelers, hair, mouths. And the typical lonely isolation of his figures both sharpens our sense of them as hieroglyphs, cryptograms, and intensifies that atmosphere of Cabala, where each image is striving to become a syllable of the world as a talismanic Word—or at least to become a Golem, bursting with extrasensory news, bulging the cage-mesh of lines.

This underswell of divination, which can be felt here and there almost as a pressure, produces wonderfully substantial, living shapes. The context of presentation, so to speak, is three-dimensionally objective—as it is throughout Baskin's art. He regards himself as first and foremost a sculptor, and in all his graphic images the "wiry, bounding line," the sheer, physical definition, is sculptural. His imagination is innately kinaesthetic. It projects itself exclusively in tensile, organic forms, which are, moreover, whole forms—images of the whole being. At the same time, as he feels out the contours and balance of these forms, he receives an x-ray of their insides. His graphic image reproduces this complex of sensations as a blueprint: the translucent womb-life of an unborn sculpture, flattened onto the paper. Or, even more aptly, as a primitive hunter's x-ray drawing of a creature's essence—its soul or divine image—with vital centres, magical, mythical or astral or future real wounds and the life-mesh meridians all in plan.

As it happens, Baskin has no interest in the worlds of occultism, or in that plane of *participation mystique* which has produced the baffling records of natural man's parapsychological gifts. But this means no more than that he trusts only his own senses. It is unusual to find a pragmatic rationality so powerfully armed and so highly mobilised as his, in a modern artist. He abhors anything that strikes him as an evasion of the real. Most Baskin observers are eventually awed by his powers of destructive derision, and any facile artistic exploitation of the dream world receives his full barrage. Whatever comes under his aesthetic scrutiny is tested first and last for its "reality." And by "reality" he means the ability to stand up in the highest, final court—"the audit of ultimate reckoning."

For Baskin, a work of art must have a "real content." As he makes clear in his various writings, by "real content" he means the "physical presence of our common reality—the common experience of our common humanity." And in the case of his own work he means, more specifically, the physical presence of "our common suffering." At this point, a captious critic might be alerted. He might say: "Considering the nature of Baskin's forms, is this claim of his consistent?" And it is true, what Baskin makes, in his work, of this "common reality" and "common suffering," the scope he embraces, the depth he searches, the specific pain he locates, the light he casts on what he finds, and his treatment of it, present us with what we might well call *uncommon* forms.

At the centre of his workshop stands the human figure, sure enough. But it is a figure in a perpetual flux of transmogrification. Other existences seem to compete for its substance. Owls, crows, angels, demons, mythical personages and half-monsters, see-ers, death apparitions—all press to assert themselves in that afflicted lump of ectoplasm at the heart of his opus. Their manifestations take up a goodly part of his output. He obviously feels compelled to give these *dramatis personae* their forms. But (remembering his own words) what sort of reality, what sort of content, can such entities deliver?

To understand the consistency which fastens his words and his images together, in this context, is to turn a key. Once that key is turned, the full psychological depth of his work can be explored.

And to turn it, perhaps, all we need is to bear in mind that Baskin is rabbinically trained, saturated with esoteric Jewish tradition. This tradition (which has indirectly supplied us, it could be argued, with the most extreme forms of scientific materialism) takes full account of all occult possibilities, and even gives most of them the benefit of the doubt. It is open, that is, on principle, to all that can happen on every imaginable level of human awareness. And it holds that what happens on one level affects all the other levels, with real consequences. It is a tradition in which the human body is the sole register, the only whole and adequate symbol, for the workings of an all-inclusive hierarchy of spirit life—an intricately organised universe of ghostly beings, conditions, powers, susceptibilities, attributes of every kind. As Jewish imagination has sustained it right up to the present, it serves as an accumulator of the full resonance of Jewish experience—an electronic archive of the inner life, as it has been lived out, and paid for, by Jews, such as no other nation possesses: a total system of coherent and workable signs. The goblins and spectres that crowd its magnetic fields are not the *ignes fatui* of folk superstition. They are minor functionaries in the oldest and most resolutely-fought court-case, still unfinished, in the judgements of God. This inheritance is as decisive in Baskin's work as it is in the achievement of that other giant among modern imaginations—Isaac Bashevis Singer. Baskin's sceptical eye, as I have said, is remarkably wide awake, but in fact it guards his inward, learned Jewishness, which is busy dreaming for him, in a rigourous, divining fashion, as it is also suffering for him. There is a patriarchal prophet among his hidden resources, as there was a Sufi master among those affable familiars of W. B. Yeats.

This tradition is the updated Witch of Endor's cave from which Baskin's forms rise. And what they soon tell us is—that they are drawn from the hard core of human pain. Each one embodies that compound of intimate, secret suffering and spiritual exultation which is Baskin's specialty. All his images, without exception, are precipitated out of this, as crystals out of a supersaturated solution. Even his birds and angels are solid and sharp with the salts and metals of it, they have the chemical composition and crystalline structure of it. Once absorbed through the eye into the nervous system they dissolve back into the real knowledge and presence of it.

Without any doubt, this is "real content." But it is not all. His images bear witness to the horror within the created glory, as our common humanity undergoes it. But there is still much more to them. Above all, and before anything else, they are beautiful. This is the first and last fact about Baskin's art: it has a peculiarly intense kind of beauty.

It is an odd paradox. He records, in what we feel to be a coolly objective way, a shocking experience of life, as it occurs somewhat behind the face, as it might return at night to one who thought he had escaped and blessedly forgotten it—returning intact, worse, more dangerously connected, more deeply involved with friend and enemy, more open to things beyond the soul's reach, but in some symbolic form, as a distorted mask simply, a sidelong look, a blank, deadpan face, or a dream shout that stays in the waking mind as a lumpish humanoid crouched there on the threshold. Yet this is the very figure he makes beautiful.

This startling, sinister beauty, characteristic of all his works, cannot easily be called "content." Yet it is something more than style, something other than the masterful technical expertise that gives his image the foot-poundage of its striking power and penetration. The subject matter of his image may shock us, and his phenomenal technique may overpower us, but this other thing does not attack in any way. It summons us very quietly. But more and more strongly. In the end it makes us seek his work out as if we needed it, and makes us cherish it, as some source of elixir, long after more documentary or photographic evidence of "our common suffering" has become a sad blur.

Again remembering Baskin's own criterion, we should ask, perhaps, just what sort of "reality" this beauty has. What weight of "necessity"—another favourite word of his— presses behind it? And being so paradoxical anyway, as a beauty created so openly and directly out of pain, it challenges us to examine it more closely.

Baskin writes of his ideal image as one that seems to have lain in the earth for generations, re-emerging now with all its temporary cultural superficies corroded away, so that only some core of elemental artistic substance remains. It is interesting to put one of his own images to this test, in imagination, so far as one can, and to superimpose a typical Baskin figure, say *The Hanged Man,* on a related image from another culture. In my own mind I associate that giant woodcut with the statue of Coatlicue, the colossal, horrendous Aztec mother and earth goddess, which stands in the Museum of Anthropology, in Mexico City.

The Hanged Man holds a special place among Baskin's graphic works. It was his first fully mature piece (1954), and it was like the herald of everything he has done since. One might say, it was the whole new thing itself, like a tight-wrapped seed.

Once we bring these two forms together, a lively field of force springs into place between them and around them, uniting them. And the Hanged Man becomes the archetypal victim of the Mother Earth Goddess in this most horrifying aspect—as a Death Goddess in fact. He becomes, like crucified Jesus, a figure nailed to his mother, sucked empty by mother, paralysed by the clasp of her extraordinary gravity, borne through timelessness in a trance of mother-possession, in death-like communion with the goddess of the source, a figure rooted in the womb, as if rooted in the earth or death. The cadenza on these themes develops itself.

But there is something through and beyond that. Something that both the Hanged Man and Coatlicue carry equally, neither male nor female, common to both, which is as well symbolised by a dangling, flayed man's corpse as by that contained eruption, that nuclear Aztec war-head.

Baskin himself might say: It is the *horror*. (And he would quote his favourite line from Conrad: "The horror! The horror!") But what exactly is it, here, that horrifies us?

It isn't only the gruesome pain of the flayed man, or the macabre grotesquerie of the divinity that requires it. The Hanged Man is certainly an image of pain. Even—of absolute pain, pain beyond flesh: ineffable, infinite affliction of being, from the dumb mouth of which the foetus hangs like some roping coagulation.

There is something beyond that pain of the Hanged Man and beyond the fact that Coatlicue is one hundred and fifty tons of rattlesnakes and skulls in a symmetrical, molecular combination.

New art awakens our resistance insofar as it proposes changes and inversions, some new order, liberates what has been repressed, lets in too early whiffs of an unwelcome future. But when this incidental novelty has been overtaken or canonised, some other unease remains. At least, where the art is serious and real (one supposes, major) it remains. An immanence of something dreadful, almost (if one dare say it) something unhuman. The balm of great art is desirable and might even be necessary, but it seems to be drawn from the depths of an elemental grisliness, a ground of echoless cosmic horror.

The mystery of music opens this horror as often as we properly hear it. Perhaps music holds the key to it. If, as we are told, mathematical law is the tree of the original gulf, rooted outside the psychological sphere, outside the human event-horizon, and if music is a sort of nest, the consolingly-shaped soul-nest, that we feathery and hairy ones weave out of the twigs of that tree (audial nerve sunk in the mingling chorales of the body's chemistry), then the horror which wells up out of music is also the sap of mathematical law, a secretion of the gulf itself—the organising and creative energy itself.

In all art, everything that isn't the music rides on the music. Without that inner musicality of every particle, art ceases to do the work and have the effect and retain the name of art. And so the very thing that makes it art, that gives it the ring of cosmic law and grips us to itself and lifts us out of our egoistic prison and connects, as it seems, everything to everything, and everything to the source of itself—is what makes it unpleasant.

Whatever this musical influx may be, human societies are apparently not too sure about it. A capricious cycle of opening to let it in, and closing to shut it out, shapes the history of every culture. It is as if it were some ambiguous substance, simultaneously holy and anathema, some sort of psychological drug flourishing in the blood-stream. Lorca gave it a name, calling it the Duende, when he described how even in one person, in one half-minute, it irrupts from the faintest titillation to the soul-rending. In his Arab-Andalusian setting he shows how naturally it can be taken for God—a divine horror—a thunderbolt beautiful and terrible.

And he makes the suggestive point—that it seems to come from "beyond death." As if he meant that it comes from "beyond life."

Yet it is the core of life, like the black, ultimate resource of the organism. Maybe that is why it rouses itself only in an atmosphere of crisis, at extreme moments. Or in the individual, it may be, who somehow lives a perpetual "extreme moment"—not of heightened powers of life, but of dead man nakedness, dead man last ditch helplessness, dead man exposure to the crowding infinities, getting to his feet only as a Lazarus, having had life stripped off him, as in those skinned figures of Baskin's, and the ego and personal life plucked out of him, through that strange wound in the chest.

This Duende-music, or music within music, or ectoplasmic essence or whatever it is, has a more familiar role as *mana*.

Mana comes to the sufferer, it is said. Maybe *mana* is the body's natural response to grave hurt—a healing. Which would make it, more than metaphorically, redemption incarnate. And all historical cultures agree, it is purchased by suffering. And it has to be paid for. Some people seem to get it—or take it—and pay later. Or pay invisibly, perhaps. Normally, payment comes first. It is a curious circumstance, a technical discovery, that deliberately self-inflicted suffering will buy *mana*. The sufferer suffers till *mana* can't hold off any longer—and so surrenders and heals the sufferer—and remains, it seems, at his, or her, disposal. Like those Indian gods who play deaf to the mortifications and ordeals and cries of the suppliant, till they can't stand it any longer—the stones of their heaven begin to sweat, their thrones begin to tremble—whereupon they descend and grant everything. And the suppliant becomes Holy, and a Healer.

Or they descend earlier and grant not quite so much.

However it is obtained, and in whatever intensity, *mana*, and the roots of music, and healing, are all mixed up in the same medicine, which oozes from that tree in the gulf.

We can only guess at the significance Coatlicue held for the men who carved her. She is a giant, composite word of Aztec hieroglyphs, a monstrous *quipu* of religious and mythological conundrums for anthropologists. But her power speaks for itself. She is a daemonic lump of *mana*, a petrified mass of grotesque music, like an irruption of dancing electrons into our sensual world—a titanic snake of solar magma, knotting a likeness of limbs and face to itself as it congealed.

It is the very image of *mana*, the embodiment of pure *mana*. *Mana* as the goddess of the source of terrible life, the real substance of any art that has substance, in spite of what we might prefer.

The Hanged Man is also an image of *mana:* all hanged gods, hung on a single rope, strung from a single hook, in the flesh of a skinned man. Not quite Coatlicue. Though she is crusted with the flayed and the self-flaying—with skulls and serpents—Coatlicue is obviously neither flayed nor strung up. She is a solid plug of magma shouldering through the basalt.

If the Hanged Man is also an image of *mana*, it is *mana* with a difference.

Other parts of Baskin's oeuvre help to define what is going on within *The Hanged Man*. Among the varied range of his images, there is a quite large and notable category that bears no taint of the supernatural, no evident burden of the symbolic. Among these are the etched insects, in the book *Diptera*, which close the present collection. If we imagine the Hanged Man at one pole, then the opposite pole might be occupied by one of these insects—maybe by the Dragonfly. It is very relevant, in any interpretation of *The Hanged Man*, to ask how this Dragonfly fits into the global wholeness of Baskin's work.

The Dragonfly does seem beautiful in an undisturbed way—at first sight. Precisely observed, densely moulded, solidly realised, compactly beautiful. As an expressive image, does the Dragonfly say more than that it is very beautiful? Is paradise all around and inside dragonflies? Or has Baskin himself escaped, for a while, from that consciousness where his other images suffer—into this little redoubt of precarious bliss?

And the Dragonfly isn't alone. Baskin's later work is richer and richer in the flora and fauna of the natural world delineated just as objectively as the Dragonfly, and always with marvellous, luminous intensity. How do such things fit into the single organism of his work? Because it *is* a single organism. I have called it global in its wholeness, but it is also organically articulated, and that *mana* circulates through every cell of it, and the whole creature has a single purpose.

The clue to the role of the Dragonfly, in his work—and of every other image in that class—is in the palpable fullness of *mana*. In the daemonic intensity—one might say, the daemonic beauty—of the object. Without any distortion of symbolic intent, the Dragonfly nevertheless performs the heroic role in this Mystery Drama. And that is, the protagonist as a consecrated being—as *the* consecrated being. What brings it into relationship with the Hanged Man is the peculiar sacramental act, the beatification, which it has undergone.

At their opposite poles, the Hanged Man and the Dragonfly can be seen as the beginning and end of a process of transformation. But the whole process is there at the beginning inside the Hanged Man, and it is still there at the end inside the Dragonfly. As if one examined these two images made of light through opposite facets of the one crystal. The same might be said for every other image that Baskin has created. Each one resonates with this same process as if they were all clones—which cells of a single organism are. And that sacramental process, which culminates in that dark radiance, which we recognise as the beauty of his art, is the essential task of his genius.

We can look into this task more narrowly, perhaps more deeply, and can come maybe to some sense of the biological weight of necessity behind it, if we think of his graphic line as an image in itself—his fundamental image.

Does this line attack, as it seems to, or does it suffer under attack, as again it seems to—or with subtle sleight of hand does it manage both simultaneously?

As a thing in itself it has a certain glamour of deadliness. An uncanny sort of grace, raptorial. Maybe all those massively-taloned birds fly up out of the line's exultation in its own hawkish-owliness.

At the same time, the line is above all delicate. And a real wound. At one moment a sensor, alert for floating particles. At the next—a deep astonished cut just about to bleed. A pain-diviner, and a pain-fathomer. The spirit of the blade of the burin, but also of the scalpel—operating, as a rule, on a naked torso, a face.

The blade and the wound: simultaneously male and female. It is a common mythological and folklore motif that the wound, if it is to be healed, needs laid in it the blade that made it.

As if the blade might cut to a depth where blood and cries no longer come—only *mana* comes.

Baskin writes, somewhere, that his subject is the wound. One could as truly say that his subject is *mana*. His real subject is the healing of the wound.

Throughout Baskin's artistic life, he has drawn strength from the kinship he feels with William Blake. One clue to this link is their preoccupation with the Book of Job. Both artists share a biblical concern for what Blake called the human form divine. It is prophetic concern. Since Blake's day, the disasters of the human condition have become more explicit, maybe more inescapable. To the apocalyptic eye (and all Baskin's work assumes an apocalyptic eye), the human form divine—formerly the responsibility of religion—is now

a universal casualty. He tries to get to his feet after the nu-
clear shock-wave—the atomisation of all supportive beliefs—
and responsibility for him is blowing in the solar wind.

That ravaged, emptied figure appears everywhere in
contemporary art. But directly abreactive art is one thing,
redemptive art quite another. Baskin's jeremiads against
contemporary artists are notorious. He sees most of them as
little more than fragmented, convulsive reflexes, after the
explosion. Or as zoologically primitive forms after some
disruption of the ozone layer: a teeming of random muta-
tions in the genetic melt-down, a forlorn hope of irradiated
chromosomes scrabbling for the new terms of adaptation, in
the new conditions of maelstrom firestorm.

But these holocaust conditions are the very ones within
which Baskin's art has evolved. Like the fourth figure in the
burning, fiery furnace, it has become visible to the human
eye, at the side of the condemned, only in this degree of
spiritual catastrophe.

What Baskin has done could seem to be inevitable—if the
resurgence of Nature's powers is inevitable. He has salvaged
that responsibility for the human form divine, and bestowed
it again—on art. An art that has been qualified by a course in
surgery. What religion once did is now, it appears, the work
of an improvised field hospital. And the Hanged Man, the
century's flayed victim, lies there on the operating table.

The human form divine has become the wound. The
biggest wood-engraving ever made up to that point in the
history of Western art, (*The Hanged Man* is nearly six feet
high), is the portrait of a total wound—head to foot one
wound.

And it is here, in this woodcut, in the actual work of the
blade, that we can find the meaning of Baskin's line. With
deep labour, he is delivering his form from the matrix. He is

liberating a body from the death that encloses it. Inevitably, one imagines a surgeon's tranced sort of alertness, as he cuts. Baskin's electrocardiograph, and the surgeon's, at the moment of incision, must be very alike. And as the scalpel cuts, *mana* flows. That is, seen from our point of vantage, beauty flows. As if the blade, in prayer, were less a honed edge, more a laying on of hands—a blessing—a caress—and a glorification. The steel, under Baskin's care, is a balm flowing into the wound.

It really is very like worship. Do you worship a wound, or rather, what is wounded, to heal it? Yet the healing does happen. We are talking about an art, after all, that has consummated its purpose. Is it less of a miracle, if it happens in art, than when it happens under the hands of the rural healer—the rough hands that pass over the wound without touching it and send a shiver through the human form, while all who witness it, when it succeeds, want to laugh and weep with amazed feeling.

And the Hanged Man really is healed. When we acknowledge the beauty, so complete, in that delineation of agony and death, we have recognised the triumph of *mana*, the musical release and emanation of *mana*, that lifts this corpse into the force-field of cosmic law—which only incidentally, and to our unaccustomed eyes, wears the illusion of horror. It is as if Coatlicue, or her equivalent, had lifted up this hanged, flayed god-man. And her *mana* suffuses him. From whichever side we look, it is a pietà. In the religion, with the dead, everliving god, it is *the* religious moment. In the woodcut *The Hanged Man*, it is *the* aesthetic moment. As if the Muse of this art were only another aspect of the mother of that god.

But in Baskin's imagination the Hanged Man is evolving further, and becoming something else too. That moment of redemption, where healing suddenly wells out of a wound that had seemed fatal, is not enough. The beauty of it has to blossom. The dead man has to flower into life. And so this skinned carcass, so wrapped and unwrapped in its pain, is becoming a strange thing—a chrysalis. A giant larva. And under Baskin's continuous concentration—the labour of his arduous life—it emerges, at last, as a Dragonfly.

This completes the cyclic process within Baskin's art.

The Hanged Man is a symbol of the first phase: *mana* nursed from agony. And the Dragonfly is a symbol of the last phase: the agony wholly redeemed, healed—and transformed into its opposite, by *mana.* The old terms of suffering have become the new terms of grace. The Hanged Man has become the Dragonfly without having ceased to be the Hanged Man. This is the healing operation of *mana,* in front of our eyes. Of a very great, concentrated density of *mana.*

There is a miracle in this, and the work seems to me miraculous, in the sense that healing is miraculous. And again, if one says: "But it's only in art," what is that "only"? The operation of art comes to the same thing, whichever way we describe it. Whether we say that it enacts, in a home-made Mystery Drama, the most important event of all—the birth, in "hard and bitter agony," of the creative, healing spirit, the nativity of the redemptive divine gift, or that it demonstrates the biological inevitability of art, as the psychological component of the body's own system of immunity and self-repair.

So when we question the peculiar beauty of Baskin's art, and ask what order or "reality," what degree of "necessity" there is behind it, the answer is to be found here: in this act of consecration made perfect.

The Hanged Man himself is in some way exultant, even jubilant. He's almost ribald, the gallows joke to end all gallows jokes.

His figure is a parable. All Baskin's figures are, in one way or another, parables—reminiscent of those Hasidic or Sufi parables: each simple-seeming confrontation is a trompe l'oeil of perspectives, at a crossroads between different planes of experience. And in this parable of the Hanged Man, after the judges have stopped laughing, and the torturers, the hangman, the skinners, the soldiers and the survivors, after they have all stopped laughing, their ears prick. The corpse, the skinless cadaver itself, has begun to laugh. Lorca did not find a more satisfying image of the Duende.

And then—in this revelatory parable—the judges cry out and fall in the dust, like Saul on the road, while the torturers, the hangman, the skinners, the soldiers and the rest, roll on the ground and grind their teeth and cry out like those tribesmen the astounded archaeologist Layard describes, hearing the epic song of the Bedouin poet in the tent.

The impact of the Hanged Man, on his own wavelength, is like a sacred shout. In some shrine, some underground chamber of the religious mystery beloved by Aeschylus, one imagines a stunning, end-of-all-things cry at the death of the god—which is also the cry of incredulity, the ecstatic outcry at his simultaneous resurrection.

Those feelings actually do flash through. The step-down transformers we've installed in our frontal lobes, at such cost, still register the input. The nerves have looked in a mirror, and the experience whizzes just past the skull, leaves a faint sweat over the brow, probably measurable electrostatic changes, even as the observer says: "I don't like it."

The Hanged Man's laughter, that flinging off of everything, deep down among the roots of the unkillable thing in nature, is the voice of *mana*.

Baskin's work in sculpture is monumental. Monumentality, as he has said himself, is one of his main sculptural preoccupations, and it affects many of his prints. The facial expression of all his figures, for instance, tends to be monumental. Typically, his large figures embody an Egyptian burden, the mass of indestructible matter, after some harrowing Aztec initiation. Humanoid, emerging out of Einstein's shadow, out of a cauldron of atoms—like a projectile from space, flayed and half-molten, some sort of cry arrested before it reaches the paralysed lips, the eyes catatonic with the shock of arrival into the skull—but taking the first human step, materialising there on the threshold, begging for a name.

This figure has immensity. The bronze-like or stony fragment of the universe, its mantle of substance, gives it immensity. And it has glory. It clutches, like some perilous crumb of radium, immortal flames of Eros. And it has tragic pathos. Its planetary physical mass, so loaded with fate and momentum, and that draughty, flamey sun-scrap of glory, are exacting their price. The pinched, stricken face is fully aware of the price. And as the features become more human, the cosmic loneliness becomes more frostily awful, and the pathos more acute.

Nevertheless this figure insists it is a Prometheus, a Job. And if it could speak, or more likely sing, we would hear the full, balanced chord of epic.

Epic is the story of *mana*. The morphology of epic, its recurrent pattern of recognisable episodes, emerges wherever the saga tells, in one metaphor or another, of the search for and the finding of *mana*.

To a surprising degree, when one examines it, Baskin's imagery can be seen to revolve around the epic archetypes. If epic has three historically familiar forms, with religious quest as the most civilised form, and heroic epic as the barbaric form, and the shaman's dream of his flight as the prototypical and, as it were, biological form, then Baskin's imagery derives abundantly from all three. Everything in his gallery of images belongs to epic's adventurous, imaginative penetration through suffering into the land of death, or into a land beyond life. The infernal or purgatorial circumstances of so many of his figures, souls in carnal torment, bodies in spiritual torment, plentiful officers of heaven and hell, mutilated torsos, terrible warriors, glimpses of Paradise, supernatural women, monstrous beings, personalities from sacred and mythical history, herbs of everlasting life, hallucinatory apparitions of death—all these obsessive themes of his are epic stock. And his most favoured images, his most personal, the forms he returns to as if to renew his energies—the birds, the bird-men, the vatic figures, and not least the death-trance as a portrait of the communion with ultimate reality, truth and the divine—all these come straight from the shaman's dream-journey, from his difficult take-off and flight, through obstacles and ordeals, to the source of renewal. In fact, these particular items have no other cultural context—except maybe for that transcendental role of the corpse, which has been requisitioned by all sacrificial religions.

All this is inevitable, since what Baskin's work has in common with all three forms of epic is that fundamental scenario of the quest for *mana.* By confining his procedure to a detailed surgery of organisms, in the spirit of the immediate crisis, he has kept his operation hard-edged and hard-headed, ironic, usually witty even when he pries deepest among the nerves. But *mana,* meanwhile, has carried him away on a long journey, down the archaic lines of the palm, and he has returned with all the traditional experiences of the shaman's entranced flight, which has always recurred, and presumably will go on recurring, spontaneously, wherever individuals are overloaded with private pain or tribal calamity. It is no coincidence that Baskin belongs to the very people which, in his generation, met the full ferocity of our mid-twentieth century head on, and rising out of their own ashes mastered it, and after two thousand years restored Israel.

The pattern of unity in Baskin's art, or that part of it which I have been able to glimpse and to sketch out, as I understand it, finds its fullest, most poignant verbal expression in the Book of Job. The fullest in our culture, at least. I say, our culture. I should say, Baskin's culture. And the Book Of Job is like the hidden master-plan behind everything he produces. It aligns all his images in their right relationships to each other and to the source of his inspiration. And it sustains the grand dimension of feeling and statement in which he casts his forms.

This kinship to the Book of Job suggests what part his art performs in the contemporary drama of Western spiritual morale, and gives us some bearing on the scale of his endeavour. As the sacerdotal trappings and hangings and dogmas melt, or evaporate, in the enlightenment of holocaust, Christianity burns down to its root in the aboriginal Jewish rock. As if the soul, which was for so long, in Western terms, "naturally Christian," had fallen from that dream of the Cross. Coming to consciousness in the ashes finds itself to be, after all, Jewish too, and cognate with naked Job, if not Job himself. Job, the human form divine, pure and simple. The naked child of an infinitely glorious, infinitely terrible Creator.

By just such shifts as these, maybe, Baskin, a healer and an Elihu of the modern cataclysm of Jewishness, comes to find, lying under his blade, the casualty of a revelation that seems universal—the human form divine of all men and women.

1983

Jean-Baptiste-Camille Corot, *A View Near Volterra*, oil on canvas, 27 ³/₈ x 37 ¹/₂ in. National Gallery of Art, Washington: Chester Dale Collection.

Notes on Corot

JAMES MERRILL

*No poet writing today has a more painterly way of observing than
James Merrill, his eye trained and nervy, his mind's eye coloring the
whole design with a palette of nuanced perceptions. But he has not
written often about paintings. "I'm somewhat prejudiced against
poems written about existing works of art," he explains. "A certain
parasitism is involved, I'm afraid: riding in on someone else's coat-
tails. Not that there aren't some beautiful ones, and not that I
haven't given in to the temptation at least once." He has given in
more than once, if we count the early "Charioteer of Delphi" and his
chipped, dimestore "Willowware Cup" with its prewar pattern of a
version of heaven: "Boat bearing the gnat-sized lovers away, / The
old bridge now bent double where her father signals / Feebly, as from
flypaper, minding less and less. / Two smaller retainers with lan-
terns light him home." But the temptation Merrill is probably al-
luding to is Giorgione's* La Tempesta, *which figures—and is bril-
liantly refigured—in the first part of his trilogy* The Changing
Light at Sandover. *It is not surprising that Corot's sketches of
Italy, where the poet lived briefly in the early 1950s, drew Merrill to
write the following essay. In those sketches, as in the Giorgione, he
discovered a quality of legend by which the world itself is a mar-
velous tale. "Prose is another matter. It can't hurt a layman, if he
writes well enough, to write about art. Proust on Vermeer and Giotto*

Reprinted with permission of the Art Institute of Chicago from *Corot, 1796–1875* (Art
Institute of Chicago, 1960), 11–15. Copyright © 1960 by James Merrill.

is splendid." Merrill proves that assertion here, but then cautions: "One would like to imagine some useful analogy between the two arts. But just try brushing-in words in Monet's manner, or Van Gogh's, or telling your student that her poem needs warmth in the lower left corner, and see how far you get. What can *be learned from pictures, perhaps, is how to bring out the mysterious tale told by interlocking forms, by things themselves—which comes through to the degree that the painter is also, in his way, a 'poet.' Chardin, for instance." Or, we might add, Corot.*

THE WRITER will always envy the painter. Even those who write well about painting, he will envy for having learned to pay close attention to appearances. And not the writer alone; it is the rare person who can look at anything for more than a few seconds without turning to language for support, so little does he believe his eyes.

Daily the painter masters new facts about the world. But years pass, and the writer is still studying his face in the mirror, wondering at what strange tendencies lie hidden beneath a familiar surface. "Pleasant enough, but what does it *mean?"* That traditional response of the layman is one he will never contrive to repress. Making it to the oeuvre of Corot, he will feel the least bit foolish. What does *it* mean? What does *he* mean? Here are the landscapes—ruins, trees, water, cows; here are the models, both with and without clothes. What can it possibly add up to but Art? The retort, by endowing the pictures with unquestionable value, gracefully waives the little matter of their significance.

He stands before a painting by Corot. As he is not himself a painter, or even if he is—painters are forever talking nowadays—he will suffer a brief, defensive spell of verbal dizziness. Phrases to be distinguished by their incoherence—linear values, tonal purity, classical heritage—will explode between himself and the canvas. When the first smoke clears, he may look more attentively; he has routed the babbling imp. And though he will end by using the dreadful phrases, seeing at last their truth if not their beauty, an observer who is by nature oriented toward language, who in the deepest sense of the cliché requires that a picture *tell a story,* must meanwhile listen for its opening words.

"Once upon a time, in a far country . . ."
The small Italian sketches are praised by those who prefer the natural to the invented, Rousseau to Chateaubriand, the early Corot to the late. They are indeed very beautiful, as well as revolutionary, with their simplifications, their early morning, open-air clarity. Let it be added, however, that they respond to a revery of the idyllic instilled in Corot by Claude and Poussin, and that, when we are moved, it is not only by their naturalism but by a revery of our own.

His rapidly-brushed Rome, the Rome he transported back to France for prudent investment, is the city of our dreams: physical, somnolent, unimperially casual and even-tempered. Its domes rise from dusky washes into the sun, or by magic from the brimming, shaded fountain on the Pincio. A pane flashes. The island of S. Bartolomeo suspends its structural Gordian knot between sky and stream. The wonderful trees are everywhere, dwarfing the monuments they frame, taking the rich light upon their bulk, like placid thunderheads. Umber shadows flood the pavements of Venice, Genoa, Florence, Naples: the eye is drawn over a balustrade and down into the radiant depths of the scene, with the same sinking delight felt on the verge of sleep. All is joyously, economically accomplished, and it is an unfortunate visitor to Italy who has not, even in this day and age, enjoyed some such delusion. Over the shoulder of an old country man sitting on a trunk, beyond a crooked window-frame, the sky, of a soft, blank brightness hard to mistake for any other, is enough to send one headlong down the stairs and out into that still barely retrievable world of awnings and ochers, sunstruck ruins, umbrella pines.

Italy—like youth, a simple word for a complicated, often idealized experience. No one would resist its appeal, as rendered in these little paintings. But each of us knows, in his way, what happens when it is over. Corot knew too. *A View near Volterra* (in the Chester Dale Collection) shows it happening in a scene so ravishing that it emerges unscathed from the jaws of allegory: the artist-prince, in peasant dress, heads his white horse (!) straight into the trees. Slowly it dawns on us what awaits him there, when he dismounts and sets up his easel. A change of light, a corresponding change of sensibility; in short, the paintings of Corot's maturity.

More than ever, as we look back on them, these Italian scenes take on a quality of legend. No need to people the glades with nymphs, or top the hill with crosses. The world itself is a marvelous tale. And as in all legend is found—what distinguishes it from myth—traces of the provincial, of genre, it is a happy accident, or no accident at all, the led the young painter to that already much-painted landscape where the peasant's cottage stands in relation to the aqueducts and arenas of the Giant. Taste, far more than credulity, is strained by the costumes of Corot's women. They belong to a world of story, it is well that they are a bit fussy and quaint.

". . . there lived a woman . . ."

One woman or hundreds of women, it makes no difference. A single impulse turned a Roman girl into a sibyl and a French girl into a Vermeer. What is strange is how we

believe in them, for all their artifice of posture and orna-
ment.

Who *are* they? The last of the Lamias? The first patients of
Freud? From the start, they fascinate and appal us by their
listlessness, their fatalism, combined with an oddly bourgeois
presence. Standing by a fountain, trusting vainly to partici-
pate in all that freshness; balancing an unplucked instru-
ment in their laps; musing without comprehension upon
book or letter, upon the enigma of a nudity or a costume
they would never have chosen, their faces drain of anima-
tion, a mortal tedium falls, glimmering downward from a
gray sun that does its best to shine and to cheer, but alas,
their painter is older now, probably indoors as well, and he
will not fake a happy light either in the world or in his own
eye. Thus the reader of the Metropolitan Museum's *The
Letter* sits in a shuttered space at the bottom of a well. No
other interpretation will do for the light that barely exposes
the musty furnishings and our heroine's unlovely, heavy-
skinned features. What has happened to interiors—of rooms
and of people alike? One has the feeling of Venice and Delft
being recreated at nightfall, on a rehearsal stage. The soli-
tude of any Renaissance woman never bothered us; she sat at
her ease on an invisible throne of philosophy and manners.
In the Lowlands, there was always a music lesson, or some
household matter to be dealt with, and we enjoyed looking
through a door at mistress and maid, off and on during the
day. The pomp and pride of one tradition, and the charming
resourcefulness of the other, are lacking in Corot's women.
The most they can do is *look* as if they were reading or able to
pick out a tune; their minds are elsewhere, we feel anxious
for them. Another *Woman Reading* (also at the Metropolitan)
has elected to sit out-of-doors in her cumbersome contadina
dress; the sun beats down muggily from a mournful zenith;
one guesses the strain she is under, the trickle of sweat

forming beneath the silken sleeve. Behind her, a tiny figure we shall see again tries and tries to steer his boat out of the rushes.

These ladies could not say, any more than Corot, what ails them. The *maladie du temps,* to be sure. But, specifically, do they not chronically suffer from their legacy (both classical and Dutch) as surely as from a "delicate constitution"? They are the last figures that a serious painter will ever render with that particular sober "studio" look—a result of training and procedure that infect his treatment of flesh and bone in much the same way as the inbred values of an Arcadian education might have done any young person in the 19th century. Their postures show what art has taught them to expect of life; their faces, what life has taught them to suspect of art. And yet they cleave to it—they are timid. They have *heard* of their shameless sister, with her parrot or her paramour, but in their eyes she is worse than any chattering bird. Better to waste away, unloved, than to break faith with their creator. In the mercy of his brush salvation lies.

Arkel to Mélisande: "I have been watching you: you were there, unconcerned perhaps, but with the strange, distraught air of someone forever expecting a great misfortune, in sunlight, in a beautiful garden."

Humble, not visionary, a virgin without child, the *Woman Reading* resists knowing herself. She would deny that the hand on which her cheek just fails to lean is constituted differently from its Raphaelesque prototype; more loosely brushed, it is nevertheless doomed to obsolescence (hence her repressive calm) by new or imminent techniques and tastes. One wants to take that hand, open those sombre eyes. Triumphs lie ahead. *She* will vanish, yes, but in her place we shall see the molecules of Pissarro, the brilliant glazes of a later reader—*L'Arlésienne.* Her nieces—she has no direct descendents—her nieces, clothed in colors as light and strokes as rapid as air, will dance all day at Bougival with bearded, floppy-hatted men. They will eat oysters! Or they will once again do *useful* things, such as bathing themselves or setting the table. If they are melancholy, it will be at their milliner's or in their music halls. (The provincial branch of the family will evidently stay on at Barbizon, ever more numerous, rich, and insufferable.)

Ah, and yet—

Lost in so much female activity will be precisely the solitary romance, the sense, however obscure, that our moments of uncomprehending loneliness are the most true; their profound dark spotlight reveals more about the human condition than any number of hours spent in dramatic relation to this or that figure or set of objects. To convey this truth, in all its narrowness, the artist may have no recourse to drama. Once seen to inhabit a setting—the saint in his cell, the siren in her loge—the supreme solitude can be shrugged off as a matter of individual preference, when it is really, as for Corot's women, a destiny, a state of soul. Some, like the *Sibyl*, are strong, requiring almost a violence of execution; others make subtler claims—consider the air of baleful French tenacity that envelops the *Young Woman* in the Hirschland Collection, all her weakness concentrated into a force; others yet are merely beautiful. But even these, at their most memorable, remain at the heart of life, which is to say, beyond any of its resources, beyond even the methodical debauchery that sheds so cold a light upon Lautrec's unhappy women. We must wait for Picasso to renew the glamour of pure identity.

Seeing this far, we should not be astonished by the *Girl with a Pink Shawl* in Boston. Flattened, simplified, positively post-impressionist in feeling, she sits against three large, quickly-done jigsaw pieces, two light, one dark. Somehow this background escapes transformation into furniture, foliage or sky. Somehow her loose white smock escapes being fitted or embroidered. A thin wash of mauve covers portions of her otherwise pale-strawberry and cream face. One hesitates to admire her, suspecting that, if one does so, it is thanks rather to a later master than to Corot. Yet she is his—awkward, virginal, unsmiling. The painting may be unfinished; her being is intact. Indeed, the rapid execution makes the difference. It suggests that she does not weigh too heavily on the artist's conscience; he has not shouldered her with *his* inheritance and *his* destiny. We are led to reflect on the degree to which these were embodied by so many of his other women.

At times Corot's mysterious heroine is literally garbed as a muse, with wreath and scroll; or lies nude, a gross-featured bacchante looking up, deadpan, at the tame leopard advancing, a child astride it, to sniff politely the lifeless bird she dangles. We may hope that such a composition is lighthearted, a spoof on certain big moments out of Titian or Poussin. But is it? She has appeared too often in pensive, humorless guises for us to be sure.

In one of the most suggestive—the Widener Collection's *Artist's Studio*—she sits with hound and mandolin, in Italianate finery, facing away from us and into a small "typical" Corot landscape. Dreamily she fingers her instrument; the dog paws her skirt in vain. She might as well be looking into a mirror, so enraptured is she by the painter's expression of her feelings.

Though we no longer readily translate scenery into emotion, the landscape that resembled oneself or one's mistress was a widely spoken Romantic language (". . . the rocky horizon seen while approaching Arbois on the main road from Dôle, was for me a clear, live image of Métilde's inner self." —Stendhal, *The Life of Henri Brulard*). Faced with Corot's most celebrated pictures—the post-Italian landscapes—to make sense of, we must not despair. Many of them, it is true, appear to have issued, like himself, from the milieu of a small tradesman who has learned the rules of mass production. But, having identified the type of scene with his Muse, we must recognize it as one that deeply stirred Corot. He returned to it, after all, again and again, often dully, always humbly and unquestioningly.

The elements of the scene are quickly named: the little glades, pockets of poetic rurality, farmhouse, stream, a far-off figure bending over the earth not so much, one feels, to gather anything, as just vaguely to keep in touch; a white-masked cow stands by like an anesthetist. These small human or animal figures at first greatly control our responses—the nostalgia of one long pent in his hectic, Balzacian metropolis, as well as the country cynic's impatience with the too easy idyll. As we go from picture to picture, we find that we can dispense with these little guides; we are learning to "read" Corot. The Boston Museum's *Beech Tree*, in which neither man nor beast appears, nevertheless vividly suggests a human, perhaps a super-human, presence. Attended by quiveringly erect younger trees, the strong, whitened trunk stands out against their familiar cloudy greens; this background is thinly painted and sets off a cluster of leaves, belonging to the subject, that might almost have been dribbled onto the canvas. At the foot of the tree a torn-off limb reinforces our impression of veiled narrative—we could be looking at a metamorphosed king.

The story grows more subjective.

The Ville D'Avray scenes, for example, place the sunlit building Corot had loved and learned to paint in Italy, deeper and deeper within the picture, frequently on the far side of still water. Young, white-trunked trees now grow in the foreground; they are seen less often massed from a vantage, than from a point in their midst. Even when fully grown, they rarely command the space; they filter, they intuit. Corot recreates for the eye, in two dimensions, something of the pleasureable hindrances of a winding progress through woods. We are left purer and warmer for the experience. At the last moment a few touches of bright color are added: earlier, they would have threatened the tone of an essentially spiritual exercise. In one picture (*Ville d'Avray* at the Metropolitan) a foliage diffuse and atmospheric overlays the entire canvas, a coarsely woven veil of branches at once dark and shining. It is a perilous moment. The artist is intoxicated by the degree to which his own powers can enter the trees, can alter, withhold, make precious the clear view beyond, which they are in danger of shutting off forever.

To the trees, then, we turn, to the water and the light, for clues to the meaning of these pictures. As with the Italian sketches and the female portraits, we feel the pull of tradition. But by now, the tiny rustics and the diaphanous vegetation bring to mind Hubert Robert more than Poussin. The mood remains Corot's—passive, trustful, melancholy; let others call it unhealthy. Those stretches of water! They sustain and extend the sky; their calm shimmer overwhelms a field; slowly, as they accumulate in scene after scene, they begin to speak of relinquishment, of escape, of an *Embarquement pour Cythère*, only ascetic, lacking the exuberant iridescence of Watteau's.

One motif recurs and recurs: the single boatman leaning over the side of his boat in what might be an effort to free it from certain reeds or bushes at the water's edge. This accomplished, he has only to cast off and glide forth across the breathless mirror. He is kept from doing so precisely by the rest of the composition, with its sum of allusions to an ideal world. The farm, the cattle, the woman and child, even the harmonious intricacy of boughs—would these not be missed, once one had given oneself up to sheer reflectiveness? Would it not, on the other hand, be braver to strike out, to dream one's own dreams for a change? Elsewhere, as before, the boatman does not need to be in sight for us to experience the delicate and crucial conflict.

The setting in motion of such insights hardly adds up to Meaning or Subject Matter (as found in, say, Millet's peasant scenes). And yet Corot's principal dilemma—loyalty to the senses or to the imagination?—does get expressed, all the more movingly for its understatement, its perverse tenuousness. There come to mind Rilke's lines:

> Were you not astonished, on Attic steles, by
> the circumspection of human gesture? were not love
> and farewell
> so lightly laid upon shoulders, they might have
> been made
> out of some other material than ourselves?

If anything can stir us in this Romantic version of classic pastoral, Corot has divined it.

His development is very subtle, hardly a development at all. We can see him applying to one period lessons learned from another: something of the convincing, pure repose of the early Italian scenes, recurs in the quite late *Venus Bathing*, and of their architectural angularity in the *Interrupted Reading* here in Chicago. But, throughout his work, his main concern was to invest places and people with the nuance of a golden or a silver age. The increasing subjectivity of his later mood can be attributed to the tarnishing of that silver in the atmosphere of his day. He was too much of an artist not to breathe it. While able, as how few dedicated painters since, to give a large contemporary public what it wanted, at the same time he could not help but reveal, particularly in his figure paintings, the inner unease of that public caught between its own sense of a way of life lost, and its imminent place at the dreamless center of the stage.

1960

Rodin, *The Thinker,* after the bombing. Photograph courtesy of the *Plain Dealer,* Cleveland.

Fragments of a "Rodin"

RICHARD HOWARD

*"I grew up 'taking' art, as we said in the Midwest," Richard
Howard remembers, "mostly painting, and continued to paint pic-
tures (mostly watercolors) through my second year in college. I began
writing about art at about the same time I began publishing poetry."
That was 1960, and those two aspects of his career have since been
inseparable. His eight books of poems contain many set pieces about
works of art:* "Purgatory, formerly Paradise" *about the Bellini
painting,* "The Giant on Giant Killing" *about Donatello's* David,
"Vocational Guidance" about Simone Martini's Annunciation,
*and others that look knowingly on painters from Starnina to
Caspar David Friedrich to Joseph Cornell. Howard has also written
poems that take up the lives of artists—and, in the case of his
monologues and closet dramas, he has literally taken those lives on.
One poem, "Contra Naturam" (in his 1974 collection* Two-Part
Inventions*) is about Rodin. To an admirer who praises him for
having given body to the god in man, for having raised pleasure to
the pitch of vision, Howard's Rodin explains that art "begins / in
an attempt to make appearance real, / and ends, if it can end, in
an attempt / to make reality appear." When Howard writes in the
following essay about "an ecstatics of art" that seeks to enrich rather
than transform the world and about "the making of an inwardness*

323

from what is outside," he might well have been describing the ambition and method of his own poems. "I do think literary people often write splendidly and irrelevantly about art," he says. "The 'value' of a poet writing about art is merely the value of any focussed intelligence considering an important human activity. Poets are no more (or less) equipped so to do than others, but they may feel an analogy, a sympathy. I think I do. I am addicted to reading the work of art historians, but of course I've read the poets on art as well: Mallarmé, Valéry, Proust. I've done so because one ransacks the world in search of eloquence in this affair: one wants the terms by which to declare one's adoration."

I

IN MARCH, 1970, an act of violence and vandalism was committed in Cleveland, Ohio, its victim a cast of Rodin's statue known as *The Thinker:* dynamite had been wedged between the grasping bronze toes, and sometime after midnight the figure was blown off its pedestal, the lower portion suffering considerable damage. Though put back in place, the statue itself has not been restored, and it looks—legs torn open, buttocks fused, the wonderful patina even more spectacular where the metal is gashed and split, a slender steel palisade boxing in the unbalanced torso—it looks like a "modern" statement now, something closer to a Reg Butler hominoid impaled on its thorns or a realization in the seething bronze of one of Francis Bacon's horrors, neatly jailed, keeping or kept at its distance, than to the celebrated figure created in 1879 and crouching, as we all know, before so many museums, colleges and courthouses across the country.

Growing up in Cleveland, I had seen this particular *Thinker* at work in front of our art museum—had seen it every week, sometimes every day, and inside the museum I had seen other statues I was told Rodin had made, particularly a pair of creamy marble clumps, *The Kiss* and *The Hand of God* (modelled, Miss McFeeley said, after the sculptor's own hand!)—which appeared very different indeed, lapped so smooth the light found nowhere to go but inward, from the rugosities of the image we visiting schoolchildren entitled, with an allegorical impulse quite as merciless as the Master's, *The Toilet.* And when I read in the papers, even in *The New York Times,* about the explosion of this childhood icon (by now I had seen its consessioner before Philosophy Hall at Columbia University, and I had visited the Rodin Museum in Philadelphia and even the Musée Rodin in Paris), I realized as surely as if I had heard the nymphs crying "the great god Pan is dead" when Christ was born, that an era was over, that a hinge had folded, and that life, as Rilke said apropos of another broken statue, must be changed.

Why, I wondered, had "they", nameless and faceless agents of Darkness, done the deed at all? No slogans scrawled on the pedestal indicated the provenance of such destruction, yet the mischief was too intricate to be no more than some midwest version of an *acte gratuit*—it lacked the adorable spontaneity of the Absurd. At first I inclined to believe *The Thinker* had been blasted because it was *thinking.* This was 1970, after all, and anti-intellectualism is scarcely a minor tributary to the stream of American life. But there was a ruinous paradox in my reasoning—indeed, had I not already noticed that the somewhat squashed effigy had a new pertinence, a deeper significance? The wound merely

enhanced the wonder of thinking. The only way to over-
come a thought is by . . . another thought. And the only vic-
tory over *The Thinker* would be, say, disposable earthworks or
primary sculpture, some emblem of unthought—not the
vandalization of a received emblem of thought.

Then, recalling that the figure had been enthroned, orig-
inally, above the lintel of *The Gates of Hell* and that Rodin in-
tended it to be called *The Poet,* for it was to represent Dante
conceiving the tormented universe of forms which writhed
beneath him, I presumed that the same negating hostility to
association, to history and to the very presentiment of the
past had functioned here as had dictated the cancellation of
the program-cover of the Republican Presidential Conven-
tion in 1956, when Rodin's *Three Shades*—chosen by a com-
mittee to illustrate Peace, Progress and Prosperity—were
discovered to be the guardians who point down into the
same swirling inferno over which *The Thinker* so creatively
broods. Yet most people have no notion that Rodin's most
popular work is not seen by them as he intended it to be
seen—as part of an encyclopedic, and unfinished, apoca-
lypse; any more than they realize that Rodin never touched
a chisel, never "carved" all those caramelized creations that
came out of his *atelier* from the hands of Italian artisans
busily producing sentimental marble facsimiles of what the
master's hands had modelled in clay, plaster and wax.

No, *The Thinker* had not been blown up because it was
thinking, or because it was thinking about Hell or history, or
because it would be fun to blow it up; *The Thinker,* I was
obliged to conclude, had been blown up because it was a
special kind of art, because it was by Rodin. What, then, had
that come to mean—"by Rodin"?

The answer might lie in a name-dropping still life with a
title lifted from Kipling, who certainly belongs in the pic-

ture: *A sonata is only a sonata, but a cigar is a good smoke.*
Under a framed lithograph of Brahms playing the piano
and puffing on a cheroot—a Brahms bearded like Whitman,
like Ibsen, like God and like Rodin himself (whose hand, I
knew, already partook of divinity)—there was a shelf of
books in our house, and the biggest book, with the same
luxuriant margins, the same gravure illustrations shielded by
a wisp of tissue-paper, the same *propos* of the Master gath-
ered as in a chalice of reverent inquirendo by Paul Gsell,
was to be found in the houses of all my parents' friends, if
not under Brahms then on top of the piano, among the
folds of an art-scarf which might have been snatched from
Isadora's chubby shoulders. This was the book republished
now by Horizon Press, and on its spine were but two words,
though they appeared in very large letters: ART, and be-
neath that, a trifle larger, RODIN.

For my family and their friends, for an aspiring middle-
class America in the first four decades, say, of this century,
the assumption was not that Rodin made art, but that Art
was what Rodin made (as Poetry, for the preceding genera-
tion, had been what Tennyson wrote). Objects which came,
or were said to come, from Rodin's hands were art because
they were made by an artist (*cherchez l'homme* is the motto of
the middle class), and they were great because they were
made by a Great Artist—not because of their intrinsic quali-
ties, formal properties, but because of a justifying aura of
comment supplied by the Master. That is how the middle
class has always recognized art: by the directives of the artist
and his ape the critic. Only an aristocracy, of course, can af-
ford to respond to such objects *unmediated;* even triumph-
ant, the bourgeoisie never asks "is that what I like?" but
only, anxiously, "what is it supposed to mean?" Rodin,
among others, told us, and we believed, we recognized. This

book is one of the places and ways in which he told us. But to determine an analogous recognition in the history of sculpture, to affix a *cachet* with the same complacent unanimity, we should have to look back as far as Canova, perhaps as far as Bernini—and that far back, no such recognition could be made by the middle classes, which were merely rising; by the time I was poring over ART by RODIN—or was it RODIN by ART?—they had risen.

Other books, as I mentioned, shared with Rodin that shelf which showed forth, until it showed up, the last word in middle-class taste, and though it appears to be period taste now (which means taste, period), who can afford to condescend to such choices when we consider our own last words? There were the works of Maeterlinck and Rostand and d'Annunzio and Anatole France (a long red row, the latter, from which I would learn, as again from Schnitzler, that *libertine* is a diminutive of liberty); there were the scores, on the piano, of Puccini and Massenet (the "Meditation" from *Thaïs* was played at my mother's wedding!); and there were certain numinous figures, living persons whose appearances and performances (often, as in the case of the Divine Sarah, identical) had to be granted the same inviolable veneration with which certain books were to be read: Nijinsky, Caruso, Duse . . . Certainly, after the Great War there was a Great Snobbery about the other side of the Atlantic, a great craving for spoils. But more than any other creative figure—even more than Richard Strauss (music, after all, even music orchestrated by Strauss, could not be *owned* in the way marble and bronze and mere clay could be owned, as chthonic trophies)—Rodin satisfied that craving, fulfilled the needs of the class and circumstance in which I grew up—the class defined, abruptly, by the circumstance of having "been"—by which was meant having been to Europe.

A class which is, today, a has-been, for it has been had—by its own possessions, despoiled by its own spoils, among which few were so proudly carted home as the statues of Auguste Rodin.

There were, of course, several Rodins. There was the Rodin who did—if indeed he did them—marble busts of Mrs. Potter Palmer and her friends for colossal sums; there was the Rodin who scandalized the townspeople of Calais by insisting that civic virtue and patriotic sacrifice were not always noble and exalted, that heroism is a form of solitude—a suffering form; there was the Rodin who questioned the very pride of the body he glorified, who in *The Old Courtesan* articulated with unendurable persistence the miscarriage of life, the futility of effort, the impotence of the mind, the weakness of the flesh; and there was the Rodin who, taking a big mouthful of water and spitting it onto the clay to keep it constantly pliable, did not always aim well and soaked George Bernard Shaw:

At the end of the first fifteen minutes, he produced by the action of his thumb a bust so living that I would have taken it away with me to relieve the sculptor of any further work. . . . But this phase vanished; within a month my bust passed successively, under my eyes, through all the stages of art's evolution. The careful reproduction of my features in their exact dimensions of life . . . went back mysteriously to the cradle of Christian art, and at this moment I had the desire to say again, stop and give me that. It is truly a Byzantine masterpiece. Then, little by little it seemed that Bernini intermingled with the work. Then, to my great horror, the bust softened in order to become a commendable eighteenth-century *morceau,* elegant enough to make one believe that Houdon had retouched a head by

Canova. . . . Once again, a century rolled by in a single night, and the bust became a bust by Rodin and it was the living reproduction of the head that reposes on my shoulders. It was a process that seemed to belong to the study of an embryologist and not to an artist.

With characteristic acuity Shaw hits on what appealed to Rodin's public—not only to his patrons who wanted to be flattered, consoled, immortalized, but to a vast audience which knew what art ought to be, though it may not have known what it liked: art was science ("the study of an embryologist"), not the genesis of a vision, not revelation but realism, but the reproduction of what we see with our own eyes. By this dispensation, art need not—always—reassure, but it must tell the truth, and that was what Rodin the evolutionary biologist claimed to do: "I am not a dreamer," he said, "but a scientist . . . There is no need to create. Genius comes only to those who know how to use their eyes and their intelligence."

This, even more than the indulger of duchesses, was the Rodin that was detonated on the steps of the Cleveland Museum of Art—the mediator of an eternal human nature (that pretext of capitalism), the mouthpiece of the bourgeois aesthetic which makes art an art of detail. Based on a quantitative representation of the universe, this aesthetic demands that the truth of any whole be no more than the sum of the individual truths which constitute it—as Rodin used to say that a statue was the sum of all its profiles. In consequence, an emphatic significance is attributed to the greatest possible quantity of details, and the mimetic surface thus produced is one of literally sensational intensity. As Albert Elsen, Rodin's most scholarly critic, puts it:

within an area confined to a few inches on the sculp-
ture, each fingertip will encounter surface inflections of

a different character; feeling one's own arm, one gains the impression that the surfaces conceived by Rodin are more richly complex.

It is an art which refuses to transform the world (choosing, as Elsen shrewdly suggests, to *enrich* it, to capitalize on our losses), which urges instead its obsessive record; indeed, an art which offers its hypertrophied mimetic surface not merely as an enrichment but as an homeopathy: to inoculate us with a contingent ill in order to forestall an essential one. This is what Roland Barthes calls the Essentialist Operation: to insinuate within an Order the complacent spectacle of its servitudes as a paradoxical but peremptory means of glorifying that Order. *The Age of Bronze, Eternal Spring, The Cathedral*—our middle-class *frisson* upon finding these "noble" titles affixed to works of a convulsive naturalism fades into acceptance, an acceptance of their ulterior and not their inherent function. To label *Dawn* (or *France* or even *Byzantine Princess*—it comes down, or climbs up, to the same) the semitransparent wax mask of Camille Claudel, the poet's sister and the sculptor's mistress, may rid us of a prejudice about the individual human countenance, but it is a prejudice which costs us dear, too dear, which costs us too many scruples, too many rebellions, and too many solitudes. To call an image of human flesh *The Thinker* is an allegorical holding-action, an alibi which manifests initially the tyranny and the injustice of that flesh, the torments it endures, the reproaches it incurs, only to rescue it at the last moment, *despite* or rather *with* the heavy fatality of its complaints, by calling it so. *Saving the appearances* by sovereign appellation, that is the Rodin who buttered up Puvis de Chavannes and his wan aristocratic allegories, that is the artist, and that the art, which passed—with its audience—from universal acclaim, from smug persuasion, in a flash of gunpowder. For it is written: I will show you fear in a handful of dust.

II

In the Print Room of the British Museum, if you have managed to murmur the proper words in the proper quarters, an attendant will set on the table before you any number of green buckram boxes, each large enough to contain an overcoat. Inside them, however, are not overcoats but the majority of the watercolors of Joseph Mallord William Turner, mounted though unframed, many with Ruskin's characteristic annotations ("nonsense picture") on the reverse—thousands and thousands of works, constituting one of the greatest achievements in art, though only a few of these pictures have been reproduced and a few more exhibited.

Here or in another such room, a deplorable scene occurred soon after the painter's death, at the age of 76, in 1851—a scene which nothing but the profusion and perfection of what is in these boxes can keep us from mourning as more than an incidental loss: according to W. M. Rossetti, Ruskin (who was not yet 35 at the time) found among these works several indecent drawings "which from the nature of their subjects it seemed undesirable to preserve", and burned them "on the authority of the Trustees" of the National Gallery. Rossetti had been helping Ruskin to sort the Turner bequest, and neither he, Ruskin, nor the Trustees were swayed by the fact that Turner evidently considered the sketches *desirable to preserve.* Nevertheless, we find in these green boxes many rapid drawings and watercolors, executed after the artist's fiftieth year, of naked lovers copulating, of naked girls embracing. According to Turner's biographer, the genitals in many sketches are plainly shown, even enlarged. These erotic works illustrated what Turner himself, in a verse written much earlier, called "the critical moment no maid can withstand/when a bird in the bush is worth two in the hand." Apparently there were many more of these caprices than the ones which survived the Rossetti/Ruskin sifting, but as in the case of the great mass of the Turner watercolors, they were not executed for sale or for exhibition—they were executed for the artist's sole delectation. Turner was the first major artist to show this division between a public and a private art—between the astonishments of Varnishing Day and the unvarnished truth of the studio.

In the archives of the Musée Rodin, there are about seven thousand drawings and watercolors by the Master; no one may see them, for as anyone knows who has attempted to undertake research in that country, France is a bureaucracy tempered by spitefulness, and though the canonical 50 years since Rodin's death have passed, the work has not been made accessible to students. About 200 drawings and water-colors are exhibited in the museum, and there are perhaps as many in other collections. Nothing, apparently, has been destroyed, but we are in something of the same case as with Turner: the world lies all before us, where to choose?

Like most of Turner's watercolors, like all of his later ones, Rodin's were painted for himself; they are a private art. So often accused of melodrama, of oratory, of sensationalism, both men, we must remember, created an entire *oeuvre* apart in which nothing happens but in which nothing is kept from happening—the art of the late Turner, of the late Rodin (who first permitted a large group of his wash-drawings to be exhibited in 1907, when he was 67), is the greatest example with which I am familiar in the history of art of an art without history, an articulation of a life that can be lived without repression, without sublimation, in eternal delight, in endless play, in the undifferentiated beatitude of bodies and earth and water and light whose realm is eter-nity, not history. The eroticism, even, of Rodin's and of

Turner's pictures has nothing to do with the drama of sex—
it is the ecstatics of a condition, not of an action, and when
we label it polymorphous-perverse we mean merely that it is
playful, exuberant, gay.

In considering the pleasant symmetries of the two artists:
that each of them ended and began a century of taste; that
each of them lived over three-quarters of a century without
ever marrying, though entertaining intractable relations
with an "unsuitable" woman; that each of them conducted
two opposing careers, the first charged with virtuoso scan-
dal—it was Hazlitt who as early as 1814 saw "a waste of mor-
bid strength, visionary absurdities, affectation and refine-
ment run mad" in Turner, and an organizer of the
American National Sculpture Society (in 1925!) who saw in
Rodin "a moral sot" and in his *Walking Man* "proof of the
working of a mind tainted with sadism"—and the second
entirely an interior rapture, no longer the assertion of self-
hood but rather the collection of an identity (motionless or
moving, rapt or reft, suggestive or stark) from the very lin-
eaments of what is *other:* this private creation of Turner and
Rodin is the highest expression Western art can show of an
identification with what is not the self but seen, the making
of an inwardness from what is outside—as I have said, an *ec-
statics* of art . . . In considering then the remarkable analo-
gies between Rodin and Turner, let us not forget that to
each genius was attached a young and voluble literary man
whose attentions were not so welcome to the artist as they
are to us: Ruskin who by his late twenties was determined to
dedicate his fortune and vocabulary (both enormous) to the
exposition of his "earthly master"; Rilke who at the same age
served as Rodin's secretary, and though ignominiously
dismissed managed to patch up the misunderstanding by
patience, admiration, servility even—and of course by one
of the most beautiful essays in the entire range of art criti-

cism, which Rodin may never have read. One sentence from each writer must suffice to manifest the degree of suffusion, the deep dye these passionate young men had taken:

> Rodin and Rodin only would follow and render that mystery of decided line, that distinct, sharp, visible but unintelligible and inextricable richness, which, examined part by part, is to the eye nothing but confusion and defeat, which, taken as a whole, is all unity, symmetry and truth.

> Turner was a worker whose only desire was to penetrate with all his forces into the humble and difficult significance of his means; therein lay a certain renunciation of Life, but in just this renunciation lay his triumph, for Life entered into his work: his art was not built upon a great idea but upon a craft, in which the fundamental element was the surface, was what is seen.

Ah no, I have the names reversed: the first sentence is by Ruskin, the second by Rilke. There is always a confusion, is there not, when literary men meddle with art?

III

Between the "wrong" Rodin mutilated on the steps of the Cleveland Museum and the undivulged Rodin I have suggested as an antidote, between the emblem of an abject ideology and the ecstatics of a released identity, it is good—it is corrective—to stand a moment before the masterpiece of Rodin's sculpture and the supreme sculptural expression of the nineteenth century, *The Gates of Hell,* begun in 1880, left unfinished (in plaster) and cast only a decade after his death. The first cast is in Philadelphia, the second in Paris, both gifts of the same American millionaire who created the

Rodin Museum in the former city and who restored Rodin's villa outside the latter, housing hundreds of original plaster studies and drawings which had been inadequately protected—a gesture never acknowledged by the French authorities. Looking at the spectacular patina of the bronze, the terrific shadows which are Dantesque indeed, one is easily distracted from the Master's intention:

> My sole idea is simply one of *color* and *effect* . . . I have revived the means employed by Renaissance artists, for example, this mélange of figures, some in low relief, others in the round, in order to obtain those beautiful blond shadows which produce all the softness . . .

Rodin had hoped to make the individual figures in wax, attaching them to the plaster frame, which would have created even subtler "blond shadows", but the technique was impracticable, and year after year the portal remained in his studio, endlessly altered, figures added, removed, shifting in scale and inclusiveness, the only fixed point being the tombs near the base of the doors, which were the last major additions before Rodin's death. Almost all the images we associate most readily—and not always with relish—with the sculptor are here, frequently in a context which challenges the connotations they have come to have for us: *The Thinker, Adam, Eve, The Prodigal Son, Crouching Woman, The Three Shades, The Old Courtesan, The Kiss, Fugit Amor, Ugolino* . . . In particular Man as *The Thinker* replaces Christ in the judgment seat, and in general chaos and flux supplant the hierarchies of doctrine. For Rodin himself, the work was as private as the swiftest of his drawings, the most summary of his clay sketches, and its inflection—though I have called it ecstatic, though I am certain it is exalted and even exultant—is catastrophic. Michelangelo called Ghiberti's doors *The Gates of Paradise,* and surely Rodin accepted the challenge in calling his own *The Gates of Hell*. They are the consummate expression of that encyclopedic impulse of the nineteenth century, that effort to gain access to prophecy by means of process, which we link to Courbet's *Atelier,* for example, and to the *Comédie Humaine* of Balzac—Balzac, of whom Rodin gives us the most *unwavering,* the most Promethean image— for their subject is not so much a version of Dante as an inversion: *La Tragédie Humaine.*

Corrective, then, to pre-empt this apocalyptic and yet intimate Rodin—apocalyptic in the sense that he creates a world of total metaphor, in which everything is potentially identical with everything else, as though it were all inside a single infinite and eternal body. The last great artist for whom art, nature and religion are identical, Rodin was faithful to what Pater calls the culture, the administration of the visible world, and he merited Revelation, which might solace his heart in the inevitable fading of that. His delights, as it says in Scripture, were with the sons of men, and in *The Gates of Hell* we read their fortune; it is ours.

1971

Edward Hopper, *House by the Railroad* (1925), oil on canvas, 24 x 29 in.
Collection, The Museum of Modern Art, New York: Given anonymously.

Crossing the Tracks
to Hopper's World

MARK STRAND

*After graduating from college, Mark Strand came to the Yale Art
School to study with Josef Albers. He stayed from 1956 until 1959,
and it was during this time, while learning to paint, that he started
writing poems. "I had no style as either a poet or a painter," he says
now, glancing back. "I wanted my paintings to look like a cross be-
tween de Kooning and Gorky, and they ended up looking like weak
Marsden Hartley." He had more luck with, and more encourage-
ment for, his poems. "While painting, I had the feeling that whatever
I was was diminished by my work, that visual experience could not
represent or take the place of other experience. So when I turned to
writing poetry it was with considerable relief. Though my poetry was
not good, I felt that it offered the opportunity for intellectual growth.
For me, writing was thinking." In the years since, Strand's poems
have thought a good deal about the estrangement and transience he
notes in Edward Hopper's work: "In a field / I am the absence / of
field." In the light of the following essay, it is more clearly evident
that the shades of Wallace Stevens and Ralph Waldo Emerson have
helped create the peculiarly American effects in both Strand and
Hopper. Strand ends this essay with an image of Hopper "being with
us, but always with his back turned." Many years later, Strand took
up that same image and applied it to himself: "Increasingly, I have*

339

*felt that I don't see a painting until I turn away from it and don't
read a poem until I close the book. What I know or retain of either
depends on what I am able to invent in their place. Oh I refer to
them, but mostly I draw on my own blindness and ignorance, in-
sight and knowledge."*

The blank concrete walls and steel constructions of
modern industry, midsummer streets with the acid
green of close-cut lawns, the dusty Fords and gilded
movies—all the sweltering, tawdry life of the American
small town, and behind all, the sad desolation of our
suburban landscape. He derives daily stimulus from
these, that others flee from or pass with indifference.

EDWARD HOPPER wrote the preceding words about
Charles Burchfield, but he might just as well have been writ-
ing about himself. He is the painter of American life at its
most hopeless and provincial. Yet he has rescued it from the
workaday rhythms in which it is demeaned and has given it a
preserving character. Buildings, people and natural objects
take on, in his work, an emblematic or pictorial unity. The
formal properties of offices, hotel rooms and bleak tene-
ment interiors reinforce the isolation of his people who
seem always in the act of entering a meaningless future—
meaningless because it is anticipated in the sterility of the
present.

The remarkable number of roads, highways, and railroad
tracks in his paintings speak for Hopper's fascination with
passage. Often, while looking at his work, we are made to
feel like transients, momentary visitors to a scene that will
endure without us and that suffers our presence with aggres-

sive reticence. His famous painting at the Museum of Modern Art, *The House by the Railroad Tracks,* is a good example of what I mean.

Separated from the house by tracks, we *feel* separated by change, by progress, by motion, and ultimately by the conditions our own mortality imposes. The house glares at us from what seems like an enormous distance. It appears so withdrawn, in fact, that it stands as an emblem of refusal, a monument to the idea of enclosure. And Hopper's famous statement of his aims—"What I wanted to do was paint sunlight on the side of a house"—seems misleading in its simplicity, for the sunlight in his paintings illuminates the secretive without penetrating it. Thus we feel separated from something essential and, as a consequence, our lives seem frivolous. When we look at his paintings we are made to feel, more than we care to, like time's creatures. Each of us would have to cross the tracks to inhabit that Victorian mansion with its coffin-like finality. And across the tracks is Hopper's forbidden land, where the present is lived eternally, where the moment is without moment, where it is always just after and just before—in this case, just after the train has passed, just before the train will arrive.

Hopper's use of light is almost always descriptive of time. In many of his paintings, duration is given a substantial and heroic geometry. In *Rooms by the Sea,* for example, an enormous trapezoid of light fills a room, denying the moment its temporality. Hopper's ability to use space convincingly as a metaphor for time is extraordinary. It demonstrates the ratio between stillness and emptiness, so that we are able to experience the emptiness of moments, hours, a whole lifetime.

His paintings frequently take place at dawn or in late afternoon in a twilight of few or no people. Again, the focus is the transitional. The times which combine elements of night and day paradoxically give the world greater solidity than it has when it is fully illuminated. Night and day in their more local manifestations as shadows and light are so arranged that they dramatize and give extra significance to buildings or parts of buildings we would otherwise take for granted. Such significance is heightened in those paintings where a house, say, stands next to trees or woods. Hopper's trees are strangely opaque; we never enter the woods in his work, nor does light. Their mystery is preserved, acting as an ominous reminder of how fragile our world of measured verticals and horizontals is.

The current show at the Whitney of selections from the Hopper Bequest is fascinating. There is not one painting in it that ranks with his masterpieces and only a few that manage to communicate that quality of loneliness and desolation we associate with many of his best known works. One of those that does is *Stairway* (no date given), a small, eerie painting which looks down a stairway leading to an open door and a dark massing of trees or hills directly outside. Not as rigorously defined spatially as his more mature paintings, it nevertheless mystifies in the same way. The open door becomes not merely a passage connecting inside and outside, but the disturbing link between nowhere and nowhere, or, again, the spatial and tangible restoration of a moment that exists between events, the events of leavetaking or arrival.

Even in the early paintings, there are a great number of roads and embankments, though they do not have the weight they will have later. *El Station* (1908) is typical Hopper subject matter, but quite insubstantial. The people, merely indicated in a few strokes, do not emerge as presences; the sunlight, convincing as itself, is without psychological depth or effect. Another painting which appears to have much in common with other, better known Hoppers is *Cape Cod Sunset* (1934), but it lacks their solidity, their monumental reticence and, in fact, displays an uncharacteristic frailty.

There are a few handsome paintings of Cobb's barns and house in Truro, but these, too, lack the forcefulness we usually associate with Hopper.

The most important aspect of the show is the watercolors, prints and drawings. Many of the watercolors move beyond being mere notation, hurried and perfunctory in gesture, and take on the strangeness, the involved quiet, of his oils. The prints also have qualities in common with the major oils. Though less austere and surely less compelling, such prints as *Evening Wind* and *American Landscape* already incorporate themes that will appear again in future Hoppers. Also exhibited are sketches and preparatory drawings for many of his well known paintings. These more than anything else in the show bring us close to his greatest work. Something of the same quality is transmitted—an oddness, a disturbing quiet, a sense of being in a room with a man who insists on being with us, but always with his back turned.

1971

Thomas Cole, *The Savage State,* from *The Course of Empire,* oil on canvas, 39 1/4 x 63 1/4 in. The New-York Historical Society, New York.

Landscape's Empire

JOHN HOLLANDER

John Hollander has written several ekphrastic poems: "Aristotle to Phyllis," "Sunday A.M. Not in Manhattan," "A Statue of Something," "August Carving." One of the earliest, a poem about the Ghent altarpiece called "The Altarpiece Finished" (which appeared in Movie-Going, *his second collection, in 1962), starts by expressing its maker's own distrust of interpretation: "I cannot see how in time it will be possible to look at / it without making all kinds of mistakes: not so much about what / means what, or about how it was all done . . . / . . . but just in thinking that something need be said at all." But interpretation is like varnish. And, says Hollander, "from Homer (the shield of Achilles) and Hesiod (the shield of Herakles) on, poets, by having to use mere words to trope pictures, have been able to illuminate painting's depths with a light neither natural nor artificial, but more penetrating than either. A light like that of the morning sun, falling on the statue of Memnon, which caused it to speak up." Hollander has also written poems about invented pictures (including "Pictures in a Gallery" and "Ode to Landscape"), which points toward another of his motives for writing about art, in verse or prose: "Because I could never draw or paint, and I loved and remembered and brooded over pictures even in childhood; the only way to make them was to describe (a) actual ones or (b) those which I invented in and by those descriptions." As a student at*

Thomas Cole, *The Arcadian or Pastoral State*, from *The Course of Empire*, oil on canvas, 39 ¹/₄ x 63 ¹/₄ in. The New-York Historical Society, New York.

Thomas Cole, *The Consummation of Empire*, from *The Course of Empire*, oil on canvas, 51 x 76 in. The New-York Historical Society, New York.

Columbia he began visiting the Thomas Cole Course of Empire
cycle at the New York Historical Society and two of the Voyage of
Life *series that hung in St. Luke's Hospital. No doubt the force of
Cole's own power of interpreting—as evident in his landscapes as in
his allegories—attracted Hollander. Cole himself once warned, "If
the Imagination is shackled, and nothing is described but what we
see, seldom will anything truly great be produced, either in Painting
or in Poetry." As Hollander's essay suggests,* The Course of Em-
pire *traces the styles of landscape painting and represents not only
the triumph of the sublime over the picturesque, of the visionary over
the historical, but the triumph of nature over civilization and of
America over Europe. Hollander "reads" these paintings the way
they read the idea of their subject. One must bring to such a reading,
he says, "the same kinds of informed knowledge about conventions,
history, iconography, allusion, conditions of commission or execu-
tion, etc. that one needs, analogously, about the language and con-
texts of a poem. And, in addition, one needs an 'eye' for form, struc-
ture, pictorial space, surface, even as one needs an 'ear' for tone and
music in verse. And finally, one must not stop with a reading (as
the art historians would have us do), but go on to interpret."*

"THE HEALTH of the eye," says Emerson, "seems to de-
mand a horizon. We are never tired, so long as we can see far
enough." But all our glimpsed horizons—in close, urban
views that the narrowing, skyscraper canyons frame, or be-
yond bare, winter expanses of dead field—can nourish only
the eye that has been weaned from the immediate, that has
been led by the truths of pictures out of a soft jail of seeing
into the wider light which is not merely observed, but read.
Painting the American landscape has been charged from the
very beginning with some of the same heavy burdens carried

Thomas Cole, *Destruction,* from *The Course of Empire,* oil on canvas, 39 $^1/_4$ x 63 $^1/_2$ in. The New-York Historical Society, New York.

Thomas Cole, *Desolation,* from *The Course of Empire,* oil on canvas, 39 $^1/_2$ x 61 in. The New-York Historical Society, New York.

by the necessity of naming American places instead of being able to rely upon names meaningful and *donnés,* as old as one's native speech, to reach out across the chasms that seem to loom between nature and language. One of these burdens was the weight of a kind of conceptual solitude, a visionary reconstitution of the landshape through the picture. The "primeval forests, virgin lakes and waterfalls" which an American painter could praise were gauded with no ruins, and twilit by no histories. Unlike "Tivolis, Ternis, Mont Blancs, Plinlimmons, hackneyed and worn by the daily pencils of hundreds," the plenitude of fresh visual surfaces which the American scenery offered was unvarnished by remembered pictures in the observing eye, and unhaunted by the ghosts of their *Sehenswürdigkeit.*

But the painter's eye could not merely accept. To exorcise bright fables from rich, dark woods, to evolve new pictorial genres and feign that they were secreted by their rocks and stones and trees, was another matter. The American imagination has struggled most with phasing out inherited fables, from Emerson's muscular turning of back on the Atlantic, to Wallace Stevens' leading equestrian statues out of the green parks, and even to W. C. Williams' fear of the unimprisoned idea. But what we inherit is ours; if for no other reason, such a struggle would have to be a continuous revolution against our own fictions as well. English romanticism rejects the literary for the truly poetic, and this seems to be echoed in the way in which painting rejects worn pictorial fictions as pejoratively literary, while embracing newer ones as they ripen into visions. To the extent that their fictions, new or old, are more or less otherwise easily available in texts, all paintings are more or less illustrations.

The texts illustrated by several traditions of American landscape painting are those which proclaim that the language of natural scenery is itself scriptural. There was enough emblematic tradition in such texts to withstand for some decades the slowly eroding claims of light, or indeed of paint, to creative authority. The search for significances in natural prospects, rather than for facts or feelings, is still an American obsession, rather than a European one: we are still the land's foster children, no longer too simple to inquire.

Even an illustration, though, may embrace supplementary fictions from some unacknowledged text; the scenarios from which our nineteenth-century landscape painting enacted its spectacles were both manifest and latent. It is only in sermons in books that one hears books in the running brooks; it was the daylong voice of Eve, imprinting its higher wave-pattern on the unmodulated rise and fall of nature's noises which made them natural music, and as Robert Frost suggested, "Never again would birds' song be the same." And so for the cooling shade of trees—as Eve's cast shadow blended into patches of dark along the unmown grass, the darkening softened (as, indeed, it hardened, past what it had been, when the foliage that painted those patches there became the first, guilty Hiding Place). If nothing else, the chronicles of human history lie unintoned alongside landscape pictures, invisibly printed *en face.* And even in the ruins and visions of Europe—projections of Claude, gleamings of Turner, shadows of Salvator Rosa—the myths that lurk in the observed land and sky and water will assert themselves.

Thomas Cole's great cyclic manifestation of *The Course of Empire* is also a chart of the course of landscape painting's evolving vision. Worked out, in a series of five paintings, between 1833 and 1836, the sequence presents its primary fictions, and yields up its secondary ones, in a manner so commandingly exemplary that we had as well school our eyes there as at our blasted northeastern countryside. Largely unvisited, across the street from the Museum of Natural History, across the park from the Metropolitan Museum, as if triangulated by nature and culture, the canvasses were half-buried in the New York Historical Society until, a few years ago, rehung. Unhackneyed and unworn by the daily visitations of few, they hang in linear serial order, showing

I   *The Savage State*
II   *The Arcadian or Pastoral*
III   *The Consummation of Empire*
IV   *Destruction,* and
V   *Desolation*

of what is the same geographical conformation—a wide bay opening to the eastward, its shores climbing up to great heights in the south. A singular peak—"a mountain of peculiar form," as Cole described his plan of it—remains invariant under the transformations that green, brown and blue of shore and water undergo, as white and gold of marble and metal, in III, will claim all but the horizon. Reading the series is both easier and harder than unravelling the precious puzzles of Victorian narrative sequences like Augustus Egg's *Past and Present:* its counterplots and connective similes appear only gradually, before the hidden texts can suggest themselves in turn.

As early as 1831 Cole had contemplated a series of paintings "that should be the history of a natural scene, as well as an epitome of Man; showing the *natural* changes of landscape, and those effected by Man in his progress from barbarism to civilization—to the state of luxury—to the vicious state or state of destruction, etc." At the beginning of the following year he had completed *A Wild Scene,* a study for *The Savage State,* representing "a general idea of a wild." In 1833, Luman Reed, a devoted and energetic connoisseur of American painting, became his patron, and commissioned the series (in the year of its completion, Reed was to die and

Cole to marry). The painter had already rendered illustrative scenery in his 1827 scene from *The Last of the Mohicans,* and while beginning his work on Reed's commission, he would envision *The Titan's Goblet,* a blending of northern and southern dreams (the tree Yggdrasill grows out at its top into a bowl containing the entire Aegean at least, with beaded structures winking at the brim), and without any comprehension of change beyond the simultaneous manifestation of architectural epochs in its tiny statues that gleam in wide sunlight. But the cyclic paintings were to dream deeper, and the dialectic of the human and the natural must needs have engaged a total sense of design in other ways. For it was not enough to create scenes from a montage of studies from nature (Tivolis and virgin lakes both), to crown *A Wild Scene*'s mountains with rocky peaks derived from a jutting pile sketched earlier. Pictures of *phases* or *states* are not like those of the landscapist's *hours*—the primary pencillings and the re-creations in studio pent. Nor indeed do they resemble either the luminist's *epiphanies*—those instants of space which eternally embody spots of time, those winkings of the light of Creation. Nor, yet again, the impressionist's *moments,* which are not in time, but in daylight, where an unimaginable touch is made palpable in the transformations of shadow. Visions of phase occupy reaches of imagined space, and they must guide the natural eye of the observer through those regions by means more supple and powerful than those of linear narrative. Philipp Otto Runge's great drawings of the four phases of day, the *Viertageszeiten* of 1803, depicted cycles of fall and redemption, movements inward and outward, in what he thought of as four dimensions of the created spirit: these phases embodied other cycles of early and late, light and darkness, promise and remembrance, seed and fruit, which, at least from the time of Oedipus' answer to the Sphinx, have identified human life-span with solar day. In a pair of canvasses from 1838 figuring *Past* and *Present,* Cole gives us a medieval tower in its full nineteenth-century panoply, a tournament being enacted in the lists nearby, another castle adorning a distant crag, giving way, in the second view, to a gorgeous, overgrown ruin, and "a solitary Shepherd feeds his flock where once stood the Royal Pavilion and the Throne of the Queen of Beauty." Catalogue copy can cheerfully gloss such sequences, but not the dialectic between pictorial modes and historical types: *Past* is gauded with the stagecraft of an academy painting, but in *Present,* Claude reconquers the plain.

The human, then, and the natural: *The Course of Empire* would invoke historical seasons, times of day and pictorial modes in mapping history onto landscape. Like the way in which, as Harold Bloom has shown, the romantic's dream internalizes the questing of old romance, the growth of culture in nature will wax and wane as the natural landscape shrinks and spreads. Even without knowing much of Cole's plan for the hanging of the series, the reading eye must abandon the purely linear order of the paintings, in which I and II (of the same size) are followed by a central III, *Consummation,* in a larger format, after which, in turn come the penultimate and final visions of destruction and desolation in the same size as the first two. *The Course of Empire* is one picture, and were New York gallery rooms as glorious and profuse as those of great vanished houses, or had the young nation some ambitious *Glyptothek* to decorate, this would have remained obvious. Overlaid upon the major curve of rise and fall are the phases of daylight, cycles of pictorial history, rotations of perspective around the pivotal prospect of the "mountain of peculiar form," and, through all, the gradual assumption of *westering,* in the sense that connects geographic space with the teleology of the terrestrial day. One thinks of the German *Abendland* that desig-

nates what, in the history of America's dreams of its own
West, has been the *Morgenland* of promise and new morrows.

A sketch of Cole's remains, showing the actual placement
of the paintings in Luman Reed's gallery: I is to be above II
on the left, III in the center above a sort of mantelpiece, and
IV and V on the right, the whole wall surmounted by three
dioramic sections of panel showing left, the rising, center,
the noonday, and right, the setting sun. Then, too, as
Ellwood Parry has ingeniously demonstrated,[1] the eight-
eenth-century aesthetic modalities of the Sublime and the
Beautiful are themselves imprinted upon this full sine-curve,
this squared-off W of down-and-up relations, and we might
even fancy that the huge canvass of *Consummation* might res-
onate in the range of that bastard category, the Picturesque,
which emerged as the tragicomedy of its epoch's theory of
light.

The times of day, the cycles of history—"there are certain
amounts of brute light and heat," accedes Emerson. "But is
there no intent of an analogy between man's life and the
seasons? And do the seasons gain no grandeur or pathos
from that analogy?" he continues, carrying us into a realm
where the fixity of emblems will not suffice to connect the
two worlds. The dialectic of the rising tower and the leveling
hill and grove subsumes others as well. Again in *Nature*
Emerson states canonically one of his major disavowals, in a
passage too easy to misread:

[1]In an unpublished dissertation on *"The Course of Empire,"* which he has
kindly permitted me to inspect, Professor Parry goes deep into Cole's
iconographic sources and studies some of their transformations into
images. My quotations in these pages, incidentally, are from Emerson's
Nature; Cole's own "Essay on American Scenery," *The American Monthly
Magazine,* N.S. Vol. I, Jan. 1836; a letter of Cole to Luman Reed on Sept. 18,
1833; an essay by James Fenimore Cooper of 1849 (these last two from
Louis L. Noble, *The Life and Works of Thomas Cole,* ed. E. S. Vessell,
Cambridge, Mass., 1964); and the English poets.

How does Nature deify us with a few and cheap elements! Give me health and a day, and I will make the pomp of emperors ridiculous. The dawn is my Assyria; the sun-rise and moon-rise my Paphos, and unimaginable realms of faerie; broad noon shall be my England of the senses and understanding; the night shall be my Germany of mystic philosophy and dreams.

There is a shadow of reversal here, a tincture of the opposite in the primary, for the American self is after all a phase of the Human, whose life dawns in Mesopotamia, and an embodying of the mind which does analytic philosophy at its noon of calm and absented desire, only to cross the Channel to become a continental in the night of pain, or want or present death. A picture of the mind must peer forth from pictures of its objects, as the tower and the mountain peak, the lone, twisted tree and Byronic hero, become figures of each other.

Here are the times of human endeavor as Cole originally planned them, in a prospectus sent to his patron in 1833:

The FIRST PICTURE, representing the savage state, must be a view of a wilderness,—the sun rising from the sea, and the clouds of night retiring over the mountains. The figures must be savage, clothed in skins and occupied in the chase. There must be a flashing chiaroscuro, and the spirit of motion pervading the scene, as though nature were just springing from chaos.

The SECOND PICTURE must be the pastoral state,—the day further advanced—light clouds playing about the mountains—the scene partly cultivated—a rude village near the bay—small vessels in the harbour—groups of peasants either pursuing their labours in the field, watching their flocks, or engaged in some simple

amusement. The chiaroscuro must be of a milder char-
acter than in the previous scene, but yet have a fresh
and breezy effect.

The THIRD must be a noonday,—a great city girding
the bay, gorgeous piles of architecture, bridge, aque-
ducts, temple—the port crowded with vessels—splendid
processions, etc.—all that can be combined to show the
fullness of prosperity: the chiaroscuro broad.

The FOURTH should be a tempest,—a battle, and the
burning of the city—towers falling, arches broken, ves-
sels wrecking in the harbour. In this scene there should
be a fierce chiaroscuro, masses and groups swaying
about like stormy waves. This is the scene of destruction
or vicious state.

The FIFTH must be a sunset,—the mountains riven—
the city a desolate ruin—columns standing isolated
among the encroaching waters—ruined temples, bro-
ken bridges, fountains, sarcophagi, etc.—no human
figure—a solitary bird perhaps: a calm and silent effect.
This picture must be as the funeral knell of departed
greatness, and may be called the state of desolation.

In the completed first painting, we are in fact looking
southeast across the bay toward what Fenimore Cooper
called "a precipitous hill, crowned with a solitary and re-
markable crag." A great gnarled tree frames the foreground
on the left; from behind its roots we see a savage brandishing
his bow, in pursuit of his wounded doe. Other hunters in the
middle distance move also toward the right of the picture,
the unopened west, toward which boats move along an estu-
ary, toward which the morning sun is reaching. Thick clouds
of night, of residual chaos rather than of impending dissolu-
tion, obscure the mountain on the right, below which, on a

kind of low, cleared plateau, a ring of innocent tepees sur-
rounds a community fire. Deer walk upon their mountains,
and the quail whistle about them their spontaneous cries.

In the Arcadian picture, the westering continues. We rec-
ognize the "solitary and remarkable crag," but see to the
right of it, hiding a horizon yet to be inferred, a far-distant
conformation of higher peaks. The unrolling of light and of
éclaircissement has revealed something higher than our
landmark, even, and beyond it. That landmark's derivation
of a balancing rock (to be seen earlier in Cole's *Last of the
Mohicans* scene), a bouldered head on a Gibraltar shoulder,
president over all that we are to see, at first appears not to
have shifted its position. But we gradually realize that we
have moved south and west: fields and meadows open up in
the foreground; at the base of a stump (not of the same tree
—but must we think so for a moment?), a Euclidoid bearded
figure proves a theorem, scratching the diagram on the
ground with a branch. To the right, a budding Pig painter-
Apelles-Giotto draws a stick figure on a rude slab of primitive
bridge. In the mid-ground a shepherd tends his flock, and
on the right, figures from Sicilian Idylls filtered through
Venetian painting pipe, pipe and dance. The ring of tepees
has given way, in the middle distance, to an unruined Stone-
henge. Salvator has given way to Claude.

—Who, in the *Consummation*'s bright noon, yields to
Turner—in his visions of Carthage—and to Cecil B. DeMille,
in architectural eclecticism, crowding and scale. We are at
mid-day of an East-West Empire, and our vantage point has
moved westward and south, so that we now face due east, our
backs to the direction which all actions, in the first two states,
had taken. Our presiding head is tiny and distant: huge ar-
chitectural fantasies, thronged with festive multitudes (we
know well who are these coming to the sacrifice: Everyone),
rise up on either shore of the bay down which we gaze. Their

summits gleam undimmed by rain or long-forgotten dew, and masonry has overbuilt hill and entrapped water. A pair of distant *pharoi* look out to sea. The deity of the City, an image of triumph expanded beyond completion, balances on the right a version of the tomb of Mausolus on the left. But she faces leftward, northward, whence barbarians will come. The triumph of the ruler, crossing the bridge in the foreground, moves leftward as well. Consummation means the death of desire; at such a summit, descent has already begun. The leftward movement that governs the last two scenes is given by the terms of design, but its reading is darkness, whose tincture lurks in the sun at its brightest.

Destruction is John Martin's Nineveh: smoke and cloud blend in a lowered sky under which we gaze eastward again down the bay amid the fires of barbaric invasion. The lighthouses are broken columns, the statues tumbled. Broken caryatids bear nothing. Skin-clad hordes have put the scene to flame and blade; broken bridges prevent escape leftward across the canvass. The sky is filled with a grim parody of the clouds of night in the condition of savagery. Most remarkable is the governing figure of Destruction: at the right, a marble Mars, bronze shield gleaming in reflected firelight, his shattered head far below his pedestal, thrusts his shield arm out leftward across the scene. *Where was he in the previous picture?* Our focus, with reference to our sad head of crag in the distance, has barely shifted northward and a hundred yards or so west. *Was he built during the intervening, unpictured period? Or were we viewing the whole broad prospect of consummation from a spot just below and south of his pedestal?* War towers over Plenty, even behind our backs; but this very eidolon will itself be in ruins before we will have known that it was to be regarded as more than a public, marble gesture.

If the darkness of *Destruction* is a reductive parody of the dispelling glooms of *The Savage State,* so the beauty of *Deso-*

lation (a moonlit view, of course, when Cole finally painted it, and not a sunset) reflects the pastoral condition. We can know the Arcadian night only in dreams of mellowed ruins, perhaps. Again, we look down the bay, but the broken columns have become surrogate tree-trunks, clothed with the foliage of shrubs. In the foreground, one major unbroken capital atop its creamy, moonlit pillar supports a nesting stork, whose mate contemplates his longevity in a pool off to the right. A delicate cascade pours leftward from a massive fragment of broken, once-pompous fountain. The element of water bathes the scene like moonlight—fire of destruction, Arcadian earth and the clearing air of the human morning all return to this. Marble and gold were a momentary shadow of a recycling light—in retrospect,

> Heaven smiles, and faiths and empires gleam,
> Like wrecks of a dissolving dream.

We return to haunted Claude; but it is a later version of ruin—until we perceive the thinness of the paint film, here at the end, our eyes dazzle: is this a passage of Courbet up the base of the dominating column?

It is only with the last scene that the prophetic dimension appears: the meditation on cyclical completion yields the vision of what lies beyond phase. Alexander Pope momentarily donned the mantle of Virgil in the Fourth Eclogue to scold the overbuilder, a vulgar anti-Maecenas whose house was a travesty of all that Burlington had stood for:

> Another age shall see the golden ear
> Embrown the Slope, and nod on the Parterre,
> Deep Harvests bury all his pride has planned,
> And laughing Ceres reassume the land.

Here, though, the eminent domain is of green, of vine and moss; here, time has restored another regent: the muse of landscape painting. The painter's brush consumes his dream, but yet more time will breed desires out of canvasses as out of *plein air* views, as

> The world's great age begins anew,
>   The golden years return,
> The earth doth like a snake renew
>   Her winter weeds outworn . . .

or, as Cole himself could write, ". . . the mind's eye may see far into futurity. Where the wolf roams, the plough shall glisten; on the gray crag shall rise temple and tower; mighty deeds shall be done in the now pathless wilderness; and poets yet unborn shall sanctify the soil."

But these texts point finally to a version of the Virgilian prophecy written four years before Pope's lines, Bishop Berkeley's "Verses on the Prospect of Planting Arts and Learning in America." Cole's vision is cyclic and unredeemable, and proclaims no realm beyond its own revolving stages. But a subtext of the series concerns, as it so often does for him, what his friend Bryant called the "wilder image" of America, and of a possible new order of American art. It is the American continent that Berkeley invokes, the "happy climes . . . / Where men shall not impose for truth and sense / The pedantry of courts and schools":

> There shall be sung another golden age,
>   The rise of empire and of arts,
> The good and great inspiring epic rage,
>   The wisest heads and noble hearts.
>
> Not such as Europe breeds in her decay;
>   Such as she bred when fresh and young,
> When heav'nly flame did animate her clay,
>   By future poets shall be sung.

—And by future painters limned. It is almost inevitable that Cole would take the title of his series from the opening of this poem's last stanza, allowing the implications of the deleted word "westward" to operate in two ways. Figuratively, it applies to the source of the painter's vision, the inspiration of a Western Muse; literally, it suggests the westering movement, from canvass to canvass, of the cycle's scenic point of view:

> Westward the course of empire takes its way;
>   The four first acts already past,
> A fifth shall close the drama with the day;
>   Time's noblest offspring is the last.

And perhaps, for a romantic painter, the last, noblest offspring must be the final vision of his *Desolation,* his own and his cycle's last age and close of day, and the fifth act (the classical cycle of the ages having been four) of his play of phase, stage, and age.

Unchanged by the moonlight of *Desolation,* only the wise mountain-topping head. In *A Wild Scene,* the mountain peaks were types of medieval ruin, leaning leftward in the painting. The balancing rock from the Cooper scene and from several sketches finally replaced them. This particular rock head appears in a drawing called *View on the Moon,* and acquires even more meaning from another one captioned: "A Shadow of a great Rock in a weary land."

Beyond the cycles of *The Course of Empire* would lie the possibilities of visionary landscape, and Cole later sought many directions through these forests. He persisted with allegorical pictures, while yet reasoning that he need not: "From yonder dark mass of foliage the village spire beams like a star. You see no ruined tower to tell of outrage—no gorgeous temple to speak of ostentation; but freedom's offspring—peace, security, and happiness, dwell there. . . ." On the other hand, he could envision the first Edward Hopper —his great painting of the Van Rensselaer mansion of 1840 transforms what would else have been a topographical view into one of those moments in which nature refills the spaces which human society has cleared—the taking out, the painterly erasures reveal a world abandoned, not merely a stage set momentarily emptied.

The grand Connecticut River *Ox Bow* of 1836 (painted while struggling with the completion of the series) was to have more consequences for subsequent American landscape painting—its wide ribbon of light lassoing the head of land whose face gazes placidly skyward, balancing the blasted trees in the left foreground, the whole washed in a sunlight which, if it does not illuminate, plainly propounds. Its manifesto was written in April of that year, in part of Cole's "Essay on American Scenery," where talking of Niagara Falls— "where the sublime and beautiful are bound together in an indissoluble chain. In gazing at it we feel as though a great void had been filled in our minds"—he moves one step further to a final acknowledgment of the axis of vision along which the scenes must ever be viewed: "Our conceptions expand—we become part of what we behold."

1977